FRED WILLARD'S *Magnificent* MOVIE TRIVIA

Put Your KNOWLEDGE of MOVIES, ACTORS, FACTS & FIRSTS to the TEST

SQUAREONE
PUBLISHERS

COVER DESIGNER: Jeannie Tudor
EDITORS: Marie Caratozzolo and Joanne Abrams
TYPESETTER: Gary A. Rosenberg
COVER PHOTOS: Courtesy of Joe Franklin
BACK COVER PHOTO: Courtesy of Guy Viau
INTERIOR PHOTOS: Courtesy of Guy Viau (page 263)
and Susan Maljan (page 265)

Square One Publishers
115 Herricks Road
Garden City Park, New York 11040
www.squareonepublishers.com

CONTENTS

To all the people involved in creating films,
which give us so much enjoyment
that even the "trivia" becomes
a form of entertainment.

ACKNOWLEDGMENTS

I'd like to thank Rudy Shur and Anthony Pomes at Square One for never giving up on me during the production of this book, and for their guidance throughout. Additionally I'd like to thank series editor Marie Caratozzolo and her wonderful team of researchers, including Joanne Abrams, Michael Weatherhead, Michele D'Altorio, Caryn Woerner, Christine Sikule, Danielle Burby, and Daniel Bubbeo. Thanks must also go to my terrific agent, Mike Eisenstadt. And finally, I'd like to extend a very special thank you to Mary—my wife and best friend—for her neverending love and support.

How to Play the Games

Welcome, friends. Are you ready to put your knowledge of movie facts and details to the test? My trivia book is built to challenge, while providing endless hours of fun and enjoyment. The games in this book have been designed in a way that allows you, the reader, to play either alone or with others. In most trivia books, when looking up the answer to a question, the reader is able to see the answers to other questions at the same time. This book doesn't allow that to happen, but you must first understand how to play the games. Ready?

THE BASICS

There are eighty games in this book, each with a dozen questions. Every game is also numbered and has been given a title that reflects the basic category of its questions, such as "The Classics," "Award Winners," "Romantic Comedies," "Breakout Roles," and "Film Firsts." Throughout, you'll also find a number of games titled "Grab Bag," which include a mix and match of questions from various categories.

THE PAGE SETUP

Each page holds four frames that are situated from the top of the page to the bottom (as seen in the example on the next page). Each frame is divided in half. The left half contains a question. The right half contains the answer to the question from a previous page. (Seem a little confusing? Not to worry—it actually sounds more complicated than it really is.) Stay with me . . .

Questions
are always on the
left side of each frame.

Answers
(to questions from previous
pages) are always on the
right side of each frame.

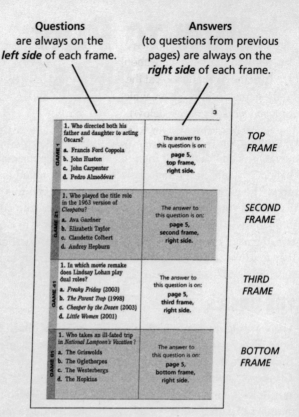

Typical Page Layout
(four frame levels on each page)

PLAYING THE GAME

The most important point to keep in mind is that the twelve questions for each game are *not* read from the top of the page to the bottom. Rather, they are found on the same frame level on succeeding pages. Let me help make this clearer with an example and some accompanying graphics.

Let's start with Game #1, which begins in the *top frame* of page 1—a *right-hand* page. Here, you will find the name and number of the game you are about to play.

Turn the page and look at the next *right-hand* page (page 3) for the game's first question, which is located on the left side of the *top frame* (see graphic below).

So where's the answer to this question? Turn the page again and continue to look at the *top frame* of the next *right-hand* page (page 5). As shown below, the answer is located on the right side of the frame. On the left side of this frame, you'll find the second question of Game #1.

Question #1 is on
left side of top frame.

Answer to Question #1 is
on next right-hand page—
right side of top frame.

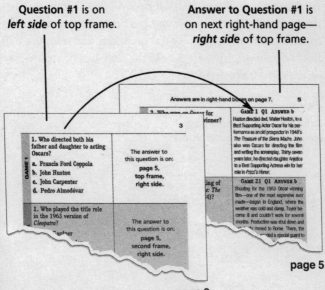

page 5

page 3

The answer to the first question of Game #1 is on the following right-hand page—and appears on the right side of the top frame. The left side of the top frame has the game's next question.

And that's how you continue—turning the page for each new question (Q), and finding its answer (A) on the following *right-hand* page (see graphic below).

Beginning with the top frame (*and staying in that top frame*), play the games, which flow from one *right-hand* page to the next until you have reached the last page. Then simply make a U-turn and continue playing the games—still in the top frame—from the back of the book to the front. While going in this direction, however, the answers to the questions will be found on consecutive *left-hand* pages.

Once you've completed the games in the top frame from the front of the book to the back, and then from the back to the front again, you'll find yourself back on page 1. Simply drop down one level to the next frame and begin playing the games found on this new level. Again, questions and answers will flow from one right-hand page to the next. Just be sure to stay on the same frame level.

Individual games are always played on the same frame level.

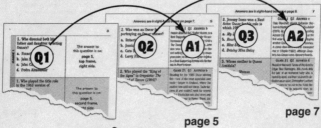

Progression of Questions and Answers

THERE'S HELP ON EVERY PAGE . . .

To be absolutely sure there's no confusion while playing the games, helpful instructions are provided on each and every page. Trust me, once you get the hang of it, you're going to love it. So kick back and get ready to be entertained, amused, and enlightened by these challenging movie questions and their fascinating fact-filled answers.

Have fun,

Fred Willard

Fred Willard

LET THE GAMES BEGIN . . .

GAME 1
Award Winners

Turn to page 3
for the first question
of Game 1.

GAME 21
Kings and Queens

Turn to page 3
for the first question
of Game 21.

GAME 41
Remakes

Turn to page 3
for the first question
of Game 41.

GAME 61
Family Flicks

Turn to page 3
for the first question
of Game 61.

**Game 21
begins on page 1,
second frame
from the top.**

GAME 20 Q12 ANSWER c
This semi-fictional crime film is told through the eyes of Henry Hill (Ray Liotta)—Brooklyn-born member of a New York crime family. The story is based on real people and events, including the 1978 Lufthansa heist at JFK airport. Of the film's six Oscar nominations, Joe Pesci was the sole winner for his portrayal of hot-tempered Tommy DeVito.

**Game 41
begins on page 1,
third frame
from the top.**

GAME 40 Q12 ANSWER c
To date, Streep has garnered sixteen Oscar nominations, putting her in the lead. (Both Jack Nicholson and Katharine Hepburn are next in line with twelve.) The legendary actress has won twice, receiving the Supporting Actress Oscar for *Kramer vs Kramer* and the Best Actress Oscar for *Sophie's Choice*. Her first nomination was for *The Deer Hunter*.

**Game 61
begins on page 1,
bottom frame.**

GAME 60 Q12 ANSWER b
Inspector Harry Callahan (Clint Eastwood) pursues the sadistic Scorpio in this first of five films in the Dirty Harry series. The villainous character was so frightening and so hated by audiences that the actor who played him, Andy Robinson, received several death threats after the film was released.

**Well, that's all, folks!
Let's play again
sometime . . .**

GAME 80 Q12 ANSWER a
Judi Dench began her career on the stage of London's Old Vic theater. Her movie roles were few in number until she portrayed M in a series of James Bond films, but between 1998 and 2007, Dench not only landed many film roles, but also earned six Oscar nominations. Dench's work in *Chocolat* resulted in one of those nominations, but not in a win.

GAME 1

1. Who directed both his father and daughter to acting Oscars?

a. Francis Ford Coppola
b. John Huston
c. John Carpenter
d. Pedro Almodóvar

The answer to this question is on:

**page 5,
top frame,
right side.**

GAME 21

1. Who played the title role in the 1963 version of *Cleopatra*?

a. Ava Gardner
b. Elizabeth Taylor
c. Claudette Colbert
d. Audrey Hepburn

The answer to this question is on:

**page 5,
second frame,
right side.**

GAME 41

1. In which movie remake does Lindsay Lohan play dual roles?

a. *Freaky Friday* (2003)
b. *The Parent Trap* (1998)
c. *Cheaper by the Dozen* (2003)
d. *Little Women* (2001)

The answer to this question is on:

**page 5,
third frame,
right side.**

GAME 61

1. Who takes an ill-fated trip in *National Lampoon's Vacation*?

a. The Griswolds
b. The Oglethorpes
c. The Westerbergs
d. The Hopkins

The answer to this question is on:

**page 5,
bottom frame,
right side.**

4 Answers are in right-hand boxes on page 2.

GAME 20

12. Which Martin Scorsese film is based on the book *Wiseguy* by Nicholas Pileggi?

a. *Mean Streets* (1973)
b. *Casino* (1995)
c. *Goodfellas* (1990)
d. *Gangs of New York* (2002)

GAME 20 Q11 ANSWER d
Telly Savalas and Clint Walker played these two members of the Dirty Dozen— a group of twelve convicted murderers recruited for a World War II suicide mission. When actor Trini Lopez (one of the "Dozen") demanded more money during filming, director Robert Aldrich had an immediate off-screen death scene written into the script for his character.

GAME 40

12. For which movie did Meryl Streep win her first Oscar?

a. *Sophie's Choice* (1982)
b. *The Deer Hunter* (1978)
c. *Kramer vs Kramer* (1979)
d. *Out of Africa* (1985)

GAME 40 Q11 ANSWER b
For her portrayal of Tessa Quayle, Weisz received the Academy Award for Best Supporting Actress. An adaptation of John le Carré's 2001 novel of the same name, the film tells the story of a man's investigation of the murder of his young activist wife. The character of Tessa is based on Yvette Pierpaoli, a noted social activist who died in 1999.

GAME 60

12. Which Dirty Harry movie features the serial killer "Scorpio"?

a. *Magnum Force* (1973)
b. *Dirty Harry* (1971)
c. *Sudden Impact* (1983)
d. *The Enforcer* (1976)

GAME 60 Q11 ANSWER d
This critically acclaimed, commercially successful comedy about a jewel heist was co-written by John Cleese of Monty Python fame. Cleese also stars in the film with Jamie Lee Curtis, Michael Palin, and Kevin Kline as members of the bumbling gang of thieves. Kline won the Best Supporting Actor Oscar for his role as the fish-swallowing Otto West.

GAME 80

12. Who plays stubborn landlord Armande Voizin in the 2000 romance *Chocolat*?

a. Judi Dench
b. Helen Mirren
c. Juliette Binoche
d. Lena Olin

GAME 80 Q11 ANSWER c
With the goal of financing friend Jeff Slater's (Bill Murray's) play *Return to the Love Canal,* actor Michael Dorsey (Dustin Hoffman) disguises himself as actress Dorothy Michaels and lands a lucrative role in a soap opera. The catch is that even Dorsey's beautiful colleague Julie Nichols (Jessica Lange) cannot be told Dorothy's true identity.

GAME 1

2. Who won an Oscar for portraying an Oscar winner?

a. Robert Downey, Jr.
b. Jessica Lange
c. Cate Blanchett
d. Larry Parks

GAME 1 Q1 ANSWER b
Huston directed dad, Walter Huston, to a Best Supporting Actor Oscar for his performance as an old prospector in 1948's *The Treasure of the Sierra Madre*. John also won Oscars for directing the film and writing the screenplay. Thirty-seven years later, he directed daughter Anjelica to a Best Supporting Actress win for her role in *Prizzi's Honor*.

GAME 21

2. Who played the "King of the Apes" in *Greystoke: The Legend of Tarzan* (1984)?

a. Casper Van Dien
b. Miles O'Keefe
c. Ron Ely
d. Christopher Lambert

GAME 21 Q1 ANSWER b
Shooting for the 1963 Oscar-winning film—one of the most expensive ever made—began in England, where the weather was cold and damp. Taylor became ill and couldn't work for several months. Production was shut down and eventually moved to Rome. There, the female extras needed a special guard to protect them from amorous Italian men.

GAME 41

2. Which American remake of a French film stars Richard Gere?

a. *Dangerous Liasons* (1988)
b. *Men Don't Leave* (1990)
c. *Twelve Monkeys* (1995)
d. *Breathless* (1983)

GAME 41 Q1 ANSWER b
Lohan plays twins who conspire to bring their divorced parents back together in this remake of the 1961 film of the same name. The original, based on the book *Lottie and Lisa* by Erich Kästner, stars Hayley Mills as the twins. The remake was the directorial debut for screenwriter Nancy Meyers and the first movie role for the twelve-year-old Lohan.

GAME 61

2. What song does Haley Mills sing in the original *Parent Trap* (1961)?

a. "Twins Are In"
b. "Let's Get Together"
c. "Seeing Double"
d. "Undeniably Identical"

GAME 61 Q1 ANSWER a
In the original screenplay of this 1983 flick, the Griswolds traveled to Disney World, but Disney executives objected to the film's negative portrayal of their theme park. For that reason, the identity of the park was changed to the fictional Walley World, and most park scenes were actually shot at Six Flags Magic Mountain in Los Angeles.

GAME 20

11. Archer Maggott and Samson Posey were members of which famous movie group?

a. *The Wild Bunch* (1969)

b. *Kelly's Heroes* (1970)

c. *The Magnificent Seven* (1960)

d. *The Dirty Dozen* (1967)

GAME 20 Q10 ANSWER d
Danny (played by Michael O'Keefe) forfeits his chance of a scholarship by helping a wealthy lout win a golf bet in this silly comedy. The story was inspired by the caddying experiences of writer Brian Doyle-Murray when he was a kid. His brother, Bill Murray, who has a role in the movie, and the film's director, Harold Ramis, also caddied as teenagers.

GAME 40

11. For which movie did Rachel Weisz win an acting Oscar?

a. *About a Boy* (2002)

b. *The Constant Gardener* (2005)

c. *Enemy at the Gates* (2001)

d. *Stealing Beauty* (1996)

GAME 40 Q10 ANSWER d
The granddaughter of novelist Ernest Hemingway, Mariel made her film debut with sister Margaux in 1976's *Lipstick*. But her most famous role to date is that of the beautiful (but very young) Tracy in Woody Allen's acclaimed romantic comedy, *Manhattan*. In fact, Mariel's performance won her an Oscar nomination for Best Actress in a Supporting Role.

GAME 60

11. In which film does Kevin Kline eat a tankful of tropical fish?

a. *The January Man* (1989)

b. *The Big Chill* (1983)

c. *I Love You to Death* (1990)

d. *A Fish Called Wanda* (1988)

GAME 60 Q10 ANSWER b
Karen Allen plays Indiana's sometime lover in Steven Spielberg's 1981 *Raiders of the Lost Ark*. In 2008's *Kingdom of the Crystal Skull*, she surprises Indiana with the news that Mutt Williams, his movie sidekick, is their son. It was Allen's role in 1978's *Animal House* that caught the eye of Spielberg, who cast her as the spirited *Raiders* heroine.

GAME 80

11. What is the subject of Bill Murray's play in the 1982 comedy *Tootsie*?

a. The Dust Bowl

b. The Great Depression

c. The Love Canal

d. Three Mile Island

GAME 80 Q10 ANSWER d
When Carell won the part of Uncle Frank, he was relatively unknown in the movie industry, and the film's producers worried about his lack of star power. But between the time that *Little Miss Sunshine* was filmed and its 2006 release, Carell appeared in the box office hit *The 40 Year Old Virgin* (2005), making the actor a hot Hollywood property.

GAME 1

3. Jeremy Irons won a Best Actor Oscar for his role in which 1990 film?

a. *My Left Foot*

b. *Reversal of Fortune*

c. *Blue Sky*

d. *Driving Miss Daisy*

GAME 1 Q2 ANSWER c

Cate Blanchett played Katharine Hepburn in Martin Scorsese's film *The Aviator* (2004). By winning the Best Supporting Actress Oscar, she made history as the first actor to win an Oscar by portraying *another* Oscar winner. Robert Downey, Jr. came close with his Oscar-*nominated* role in *Chaplin* (1992), although Chaplin's two Oscars were *Honorary* Awards.

GAME 21

3. Whose mother is Queen Amidala?

a. Wonder Woman

b. Luke Skywalker

c. Flash Gordon

d. Darth Vader

GAME 21 Q2 ANSWER d

Based on the novel *Tarzan of the Apes* by Edgar Rice Burroughs, this movie tells the tale of an orphaned baby who is raised by apes, and then returned to civilization as an adult. Christopher Lambert (best known for his role in the 1986 film *Highlander* and its sequels) stars as Tarzan, although interestingly, the name Tarzan is never used in the film.

GAME 41

3. In which film is Clark Gable cast as a big game hunter?

a. *Mogambo* (1953)

b. *Maracaibo* (1958)

c. *Topkapi* (1964)

d. *Elephant Walk* (1954)

GAME 41 Q2 ANSWER d

Jean-Luc Godard's 1959 film *À Bout de Souffle* is set in Paris and stars Jean-Paul Belmondo and Jean Seberg as a French criminal and his American girlfriend. The 1983 remake is set in LA and stars Gere and Valérie Kaprisky as an American criminal and his French girlfriend. Gere also stars in 1993's *Somersby*, another remake of a French film.

GAME 61

3. Who directed the 1989 film *Parenthood*?

a. Rob Reiner

b. Nora Ephron

c. Steven Spielberg

d. Ron Howard

GAME 61 Q2 ANSWER b

Written by brothers Robert and Richard Sherman, "Let's Get Together" was sung as a duet by *Parent Trap* characters Sharon and Susan—both of whom were played by Haley Mills. When the song debuted as a single, it quickly became a Top 10 hit. This led to a brief recording career for Mills, who was to produce only one other hit tune, "Johnny Jingo."

GAME 20

10. Danny is a squeaky clean young man who hopes to earn a college scholarship in:

a. *Pretty in Pink* (1986)

b. *Ferris Bueller's Day Off* (1986)

c. *The Breakfast Club* (1985)

d. *Caddyshack* (1980)

GAME 20 Q9 ANSWER b
They played father and son in this story about a family living on a Montana Ranch in the early 1900s. A year after *Legends*, both men were nominated for Oscars—Hopkins for the title role in *Nixon* (he lost to Nicolas Cage for *Leaving Las Vegas*), and Pitt for his supporting role in *Twelve Monkeys* (he lost to Kevin Spacey for *The Usual Suspects*).

GAME 40

10. Who plays Woody Allen's school-age girlfriend in 1979's *Manhattan*?

a. Uma Thurman

b. Mira Sorvino

c. Christina Ricci

d. Mariel Hemingway

GAME 40 Q9 ANSWER b
In this sequel to 1984's *The Terminator*, Robert Patrick is the shape-shifting android antagonist. The T-1000—considered a technological leap over the 800-Series Terminator, portrayed by Arnold Schwarzenegger—was voted one of the top 100 villains of all time by the Online Film Critics Society.

GAME 60

10. Which film character's love interest is Marion Ravenwood?

a. Butch Cassidy

b. Indiana Jones

c. Mr. Chips

d. Allan Quatermain

GAME 60 Q9 ANSWER d
This epic film starring Peter O'Toole is based on the life of Thomas Edward Lawrence, a British Army official who was instrumental in leading an Arab revolt against the Turks during WWI. Considered a cinematic masterpiece, the movie won seven Oscars, including Best Picture and Best Director (David Lean). O'Toole received a Best Actor nod.

GAME 80

10. Who plays Abigail Breslin's troubled uncle in *Little Miss Sunshine*?

a. Greg Kinnear

b. Paul Dano

c. Alan Arkin

d. Steve Carell

GAME 80 Q9 ANSWER b
Although Perkins is best known for his role in Alfred Hitchcock's 1960 classic *Psycho*, he appeared in dozens of films, as well as on stage. In *Friendly Persuasion*, Perkins plays Josh Birdwell, a young man who must choose between the pacifist teachings of his Quaker community and the need to protect his home against invading Confederate soldiers.

GAME 1

4. Which *Rosemary's Baby* actor won an Oscar for his/her work in the film?

a. Ruth Gordon
b. Mia Farrow
c. John Cassavetes
d. Ralph Bellamy

GAME 1 Q3 ANSWER b
Running that year against heavyweight Robert De Niro for his Oscar-nominated performance in Penny Marshall's film *Awakenings*, Jeremy Irons won the award for his icy portrayal of wealthy British socialite Claus von Bülow (who was accused of trying to kill his wife). This film also received an Oscar nomination for Best Director (Barbet Schroeder).

GAME 21

4. In which country does the 1956 musical *The King and I* take place?

a. Nepal
b. Persia
c. Singapore
d. Siam

GAME 21 Q3 ANSWER b
Natalie Portman debuted as this "Star Wars" queen in *The Phantom Menace* (1999), with Hayden Christenson cast as her doomed husband, Anakin Skywalker. Portman had appeared in her first feature film at age thirteen, and was still so young when *Phantom Menace* was made that she had to miss the New York premiere party to study for her high school finals.

GAME 41

4. Which Martin Scorsese film is a remake?

a. *Casino* (1995)
b. *The Aviator* (2004)
c. *Cape Fear* (1991)
d. *Taxi Driver* (1976)

GAME 41 Q3 ANSWER a
Mogambo is a remake of 1932's *Red Dust*, and Gable stars as the male lead in both films—despite the twenty-one year span between them! He stars with Jean Harlow in *Red Dust*, which takes place on a rubber plantation in Indochina, and with Ava Gardner in *Mogambo*, which is set in Kenya. For her role, Gardner received a Best Actress Oscar nod.

GAME 61

4. What is the name of Macaulay Culkin's character in *Home Alone*?

a. Tommy
b. Justin
c. Mark
d. Kevin

GAME 61 Q3 ANSWER d
The storyline of *Parenthood* was partly based on the parenting experiences of director Ron Howard, screenwriters Lowell Ganz and Babaloo Mandel, and film producer Brian Grazer. The resulting comedy-drama touched parents and singles alike. In fact, it was so well received by both viewers and critics that so far, it has generated two TV adaptations.

GAME 20

9. Which film united Anthony Hopkins and Brad Pitt?

a. *The Bounty* (1984)

b. *Legends of the Fall* (1994)

c. *A River Runs Through It* (1992)

d. *Bram Stoker's Dracula* (1992)

GAME 20 Q8 ANSWER d
John Goodman portrayed the legendary baseball great George Herman "Babe" Ruth in the 1992 film *The Babe*. William Bendix played him in the *The Babe Ruth Story* (1948). Also nicknamed "the Great Bambino," Ruth appeared as himself in *Pride of the Yankees* (1942), and in a number of 1930s movie shorts including *Home Run on the Keys.*

GAME 40

9. Which film features a liquid metal killing machine called the T-1000?

a. *Total Recall* (1990)

b. *Terminator 2: Judgment Day* (1991)

c. *RoboCop* (1987)

d. *Aliens* (1986)

GAME 40 Q8 ANSWER c
Audrey Hepburn plays the charming gold digger in 1961's *Breakfast at Tiffany's*, which was adapted from the Truman Capote novella of the same name. Holly Golightly is considered Hepburn's most memorable and identifiable role—a role for which she received a Best Actress Oscar nomination. She lost that year to Sophia Loren for her role in *Two Women.*

GAME 60

9. In which film are there no females in credited roles?

a. *Cool Hand Luke* (1967)

b. *The Shawshank Redemption* (1994)

c. *The Dirty Dozen* (1967)

d. *Lawrence of Arabia* (1962)

GAME 60 Q8 ANSWER b
In this Ridley Scott film starring Harrison Ford and Rutger Hauer, blade runners are retired police assassins who destroy dangerous cyborgs called "replicants." After *Blade Runner's* release, many of the companies whose logos appeared in the film experienced some form of bad luck. This gave rise to what became known as the "Blade Runner Curse."

GAME 80

9. Which film cast Anthony Perkins as a reluctant Civil War soldier?

a. *The Red Badge of Courage* (1951)

b. *Friendly Persuasion* (1956)

c. *Five Miles to Midnight* (1962)

d. *Shenandoah* (1965)

GAME 80 Q8 ANSWER b
As the daughter of TV actress Majorie Lord and film and TV actor John Archer, Anne Archer grew up in and around show business. Her portrayal of the long-suffering Beth won her an Academy Award nomination for Best Actress in a Supporting Role, but the Oscar went to Olympia Dukakis for her performance in 1987's romantic comedy *Moonstruck.*

GAME 1

5. Which movie's entire cast was nominated for Oscars?

a. *The War of the Worlds* (2005)

b. *Camille* (1936)

c. *Queen Christina* (1933)

d. *Sleuth* (1972)

GAME 1 Q4 ANSWER a
Ruth Gordon spent many years writing Hollywood screenplays with her husband and fellow writer Garson Kanin (including the Oscar-nominated 1949 "Tracy and Hepburn" comedy *Adam's Rib*). She finally won a Best Supporting Actress Oscar for her role as tacky Satan-worshipping neighbor Mrs. Minnie Castevet in this 1968 chiller.

GAME 21

5. In *The Princess Diaries 2* (2004), what must Mia do before becoming queen?

a. Study law at Princeton

b. Live a year in a convent

c. Travel around the world

d. Get married

GAME 21 Q4 ANSWER d
Yul Brynner won the Oscar for his role as the King of Siam in this film classic (as well as a Tony for the stage version). The movie is banned in Thailand (formerly Siam) due to historical inaccuracies and perceived disrespect to the monarchy. In 1999, Chow Yun-Fat played the King in *Anna and the King*—an updated movie version starring Jodie Foster.

GAME 41

5. Which singer stars in the 1980 remake of *The Jazz Singer*?

a. Kenny Rogers

b. Neil Diamond

c. Kris Kristofferson

d. Neil Sedaka

GAME 41 Q4 ANSWER c
Robert De Niro received an Oscar nomination for his role as Max Cady, the out-for-revenge ex-con, in this remake of the 1962 film of the same name. Robert Mitchum plays the evil Cady in the original. Another Scorsese remake is his 2006 multiple Oscar winner *The Departed*—a remake of the 2002 Hong Kong crime thriller *Infernal Affairs*.

GAME 61

5. Which comedy features a dad who cross-dresses in order to see his children?

a. *Dave* (1993)

b. *The Sure Thing* (1985)

c. *Mrs. Doubtfire* (1993)

d. *What About Bob?* (1991)

GAME 61 Q4 ANSWER d
The idea for this 1990 flick was born during the filming of *Uncle Buck* (1989), when director John Hughes watched Culkin perform a deadpan interrogation through a mail slot. Even though the part of Kevin was created for Culkin, *Home Alone* director Chris Columbus auditioned hundreds of other children before deciding that Culkin was the best choice.

GAME 20

8. Which real person has been portrayed on film by John Goodman and William Bendix?

a. Henry VIII

b. William Howard Taft

c. Huey Long

d. Babe Ruth

GAME 20 Q7 ANSWER c
Robert De Niro earned an Oscar nomination portraying Cady, the obsessed tormentor of Sam Bowden (played by Nick Nolte). Robert Mitchum played Cady in the original *Cape Fear* (1962) and returned in the remake as Lieutenant Elgart. Gregory Peck starred in the original movie as Bowden and played Cady's lawyer in the 1991 version.

GAME 40

8. Pearls and cigarette holders are hallmarks of which screen character?

a. Dolly Levi

b. Kitty Foyle

c. Holly Golightly

d. Annie Hall

GAME 40 Q7 ANSWER b
Norton's Smoochy the Rhino (a parody of Barney the Dinosaur) is hired to replace corrupt children's TV show host Rainbow Ralph (Robin Williams) when it becomes known that Ralph has been accepting bribes from parents. Danny DeVito directed and starred in this 2002 dark comedy, which was widely panned by critics and a box office flop.

GAME 60

8. In the futuristic 1982 film, what is a *Blade Runner*?

a. A clone

b. A bounty hunter

c. A gangster

d. A prisoner of war

GAME 60 Q7 ANSWER c
In *Mad Max* (1979), Max seeks revenge on a gang that attacks his wife, son, and a friend. In *Cape Fear* (1962, 1991) a criminal seeks revenge on his lawyer for overlooking a piece of evidence that may have prevented his conviction. In *Death Wish* (1974), a man becomes a vigilante after street thugs murder his wife and rape his daughter.

GAME 80

8. Who plays betrayed wife Beth Gallagher in 1987's *Fatal Attraction*?

a. Debra Winger

b. Anne Archer

c. Kelly McGillis

d. Glenn Close

GAME 80 Q7 ANSWER a
A parody of the Q and M characters in the James Bond films, agent Basil Exposition provides Austin Powers (Mike Myers) with his missions and gives him all kinds of remarkable gadgets, such as a time machine car. According to the 2002 film *Austin Powers in Goldmember*, Powers and Exposition met while attending the British Intelligence Academy.

GAME 1

6. Which of these Oscar-winning films is about a fictional character?

a. *The Last Emperor* (1987)

b. *Lawrence of Arabia* (1962)

c. *A Man for All Seasons* (1966)

d. *Ben-Hur* (1959)

GAME 1 Q5 ANSWER d
"Sir" Michael Caine and "Sir" Laurence Olivier were the only cast members in this 1972 film based on Anthony Shaffer's play and directed by multiple Oscar-winner Joseph L. Mankiewicz. Both actors cancelled each other out for Oscars, as the Best Actor award went to Jack Lemmon for his role in the drama *Save the Tiger*.

GAME 21

6. Who had the title role in the 2006 film *Marie Antoinette*?

a. Kiera Knightly

b. Kate Winslet

c. Ann Hathaway

d. Kirsten Dunst

GAME 21 Q5 ANSWER d
In this sequel to the 2001 film, Anne Hathaway reprises her role as Princess Mia. The movie features the first singing performance in seven years by Julie Andrews, who had throat surgery in 1997. Because Hathaway was committed to the film, she couldn't take the role of Christine in a 2004 movie adaptation of *Phantom of the Opera*.

GAME 41

6. Which actress has *not* played the female lead in any *King Kong* films?

a. Fay Wray

b. Naomi Watts

c. Jessica Lange

d. Michelle Pfeiffer

GAME 41 Q5 ANSWER b
Diamond is the son of a Jewish cantor who breaks family tradition to become a pop singer in this second big-screen remake of the 1927 original—the first is the 1952 film with Danny Thomas. The original, starring Al Jolson, is noted for being the first full-length "talkie," which had sound-synchronized speech and singing sequences.

GAME 61

6. Who wrote the books on which *The Chronicles of Narnia* movies are based?

a. C.S. Lewis

b. Daniel Handler

c. Roald Dahl

d. J.K. Rowling

GAME 61 Q5 ANSWER c
In *Mrs. Doubtfire*, Robin Williams plays a divorced dad who disguises himself as a nanny so he can spend more time with his kids. Williams' makeup took about four and a half hours each day to complete, and included eight separate pieces to cover his face alone. The impressive results won the film a 1993 Academy Award for Best Makeup.

GAME 20

7. How is the evil Max Cady finally disposed of in the 1991 film *Cape Fear*?

a. Shot to death
b. Falls off a cliff
c. Drowns in a lake
d. Burns in a fire

GAME 20 Q6 ANSWER c
Starring Billy Bob Thornton as Coach Gary Gaines, this movie is based on the H.G. Bissinger book, which documents the small-town team from Odessa, Texas, as it makes a run for the 1988 State Championship. The film centers on the town's obsession with the team and its "win-at-all-costs" attitude. The movie led to the NBC series of the same name.

GAME 40

7. Who plays the fuchsia-colored rhino in *Death to Smoochy*?

a. Russell Crowe
b. Edward Norton
c. Eric Stoltz
d. Chris Tucker

GAME 40 Q6 ANSWER c
Hannah, who plays a mermaid in this romantic fantasy, takes the name from Madison Avenue while walking the streets of Manhattan. At the time, Madison was a relatively unknown girl's name, but its popularity has risen significantly since *Splash's* release. To date, it is one of the top ten names for girls born in the twenty-first century.

GAME 60

7. What theme is shared by *Mad Max, Cape Fear,* and *Death Wish*?

a. Unrequited love
b. Coming of age
c. Revenge
d. Time travel

GAME 60 Q6 ANSWER c
This epic Western has the unfortunate reputation of being one of the biggest film disasters in history. Its failure all but destroyed the credibility of director Michael Cimino, who was deemed self-indulgent and financially irresponsible. The film lost so much money, it lead to the sale of United Artists studio, which was purchased by MGM.

GAME 80

7. Who plays Basil Exposition in the *Austin Powers* film series?

a. Michael York
b. Michael Caine
c. Robert Wagner
d. Rob Lowe

GAME 80 Q6 ANSWER c
This Howard Hawks film introduced nineteen-year-old Lauren Bacall not only to moviegoers, but also to future husband Humphrey Bogart. Later Bogart-and-Bacall films would include *The Big Sleep* (1946), *Dark Passage* (1947), and *Key Largo* (1948). The two actors also made a closing-scene cameo in the 1946 comedy *Two Guys from Milwaukee*.

GAME 1

7. Marlee Matlin and Geena Davis each won Oscars starring opposite which actor?

a. Jeff Goldblum

b. Dustin Hoffman

c. Jimmy Fallon

d. William Hurt

GAME 1 Q6 ANSWER d
Judah Ben-Hur is the character of a novel published in 1880 by author Lewis Wallace. Charlton Heston won an Oscar for the title role in *Ben-Hur,* while Paul Scofield won an Oscar for his role as Sir Thomas More in *A Man for All Seasons.* Peter O'Toole played British general T.E. Lawrence in *Lawrence of Arabia.*

GAME 21

7. In the *Lord of the Rings* trilogy, who plays Galadriel, Queen of the Elves?

a. Emma Thompson

b. Cate Blanchett

c. Penelope Cruz

d. Liv Tyler

GAME 21 Q6 ANSWER d
Sofia Coppola, the film's writer and director, is the daughter of director Francis Ford Coppola. She cast a number of actors in the movie who are children of well-known people in the film industry, including Jason Schwartzman, who is the son of actress Talia Shire and producer Jack Schwartzman; and Danny Huston, the son of director John Huston.

GAME 41

7. *Heaven Can Wait* (1978) is a remake of which 1941 classic?

a. *Here Comes Mr. Jordan*

b. *Back Street*

c. *The Great Lie*

d. *Meet John Doe*

GAME 41 Q6 ANSWER d
The gigantic ape is smitten by Ann Darrow, a beautiful blond movie star, who meets Kong on Skull Island. In the original 1933 film, it is Fay Wray who plays Darrow. In the 1976 Dino De Laurentiis remake, Jessica Lange has the part in her first movie role. Naomi Watts befriends the big ape in the 2005 Peter Jackson-directed version.

GAME 61

7. From which country do the von Trapps escape in *The Sound of Music*?

a. Germany

b. Czechoslovakia

c. Austria

d. Italy

GAME 61 Q6 ANSWER a
C.S. Lewis wrote his fantasy novels about the Pevensie children during the 1950s. Lewis never wanted his books to be turned into films because he felt that no film could realistically represent the more fantastical elements of the stories. Permission to make the Disney Studio Narnia movies was provided by Douglas Gresham, one of Lewis's stepsons.

6. *Friday Night Lights* (2004) focuses on which high school football team?

a. South Kingstown Rebels
b. Compton Comets
c. Permian Panthers
d. Toledo Rockets

GAME 20 Q5 ANSWER b
Brody played screenwriter Jack Driscoll in this remake of the 1933 film (Jeff Bridges starred in a 1976 version). Director Peter Jackson's only choice for the role, Brody signed a contract before the script was completed. He also did his own stunt driving. The movie won three Oscars and became one of Universal Pictures highest grossing films.

6. What's the name of Daryl Hannah's character in *Splash* (1984)?

a. Taylor
b. Diandra
c. Madison
d. Veronica

GAME 40 Q5 ANSWER c
In *Phone Booth*, Farrell's character answers a call in a public phone booth, and is subsequently held hostage by a sniper. The movie, which was set to be released in November 2002, was pushed back to April 2003. This was because of the "Beltway Sniper" attacks, which had just occurred in October 2002 in Virginia, Maryland, and Washington, DC.

6. Which 1980's flop stars Christopher Walken and Kris Kristofferson?

a. *Howard the Duck* (1986)
b. *Ishtar* (1987)
c. *Heaven's Gate* (1980)
d. *Shanghai Surprise* (1986)

GAME 60 Q5 ANSWER c
She plays the two-timing Lori, who is out to kill her secret agent husband in this science fiction-action film. Stone's grueling training for the role resulted in her induction into the Stunt Woman Association as an honorary member. Shwarzenegger was so impressed with how diligently she trained, he would refer to her as the "Female Terminator."

6. Which film features the line, "You know how to whistle, don't you, Steve"?

a. *Dark Passage* (1947)
b. *Key Largo* (1948)
c. *To Have and Have Not* (1944)
d. *The Big Sleep* (1946)

GAME 80 Q5 ANSWER c
Max Steiner, the Vienna-born composer of *Gone With the Wind's* memorable score, worked in Hollywood from the 1930s through the 1960s. Other well-known films that feature a Steiner score include *Now, Voyager* (1942), *Casablanca* (1942), *The Treasure of the Sierra Madre* (1948), *The Caine Mutiny* (1954), and *A Summer Place* (1959).

GAME 1

8. Helen Hunt won the 1998 Best Actress Oscar for her performance in which film?

a. *Cast Away*

b. *Twister*

c. *As Good As It Gets*

d. *What Women Want*

GAME 1 Q7 ANSWER d
Marlee Matlin won a Best Actress Oscar opposite William Hurt in *Children of a Lesser God* (1986), while Geena Davis won a Best Supporting Actress Oscar opposite Hurt in writer/director Lawrence Kasdan's film *The Accidental Tourist* (1988). That film also featured actress Kathleen Turner, Hurt's costar from Kasdan's 1981 film *Body Heat*.

GAME 21

8. Which "King" movie centers on the character Rupert Pupkin?

a. *King Creole* (1958)

b. *King of Kings* (1961)

c. *The King of Comedy* (1982)

d. *The Lion King* (1994)

GAME 21 Q7 ANSWER b
Blanchett claimed that her favorite part of playing Galadriel was wearing the pointed elf ears. In fact, she has jokingly said it's the reason she took the role! After completing the trilogy, she had the ears bronzed. (Eary, no?) A seasoned Oscar-nominated actress, Blanchett won the award for her portrayal of Katharine Hepburn in *The Aviator* (2004).

GAME 41

8. Which "blue" movie was the remake of an earlier film?

a. *Blue Hawaii* (1961)

b. *The Blue Lagoon* (1980)

c. *Blue Velvet* (1986)

d. *Blue Thunder* (1983)

GAME 41 Q7 ANSWER a
The movie, based on the play *Heaven Can Wait* by Harry Segall, stars Robert Montgomery as a boxer who is taken to heaven before his time. The film led to the 1947 sequel *Down to Earth* and two remakes—1978's *Heaven Can Wait,* starring Warren Beatty, and 2001's *Down to Earth,* starring Chris Rock. It also inspired the hit TV series *Quantum Leap.*

GAME 61

8. Which movie is *not* composed of computer-generated graphics?

a. *A Bug's Life* (1998)

b. *Lilo & Stitch* (2002)

c. *Finding Nemo* (2003)

d. *Monsters, Inc.* (2001)

GAME 61 Q7 ANSWER c
In the 1965 movie, the von Trapps hike across the Alps to Switzerland, but this would have been geographically impossible; they would have ended up in Germany instead. The real von Trapps simply took a train to Italy since Captain von Trapp was also an Italian citizen. The family eventually traveled to the US and settled in Stowe, Vermont.

GAME 20

5. Who starred in the 2005 hit remake of *King Kong*?

a. Keanu Reeves
b. Adrien Brody
c. Jeff Bridges
d. Johnny Depp

GAME 20 Q4 ANSWER a
NBA star Ray Allen plays Jesus, the top US college basketball recruit. Denzel Washington plays his father, who is let out of prison to convince Jesus to sign with the governor's alma mater. Washington has also appeared in two other Spike Lee films—*Mo' Better Blues* and *Malcolm X*, for which he received a Best Actor Oscar nomination.

GAME 40

5. Where does Colin Farrell get trapped in the 2003 film of the same name?

a. Elevator
b. Coal mine
c. Phone booth
d. Bus

GAME 40 Q4 ANSWER d
Laurie received a Best Actress Oscar nomination for her portrayal of Sarah Packard. After taking a fifteen-year break, Laurie returned to the big screen in 1976's *Carrie*, scoring a Supporting Actress Oscar nod for her role as Carrie's mother. She earned another nomination in the same category for 1987's *Children of a Lesser God*.

GAME 60

5. Who plays Arnold Schwarzenegger's wife in 1990's *Total Recall*?

a. Kim Basinger
b. Annette Bening
c. Sharon Stone
d. Marisa Tomei

GAME 60 Q4 ANSWER b
She is the sexy ukulele-playing member of an all-girl band in this Billy Wilder comedy classic, which also stars Tony Curtis and Jack Lemmon. During filming, Monroe reportedly had a hard time remembering her lines, so they had to be displayed off-camera. In 2000, the American Film Institute ranked *Some Like It Hot* #1 on its list of best comedies.

GAME 80

5. Which film includes the musical composition known as "Tara's Theme"?

a. *Doctor Zhivago* (1965)
b. *Breakfast at Tiffany's* (1961)
c. *Gone With the Wind* (1939)
d. *Casablanca* (1942)

GAME 80 Q4 ANSWER d
The husband-stealing character Addie Ross never appears on camera, but her voice is heard a number of times as a means of narration. Celeste Holm's work as the voice-over actress was uncredited, and 20th Century Fox kept it a secret when the film was released so that the studio could promote the movie by holding "Who is Addie?" contests.

GAME 1

9. Which screwball comedy won the Best Director Oscar for Leo McCarey in 1937?

a. *Bringing Up Baby*
b. *The Awful Truth*
c. *It Happened One Night*
d. *The Lady Eve*

GAME 1 Q8 ANSWER c
Hunt won the Oscar for her work in this heartwarming film from James L. Brooks, who won three Oscars for producing, directing, and writing the 1984 feature film *Terms of Endearment. As Good as It Gets* also won a Best Actor Oscar for Jack Nicholson and a Best Supporting Actor Oscar nomination for Greg Kinnear.

GAME 21

9. Who provided the voice of Queen Lillian in *Shrek 2* and *Shrek the Third*?

a. Susan Sarandon
b. Barbra Streisand
c. Carrie Fisher
d. Julie Andrews

GAME 21 Q8 ANSWER c
In this dark Martin Scorsese film, Robert De Niro is the pathetic Pupkin, whose dream to be a stand-up comic causes him to kidnap comedian Jerry Langford (Jerry Lewis). During filming, De Niro made a slew of anti-Semitic remarks to provoke Lewis's anger (a method-acting trick). Initially, Lewis was appalled, but it resulted in his credible performance.

GAME 41

9. In 2001's *Ocean's 11* remake, which casino was *not* targeted in the heist?

a. Bellaggio
b. Sands
c. Mirage
d. MGM Grand

GAME 41 Q8 ANSWER b
The film, starring Brooke Shields and Christopher Atkins as two children shipwrecked on an tropical island, is a remake of the 1949 film of the same name starring Jean Simmons and Donald Houston. Both are based on the novel *The Blue Lagoon* by Henry De Vere Stacpoole. Conservative groups criticized the film for its nudity and teen sexuality.

GAME 61

9. Who narrates the story of the Hanson family in 1948's *I Remember Mama*?

a. Irene Dunne
b. Barbara Bel Geddes
c. June Hedin
d. Peggy McIntyre

GAME 61 Q8 ANSWER b
Produced by Walt Disney Pictures, *Lilo & Stitch*—which is about a girl (Lilo) who adopts a fugitive alien (Stitch) from an animal shelter—uses not only traditional hand-drawn animation, but also hand-painted watercolor backgrounds, which hadn't been employed in years. The resulting film received a positive response from both moviegoers and critics.

GAME 20

4. In which Spike Lee movie is the lead character Jesus Shuttlesworth?

a. *He Got Game* (1998)

b. *Jungle Fever* (1998)

c. *Do the Right Thing* (1989)

d. *Crooklyn* (1999)

GAME 20 Q3 ANSWER c
In the psychological thriller *One Hour Photo,* Williams plays Seymour "Sy" Parrish, who becomes obsessed with a young suburban family after developing their pictures. Jack Nicholson was first asked to play the role, but turned it down. Williams, who had initially been cast as the store manager, requested the part of Sy after rereading the script.

GAME 40

4. Who played Paul Newman's girlfriend in 1961's *The Hustler*?

a. Anne Francis

b. Ann-Margret

c. Tuesday Weld

d. Piper Laurie

GAME 40 Q3 ANSWER a
The often turbulent relationship between an aging professor and his daughter is explored by acting legend Henry Fonda and real-life daughter Jane in this 1981 film. For his distinguished performance, Fonda won his only Oscar, which he received shortly before his death. Jane accepted the award for her dad, who was too ill to attend the ceremony.

GAME 60

4. Who is Marilyn Monroe's character in 1959's *Some Like It Hot*?

a. Cherry Red

b. Sugar Kane

c. Lorelei Lee

d. Holly Golightly

GAME 60 Q3 ANSWER d
The film is based on a real Pennsylvania crime family that operated in the 1960s and 1970s. Walken plays the leader of the crew, whose estranged son, played by Sean Penn, becomes an informant against him. Penn's real-life brother, Chris Penn, plays his brother in the film, and actress Eileen Ryan (their real-life mom), is cast as their grandmother.

GAME 80

4. Who provides the voice of Addie Ross in 1949's *A Letter to Three Wives*?

a. Anne Baxter

b. Bette Davis

c. Lauren Bacall

d. Celeste Holm

GAME 80 Q3 ANSWER a
In his debut film role, McQueen—then billed as Steven McQueen—plays Steve Andrews, a creative thinker who decides to freeze the blob with carbon dioxide before it can finish eating the town. Despite this intriguing plot, it was not until McQueen starred in the late-1950s TV show *Wanted: Dead or Alive* that *The Blob* became a popular drive-in movie.

10. Warner Baxter won a Best Actor Oscar in 1929 playing what adventure hero?

a. Allan Quatermain

b. The Cisco Kid

c. Tarzan

d. John Carter

GAME 1 Q9 ANSWER b

This was the first of two Best Director Oscars that McCarey won in his career—he won again in 1944 for the Bing Crosby picture *Going My Way*. Earlier in his career, Leo McCarey brought together Laurel & Hardy as a comedy duo and directed the Marx Brothers in their classic 1933 film *Duck Soup*.

10. Who played King Arthur in the 1975 film *Monty Python and the Holy Grail*?

a. Graham Chapman

b. John Cleese

c. Eric Idle

d. Terry Gilliam

GAME 21 Q9 ANSWER d

Although the talented Julie Andrews isn't a queen in real life, she was named a Dame by Queen Elizabeth II on New Year's Eve 1999. Early in her career, she was cast in the title role of the 1964 Disney movie *Mary Poppins*—and earned an Oscar for it. In *Shrek the Third*, her character hums "A Spoonful of Sugar"—a popular *Mary Poppins* song.

10. *Against All Odds* (1984) is a remake of which classic film noir?

a. *Out of the Past* (1947)

b. *The Big Sleep* (1946)

c. *Touch of Evil* (1958)

d. *Crisscross* (1949)

GAME 41 Q9 ANSWER b

The Sands was one of the casinos targeted in the original 1950 film starring "Rat Packers" Frank Sinatra, Dean Martin, Sammy Davis, Jr., Peter Lawford, and Joey Bishop. When Lawford, who owned the rights to the story, first told Sinatra of the movie possibility, supposedly Sinatra joked, "Forget the movie, let's pull the job!"

10. What kind of candy does E.T. eat in *E.T.: The Extra-Terrestrial* (1982)?

a. M&M's

b. Skittles

c. Raisinets

d. Reese's Pieces

GAME 61 Q9 ANSWER b

Playing Katrin Hanson, the eldest daughter of "Mama" Marta Hanson, Bel Geddes narrates this charming story of a Norwegian family living in San Francisco at the start of the twentieth century. Irene Dunne has the role of the wise and loving mother, and Peggy McIntyre and June Hedin portray Katrin's younger sisters, Christine and Dagmar.

22 Answers are in right-hand boxes on page 20.

GAME 20

3. Who had a 2002 film role as a creepy photo lab technician?

a. Jack Nicholson
b. Gary Busey
c. Robin Williams
d. Nick Nolte

GAME 20 Q2 ANSWER d
Danny DeVito and Michelle Pfeiffer play the two "baddies." In *Batman,* Jack Nicholson is the Joker, while Heath Ledger portrays a dark version of his character in *The Dark Knight*—a role that earned him a posthumous Oscar. Jim Carrey is the Riddler in *Batman Forever,* and Arnold Schwarzenneger is Mr. Freeze in *Batman & Robin.*

GAME 40

3. What was Henry Fonda's last movie?

a. *On Golden Pond*
b. *Midway*
c. *Meteor*
d. *Wanda Nevada*

GAME 40 Q2 ANSWER c
This time around, Kevin McCallister (Culkin) mistakenly boards a plane to New York as the rest of his family flies to Miami. Many actors from the first film reprised their roles in this 1992 sequel, including Joe Pesci and Daniel Stern as the villains. *Home Alone 2* was one of the year's most successful films, grossing over $350 million worldwide.

GAME 60

3. In which movie are Christopher Walken and Sean Penn father and son?

a. *Dead Man Walking* (1995)
b. *The Dead Zone* (1983)
c. *Murder One* (1988)
d. *At Close Range* (1986)

GAME 60 Q2 ANSWER a
This film details the famous 1974 heavyweight championship match between Muhammad Ali and George Foreman. Often cited as one of the best boxing documentaries, it won the Oscar for Best Documentary Feature. At the Academy Awards ceremony, Ali and Foreman accepted the Oscar together, signifying that they had made amends since the match.

GAME 80

3. Who figures out how to stop *The Blob* in the 1958 sci-fi classic?

a. Steve McQueen
b. Gene Barry
c. Charlton Heston
d. Hugh Marlowe

GAME 80 Q2 ANSWER b
Although Connery received an Oscar for his portrayal of policeman Jimmy Malone, he was criticized for using a Scottish accent despite Malone's Irish background. In fact, Connery has famously retained his Highland accent whether playing British agent James Bond in *Goldfinger* (1964) or Russian captain Marko Ramius in *The Hunt for Red October* (1990).

GAME 1

11. What was the Oscar-winning song from the 2007 Irish film *Once*?

a. "A Kiss at the End of the Rainbow"

b. "Falling Slowly"

c. "The Continental"

d. "Into the West"

GAME 1 Q10 ANSWER b

Distinguished in film history as the first Western to use sound, *In Old Arizona* featured Baxter's Oscar-winning role as The Cisco Kid. Baxter was the second actor ever to win a Best Actor Oscar. The first was Emil Jannings, who won the award in 1928 at the first Academy Awards ceremony for his role in *The Last Command.*

GAME 21

11. In the 2006 movie *The Queen*, Helen Mirren portrays:

a. Bloody Mary

b. Elizabeth II

c. Marie Antoinette

d. Aretha Franklin

GAME 21 Q10 ANSWER a

This cult comedy classic, which served as inspiration for the 2005 Tony Award-winning musical *Spamalot,* spoofs the legends of King Arthur in his mission to find the Holy Grail. Though often overshadowed by his fellow Monty Python members on their BBC-TV series, Chapman was the star both of this film and the group's 1979 film *Life of Brian.*

GAME 41

11. In the 1999 *Thomas Crown Affair* remake, what does Crown steal?

a. CIA documents

b. The Hope Diamond

c. Monet painting

d. Gutenberg Bible

GAME 41 Q10 ANSWER a

Robert Mitchum, Kirk Douglas, and Jane Greer star in the original film, which is considered a perfect example of film noir and was added to the US National Film Registry. Jeff Bridges, James Woods, and Rachel Ward star in the 1984 remake, which earned Phil Collins an Oscar for Best Original Song—"Against All Odds (Take a Look at Me Now)."

GAME 61

11. In which movie are three children sent to live with an apprentice witch?

a. *Bedknobs and Broomsticks* (1971)

b. *Practical Magic* (1998)

c. *Hocus Pocus* (1993)

d. *The Witches* (1990)

GAME 61 Q10 ANSWER d

Director Steven Spielberg first wanted to use M&M's in his movie, but the Mars company said no. The director then approached the Hershey Company about their flagship product, Hershey's Kisses, but again, Spielberg was refused. Fortunately, Hershey's did allow Reese's Pieces to appear in the film, a decision that caused sales of the candy to climb.

GAME 20

2. In which "Batman" movie are Penguin and Catwoman the villains?

a. *Batman* (1989)

b. *Batman & Robin* (1997)

c. *Batman Forever* (1995)

d. *Batman Returns* (1992)

GAME 20 Q1 ANSWER c
This intense drama focuses on an elite team of soldiers based in Iraq, whose job is to disarm bombs in the heat of combat. Along with *Avatar*, it lead the 2010 Oscar nominations with nine. The movie won six, including Best Picture and Best Director (Kathryn Bigelow). Interestingly, Bigelow was once married to James Cameron, director of *Avatar*.

GAME 40

2. In which city does Macaulay Culkin's character get lost in *Home Alone 2*?

a. Los Angeles

b. Paris

c. New York City

d. Budapest

GAME 40 Q1 ANSWER c
In this horror/sci-fi flick, Stewart plays an alien-possessed science teacher who tries to infect his students with a parasite. The movie was penned by Kevin Williamson, who is known for his work on the films *Scream* (1996) and *I Know What You Did Last Summer* (1997). Williamson also worked on TV's *Dawson's Creek* and *The Vampire Diaries*.

GAME 60

2. What is the genre of the 1996 movie *When We Were Kings*?

a. Documentary

b. Romantic comedy

c. Science fiction

d. Mystery

GAME 60 Q1 ANSWER b
It is widely believed that this film is based on an actual 1940's experiment in which the US Navy attempted to make a destroyer undetectable to radar. (The Navy denies the experiment ever occurred.) In the film, the experiment fails horribly and the only two survivors are, as a result, transported from 1943 to 1984.

GAME 80

2. Who won the Best Supporting Actor Oscar for 1987's *Untouchables*?

a. Robert De Niro

b. Sean Connery

c. Andy Garcia

d. Charles Martin Smith

GAME 80 Q1 ANSWER a
New York City-born actor Viggo Peter Mortensen was cast in both 1984's *Swing Shift* and 1985's *The Purple Rose of Cairo*, but in both cases, Mortensen's scenes ended up on the cutting room floor. That's why film audiences didn't see the actor until he portrayed genial Amish farmer Moses Hochleitner in the Oscar-winning thriller *Witness*.

GAME 1

12. What was the first "color" film to win a Best Picture Oscar?

a. *How Green Was My Valley*
b. *Mutiny on the Bounty*
c. *Gone With the Wind*
d. *Rebecca*

GAME 1 Q11 ANSWER b
"Falling Slowly" was written for *Once* by real-life musicians Glen Hansard and Markéta Irglová, who starred in the film. The Oscar-nominated song "A Kiss at the End of the Rainbow" was written for Christopher Guest's 2003 film *A Mighty Wind* by Michael McKean and his wife Annette O'Toole.

GAME 21

12. Who played the Acid Queen in the 1975 movie *Tommy*?

a. Ann-Margret
b. Grace Jones
c. Tina Turner
d. Debbie Harry

GAME 21 Q11 ANSWER b
Mirren's Oscar-winning performance in the film—a fictional account of the Royal Family's reaction after the death of Princess Diana—received a five-minute standing ovation at the Venice Film Festival, where the movie premiered. The real Queen Elizabeth II refused to watch the movie, not wanting to relive "one of the worst weeks of her life."

GAME 41

12. In which remake are the guys Memphis, Mirror Man, and The Sphinx?

a. *Bourne Supremacy* (2004)
b. *Fast and the Furious* (2001)
c. *Mission: Impossible* (1996)
d. *Gone in 60 Seconds* (2000)

GAME 41 Q11 ANSWER c
In the original 1968 film, Steve McQueen plays the bored millionaire who amuses himself by stealing, while Pierce Brosnan is cast in the remake. Crown robs a bank in the first film and commits an art heist in the second. The original earned a Best Original Song Oscar for "The Windmills of Your Mind" by Michel Legrand, and Alan and Marilyn Bergman.

GAME 61

12. In which movie are the parents motion study experts?

a. *Please Don't Eat the Daisies* (1960)
b. *Meet Me in St. Louis* (1944)
c. *Cheaper by the Dozen* (1950)
d. *The Second Time Around* (1961)

GAME 61 Q11 ANSWER a
The witch, who is learning her craft via a correspondence course, is Eglantine Price, played by Angela Lansbury. According to Leonard Maltin's *The Disney Films*, before Lansbury was cast in the role of the witch-in-training, Disney studios considered other actresses for the part, including Julie Andrews, Lynn Redgrave, Leslie Caron, and Judy Carne.

GAME 20

1. Which of the following movies is *not* based on a book?

a. *The Blind Side* (2009)

b. *Shutter Island* (2010)

c. *The Hurt Locker* (2008)

d. *Taking Woodstock* (2009)

The answer to this question is on:

page 24, top frame, right side.

GAME 40

1. Which popular comedian played a teacher in *The Faculty* (1998)?

a. Chris Rock

b. Bill Maher

c. Jon Stewart

d. Jay Mohr

The answer to this question is on:

page 24, second frame, right side.

GAME 60

1. What is the subject of 1984's *The Philadelphia Experiment*?

a. Space exploration

b. Time travel

c. Medical research

d. Cloning

The answer to this question is on:

page 24, third frame, right side.

GAME 80

1. Who made his film debut in 1985's *Witness*?

a. Viggo Mortensen

b. Alexander Godunov

c. Lukas Haas

d. Danny Glover

The answer to this question is on:

page 24, bottom frame, right side.

GAME 2

Horror Movies

*Turn to page 29
for the first question.*

Turn to page 29
for the first question.

GAME 22

Locations, Locations, Locations

*Turn to page 29
for the first question.*

GAME 42

God and the Devil

*Turn to page 29
for the first question.*

GAME 62

Ghosts and the Paranormal

*Turn to page 29
for the first question.*

GAME 1 Q12 ANSWER c

With eight Oscars to its credit along with two Honorary awards, 1939's *Gone With the Wind* stands as the crowning career achievement of legendary Hollywood producer David O. Selznick. The next Hollywood film shot in color to win the Best Picture Oscar would be Gene Kelly's musical *An American in Paris* (1951) directed by Vincente Minnelli.

GAME 21 Q12 ANSWER c

Tina Turner was just one of many rockers in this movie based on The Who's rock opera of the same name. Elton John and Eric Clapton also appeared, along with the members of The Who (Roger Daltry, Keith Moon, John Entwhistle, Pete Townsend). Tina Turner's role (originally for David Bowie) led to her second solo album, aptly named *Acid Queen*.

GAME 41 Q12 ANSWER d

The 1974 original and the 2000 remake center on a group of car thieves who must steal a certain number of cars within a few days. The original (noted for wrecking 93 cars during a chase scene) was written, directed, and produced by H.B. Halicki, who also starred in it. While filming a 1989 sequel, he was killed while performing one of the stunts.

GAME 61 Q12 ANSWER c

In 1950's *Cheaper by the Dozen*, Myrna Loy and Clifton Webb play real-life motion study experts Frank and Lillian Gilbreth. The Gilbreths, who often used their children as guinea pigs in their time motion experiments, believed that every manual activity can be reduced to a set of basic movements called "therbligs"—a scrambled version of "Gilbreth."

28

GAME 20

GRAB BAG

*Turn to page 26
for the first question.*

GAME 40

GRAB BAG

*Turn to page 26
for the first question.*

GAME 60

GRAB BAG

*Turn to page 26
for the first question.*

GAME 80

GRAB BAG

*Turn to page 26
for the first question.*

GAME 19 Q12 ANSWER a
Cary Guffey was only four years old when filming began on this sci-fi classic. In an effort to capture a realistic performance from the young actor, director Steven Spielberg surprised him with hidden toys, and even asked a few crew members to wear silly costumes off camera. It worked so well, the toddler ended up with the nickname "One-Take Cary."

GAME 39 Q12 ANSWER c
Set in the mid-1950s, this Canadian comedy is about a group of high school boys who are intent on losing their virginity. Kim Cattrall (Samantha of *Sex and the City* fame) had one of her first major roles in this film as the sexy "Lassie" Honeywell. The movie spawned two sequels—*Porky's II: The Next Day* (1983) and *Porky's Revenge* (1985).

GAME 59 Q12 ANSWER c
Gibson's portrayal of a paranoid Manhattan taxi driver in *Conspiracy Theory* is reminiscent of Robert De Niro's performance as the delusional Travis Bickle in Martin Scorsese's *Taxi Driver* (1976). And just as Martin Scorsese has a cameo as a cab passenger in his film, director Richard Donner also has a cameo as a passenger in *Conspiracy Theory*.

GAME 79 Q12 ANSWER a
When filming *Date Movie*, I worked with Jennifer Coolidge, with whom I have appeared in Christopher Guest's "mockumentary" films. Our performances were deliberate parodies of the characters played by Dustin Hoffman and Barbra Streisand in the 2004 comedy *Meet the Fockers*. Coolidge and I also appeared in *Austin Powers: The Spy Who Shagged Me* (1999).

28

GAME 2

1. Through what item does a spirit abduct a child in *Poltergeist* (1982)?

a. TV screen

b. Fireplace chimney

c. Swimming pool

d. Telephone

The answer to this question is on:

page 31, top frame, right side.

GAME 22

1. In which city does *Ferris Bueller's Day Off* (1986) take place?

a. Los Angeles

b. New York

c. Chicago

d. International Falls

The answer to this question is on:

page 31, second frame, right side.

GAME 42

1. Which film features a devil named Daryl Van Horne?

a. *The Witches of Eastwick* (1987)

b. *Angel Heart* (1987)

c. *The Exorcist* (1973)

d. *The Prophecy* (1995)

The answer to this question is on:

page 31, third frame, right side.

GAME 62

1. In which cinematic ghost story does Nicole Kidman star?

a. *Always* (1989)

b. *The Others* (2001)

c. *Sleepy Hollow* (1999)

d. *Gothika* (2003)

The answer to this question is on:

page 31, bottom frame, right side.

GAME 19

12. Who is abducted by aliens in 1977's *Close Encounters of the Third Kind*?

a. A small boy

b. A death row convict

c. A college student

d. A homemaker

GAME 39

12. Which racy teen flick is set in South Florida's Angel Beach?

a. *Risky Business* (1983)

b. *Road Trip* (2000)

c. *Porky's* (1982)

d. *Superbad* (2007)

GAME 39 Q11 ANSWER b
Reid plays a college newspaper reporter who is doing a story on Van Wilder (Ryan Reynolds)—a student who has been in college seven years. Reid is known for her roles in *American Pie* (1999) and *Josie and the Pussycats* (2001), while costar Reynolds has starred in *Definitely, Maybe* (2008), *The Proposal* (2009), and *X-Men Origins: Wolverine* (2009).

GAME 59

12. What is Mel Gibson's occupation in 1997's *Conspiracy Theory*?

a. Reporter

b. Lawyer

c. Taxi driver

d. Schoolteacher

GAME 59 Q11 ANSWER c
Released in April 1974, a few months after the televised Watergate Committee hearings, Francis Ford Coppola's film stars Gene Hackman as a San Francisco surveillance expert. His character, Harry Caul, is tormented by the deaths that occurred as a result of a bugging job he took in New York.

GAME 79

12. Which character do I play in the parody film *Date Movie* (2006)?

a. Bernie Fockyerdoder

b. Harold Flaherty

c. Ed Harken

d. Terrence Williams

GAME 79 Q11 ANSWER c
In 1984, Harry Shearer appeared with Christopher Guest and Michael McKean in Rob Reiner's heavy-metal "rockumentary" *This Is Spinal Tap*. I had a brief part in that movie as an Air Force lieutenant who books the group for an officer's dance. Harry Shearer's first appearance in a Christopher Guest film was in 2003's *A Mighty Wind*.

GAME 2

2. Who played Father Merrin in the classic horror film *The Exorcist* (1973)?

a. Jason Miller
b. Richard Burton
c. Max von Sydow
d. Nicol Williamson

GAME 2 Q1 ANSWER a
Steven Spielberg co-produced and co-wrote this scary film that did for televisions what *Jaws* (1975) did for sharks. *Poltergeist* was actually directed by Tobe Hooper, who rose to fame with his 1974 horror classic *The Texas Chain Saw Massacre*. Although Hooper is credited, Spielberg made many of the directorial decisions for *Poltergeist*.

GAME 22

2. Which movie takes place in Miami's South Beach?

a. *Cocoon* (1985)
b. *The Birdcage* (1996)
c. *Body Heat* (1981)
d. *Flipper* (1996)

GAME 22 Q1 ANSWER c
This John Hughes classic starring Matthew Broderick was shot in a number of famous "Windy City" locales, like the Sears Tower, Wrigley Field, and the Art Institute. Other notable films that are set in Chicago include *Risky Business* (1983), *The Blues Brothers* (1983), and, of course, 2002's *Chicago* (although most of its filming was shot in Toronto).

GAME 42

2. In *Bruce Almighty* (2003), what is Jim Carrey's occupation?

a. Dentist
b. Firefighter
c. Lawyer
d. TV reporter

GAME 42 Q1 ANSWER a
Jack Nicholson plays the devil in this Oscar-nominated movie, based on John Updike's 1984 novel of the same name. He seduces three women, played by Cher, Susan Sarandon, and Michelle Pfeiffer, who have just discovered they have supernatural powers. The story also spawned a British musical and a short-lived television show.

GAME 62

2. Which Christina Ricci movie has the tagline "Get an Afterlife"?

a. *Casper* (1995)
b. *Ghost Dad* (1990)
c. *Beetlejuice* (1988)
d. *Defending Your Life* (1991)

GAME 62 Q1 ANSWER b
Kidman initially told director Alejandro Amenábar to look for another actress to play the part of Grace Stewart in this spooky tale. Having just played the role of Satine in the wild and exuberant musical *Moulin Rouge!* that same year, she feared she might not be able to address the dark and serious mood of the horror film accurately.

GAME 19

11. Which beverage causes E.T. to get drunk in the 1982 film?

a. Wine

b. Scotch

c. Champagne

d. Beer

GAME 19 Q10 ANSWER b

To depict the barren landscape of Skywalker's home world, director George Lucas filmed *Star Wars* (1977) in various spots around Tunisia. He even named the planet after the country's southern city of Tataouine. While shooting, a powerful sandstorm destroyed the sets in the desert outside the town, shutting down production for two days.

GAME 39

11. Which actress stars with Ryan Reynolds in *Van Wilder* (2002)?

a. Alyson Hannigan

b. Tara Reid

c. Shannon Elizabeth

d. Natasha Lyonne

GAME 39 Q10 ANSWER c

Robert Carradine and Anthony Edwards star as the lovable nerds in this movie, which was filmed at the University of Arizona. To test their "nerd" makeup and wardrobe, the two actors attended the school's rush week, when fraternities reviewed potential pledges. The leader of the first frat house took one look and immediately rejected them both.

GAME 59

11. Which political drama does *not* take place in Washington, DC?

a. *Advise & Consent* (1962)

b. *The Seduction of Joe Tynan* (1979)

c. *The Conversation* (1974)

d. *No Way Out* (1987)

GAME 59 Q10 ANSWER c

For her role as the defamed Ohio senator Laine Hanson in this 2000 film costarring Jeff Bridges, Gary Oldman, and Christian Slater, Allen received her first Oscar nomination for Best Actress. In another political film, Oliver Stone's 1995 *Nixon,* she received her first Best Supporting Actress Oscar nomination for her role as First Lady Pat Nixon.

GAME 79

11. Who is *not* one of my co-stars in *Best in Show* (2000)?

a. Ed Begley, Jr.

b. Catherine O'Hara

c. Harry Shearer

d. Parker Posey

GAME 79 Q10 ANSWER d

Silver Streak is the first of two movies starring Richard Pryor and Gene Wilder and directed by Oscar-nominated filmmaker Arthur Hiller. I got in some good laughs in that film as a lowly and slightly confused Chicago railroad worker named Jerry Jarvis. The film also features a musical score by four-time Oscar winner Henry Mancini.

GAME 2	**3.** Which year is shown in the photo at the end of *The Shining* (1980)? **a.** 1900 **b.** 1910 **c.** 1912 **d.** 1921	**GAME 2 Q2 ANSWER c** Max von Sydow was in his early forties when he played the much-older part of Father Merrin—called upon by Father Damian Karras (Jason Miller) to help exorcise a demon from Regan MacNeil (Linda Blair). Richard Burton played a priest in *The Exorcist II* (1977), while Nicol Williamson played one in *The Exorcist III* (1990).

GAME 22	**3.** Which epic film was shot in Morocco, Italy, and England? **a.** *The Last Emperor* (1987) **b.** *Saving Private Ryan* (1998) **c.** *Gladiator* (2000) **d.** *Braveheart* (1995)	**GAME 22 Q2 ANSWER b** In this Mike Nichols-directed comedy, Robin Williams plays the owner of a drag cabaret in which his domestic partner (Nathan Lane) regularly appears as the featured performer "Starina." The other answer choices are all set in various Florida locations. *Cocoon* takes place in St. Petersburg; *Body Heat*, in Palm Beach; and *Flipper*, in the Florida Keys.

GAME 42	**3.** What is the name of the devil child in *The Omen* (1976)? **a.** Nolan **b.** Ruben **c.** Damien **d.** Regan	**GAME 42 Q2 ANSWER d** Carrey plays Bruce Nolan, who complains that God isn't doing His job properly. So God (Morgan Freeman) gives Bruce some of His powers and challenges him to do a better job. The movie, which costars Jennifer Aniston as Bruce's girlfriend, was banned in Egypt, due to pressure from Islamic groups that objected to God looking like an ordinary man.

GAME 62	**3.** Who plays a bounty hunter for Satan in 2007's *Ghost Rider*? **a.** Howie Long **b.** Nicolas Cage **c.** Viggo Mortensen **d.** Gerard Butler	**GAME 62 Q2 ANSWER a** The feature was praised for its entertaining visual effects and was the first to use computer-generated imagery to animate a title character. In addition to bringing Casper to "life," computers were also used to create the ghosts of Stretch, Stinkie, and Fatso, the last of whom was voiced by future *Everybody Loves Raymond* star Brad Garrett.

GAME 19

10. Which sci-fi character hails from the planet Tatooine?

a. Ming the Merciless
b. Luke Skywalker
c. Commander Khan
d. Flash Gordon

GAME 19 Q9 ANSWER c
Raising the stakes of the original *Predator* (1987), visual effects wiz Stan Winston was able to incorporate even more interesting weaponry into this 1990 sequel. Among the devices used by the alien are a retractable spear, detachable pincers, and Frisbee blades. It became the first film to get an NC-17 rating, before being re-cut to achieve an R.

GAME 39

10. *Lambda Lambda Lambda* is a fraternity in which comedy?

a. *Dumb and Dumber* (1994)
b. *Back to School* (1986)
c. *Revenge of the Nerds* (1984)
d. *Animal House* (1978)

GAME 39 Q9 ANSWER d
In this dark comedy, the kidnapping goes awry when the girls accidentally kill their friend, who chokes to death on a jawbreaker. Starring Rose McGowan, Rebecca Gayheart, and Julie Benz, *Jawbreaker* features a cameo by McGowan's then-boyfriend, rocker Marilyn Manson. The film was met mainly with negative reviews.

GAME 59

10. Who plays a senator and would-be vice president in *The Contender*?

a. Geena Davis
b. Glenn Close
c. Joan Allen
d. Jane Alexander

GAME 59 Q9 ANSWER c
A year after starring in *Jaws* (1975), Roy Scheider costarred in *Marathon Man* as the secret-agent brother to Dustin Hoffman's character—a Columbia University graduate student. Scheider's character is killed by the Nazi villain Dr. Christian Szell. For his role as the evil Nazi, Laurence Olivier earned a Best Supporting Actor nomination.

GAME 79

10. In which Richard Pryor/ Gene Wilder comedy do I appear?

a. *Another You* (1991)
b. *See No Evil, Hear No Evil* (1989)
c. *Stir Crazy* (1980)
d. *Silver Streak* (1976)

GAME 79 Q9 ANSWER b
Roxanne is a modern-day version of Edmond Rostand's classic, *Cyrano de Bergerac*. I portrayed Mayor Deebs, Steve Martin was Fire Chief C.D. Bales, Brian George played plastic surgeon Dave Schepsi, Rick Rossovich was shy firefighter Chris McConnell, and beautiful Daryl Hannah took the title role of astronomer Roxanne Kowalski.

GAME 2

4. In how many movies did Béla Lugosi appear as the vampire Dracula?

a. One

b. Two

c. Five

d. Eight

GAME 2 Q3 ANSWER d

The full date is July 4, 1921, and the photo shows Jack Nicholson dressed up with fellow partygoers at the Overlook Hotel. Other puzzling numbers appear throughout this Stanley Kubrick-directed film, such as the hotel room number "237," Danny's cryptic "Apollo 11" sweater, and even the 1971 film *Summer of '42* that's shown on a hotel TV.

GAME 22

4. In which city does *Bullitt* (1968) take place?

a. Chicago

b. Houston

c. New York

d. San Francisco

GAME 22 Q3 ANSWER c

The opening battle scenes in this Ridley Scott film were shot in the Bourne Woods of Surrey, England. When Scott learned that the area had been slated for deforestation, he offered to burn it to the ground during filming, and the Royal Forestry Commission gladly accepted. *Gladiator* won five Oscars including Best Picture and Best Actor (Russell Crowe).

GAME 42

4. Which actor has *not* portrayed the devil on film?

a. Anthony Hopkins

b. Gabriel Byrne

c. Bill Cosby

d. Viggo Mortensen

GAME 42 Q3 ANSWER c

Harvey Stephens was six years old when he played Satan's son. During filming, the project seemed to be cursed. The dogs used in the movie attacked their trainers; the plane that actor Gregory Peck took to the filming site was hit by lightning; director Richard Donner's hotel was bombed; and several crew members were involved in a head-on car crash.

GAME 62

4. In which ghost story are the spirits referred to as the "TV people"?

a. *Ghostbusters* (1984)

b. *The Sixth Sense* (1999)

c. *Heaven Can Wait* (1978)

d. *Poltergeist* (1982)

GAME 62 Q3 ANSWER b

A life-long comic book fan, Nicolas Coppola took his namesake from Marvel character Luke Cage to avoid the appearance of nepotism early in his career. Prior to becoming the Ghost Rider, Cage was also chosen to play Superman in an unproduced Tim Burton film, and actually named his own son Kal-El after the Man of Steel's Kryptonian alias.

GAME 19

9. What do the aliens give Danny Glover's character in *Predator 2*?

a. A medal

b. A bomb

c. A pistol

d. A necklace

GAME 19 Q8 ANSWER c
Howard began his showbiz career as an actor in the 1960s, playing young Opie Taylor on *The Andy Griffith Show*. He continued to appear on television in the '70s as a cast member of the wildly popular *Happy Days*, but soon transitioned to the director's chair. Now an accomplished filmmaker, his hits include *Apollo 13* (1995) and *A Beautiful Mind* (2001).

GAME 39

9. Which film involves a fake kidnapping by a clique of high school girls?

a. *Go* (1999)

b. *Heathers* (1988)

c. *Mean Girls* (2004)

d. *Jawbreaker* (1999)

GAME 39 Q8 ANSWER d
Murray's film debut (and first leading role) was in this Ivan Reitman-directed movie, which was filmed at a real summer camp in Ontario. Many of the extras were actual campers and counselors, and most locations in the film were actual camp sites. The movie has had several sequels, but neither Murray nor Reitman were attached to any of them.

GAME 59

9. Who plays Dustin Hoffman's brother in the 1976 thriller *Marathon Man*?

a. Sean Connery

b. Jon Voight

c. Roy Scheider

d. Warren Beatty

GAME 59 Q8 ANSWER b
De Palma grew up in Philadelphia, so it was a homecoming for him to shoot *Blow Out* there. The film's plot echoes America's memories of the 1963 assassination of President John F. Kennedy, as well as Senator Edward Kennedy's 1969 car accident off Chappaquiddick Island that resulted in the death of Mary Jo Kopechne.

GAME 79

9. What is my role in the 1987 hit comedy *Roxanne*?

a. Fire Chief Bales

b. Mayor Deebs

c. Dr. Dave Schepsi

d. Firefighter Chris McConnell

GAME 79 Q8 ANSWER a
Americathon 1998 also features an appearance by Elvis Costello and is based on a play by Phil Proctor and Peter Bergman—half of the legendary Firesign Theatre comedy team. *Collision Course* pairs *Tonight Show* host Jay Leno with Pat Morita of *Karate Kid* fame, while *Real Men* costars John Ritter and Jim Belushi.

GAME 2

5. Piper Laurie plays the mother from hell in which horror classic?

a. *The Birds* (1963)

b. *Carrie* (1976)

c. *Rosemary's Baby* (1968)

d. *The Omen* (1976)

GAME 2 Q4 ANSWER b
Nine years after the 1922 German silent film *Nosferatu*, Béla Lugosi's performance as Count Dracula in the 1931 movie from Universal Pictures made his career. Although he is remembered best for playing Dracula, Lugosi played the character only twice: first in the 1931 movie and then later in the 1948 comedy *Abbott & Costello Meet Frankenstein*.

GAME 22

5. Where does a smitten songwriter follow a blonde beauty in *10*?

a. Mexico

b. French Riviera

c. Hawaii

d. Key West

GAME 22 Q4 ANSWER d
Steve McQueen's high-speed chase up and down the streets of San Francisco is one of this movie's most memorable scenes. Mostly filmed from inside McQueen's '68 Mustang, the chase made audiences feel as if they were actually in the car, which reached speeds of up to 110 mph and simulated a wild roller coaster ride. It took three weeks to film.

GAME 42

5. Who played the girl with the holy vision in *The Song of Bernadette* (1943)?

a. Deanna Durbin

b. Jennifer Jones

c. Gene Tierney

d. Veronica Lake

GAME 42 Q4 ANSWER a
Although Hopkins has played a number of unsavory characters, like Adolf Hitler and Hannibal "the Cannibal" Lecter, the devil isn't one of them. Gabriel Byrne played Satan in search of a bride in *End of Days* (1999); Viggo Mortensen was Lucifer in *The Prophecy* (1994); and Bill Cosby had the role in the family comedy *The Devil and Max Devlin* (1981).

GAME 62

5. Which activity is involved in a romantic scene from the 1990 film *Ghost*?

a. Weeding a garden

b. Playing the piano

c. Spinning clay

d. Cooking breakfast

GAME 62 Q4 ANSWER d
Despite the "TV people" euphemism, poltergeists are more aptly translated from the German as "rattling spirits." It was a familiarity with these noisy ghosts that drew director Tobe Hooper to the project. As a young man, Hooper is said to have witnessed numerous supernatural occurrences in his own home after the death of his father.

GAME 19

8. Where are the alien pods stored Ron Howard's 1985 movie *Cocoon*?

a. A marble crypt
b. A dank basement
c. A swimming pool
d. A butcher's freezer

GAME 19 Q7 ANSWER b
Jeff Bridges earned an Oscar nomination for his portrayal of an alien who must travel to Arizona to meet his mothership. Though it was Bridges' third time being nominated, the award went to F. Murray Abraham for *Amadeus* (1984). After being selected twice more as a nominee, he finally won the honor for his leading role in 2009's *Crazy Heart*.

GAME 39

8. Who stars in the summer camp comedy *Meatballs* (1979)?

a. Chevy Chase
b. Dan Aykroyd
c. John Belushi
d. Bill Murray

GAME 39 Q7 ANSWER c
Due to a magical earring mix-up, Jessica —a popular high school cheerleader— switches bodies with a thirty-year-old criminal named Clive (Rob Schneider). Producer Adam Sandler has a small role as the "Mambuza Bongo Player," based on one of Schneider's *Saturday Night Live* characters. Ashlee Simpson also appears in this movie—her first.

GAME 59

8. In which city does Brian De Palma's 1981 film *Blow Out* take place?

a. New York
b. Philadelphia
c. Chicago
d. Atlantic City

GAME 59 Q7 ANSWER d
Political consultant James Carville was executive producer of this remake, which is based more on the acclaimed 1946 novel by Robert Penn Warren than the first film adaptation that was released in 1949. The original film won three Oscars for Best Picture, Best Actor (Broderick Crawford), and Best Supporting Actress (Mercedes McCambridge).

GAME 79

8. Which movie pairs me with John Ritter, Harvey Korman, and Jay Leno?

a. *Americathon 1998* (1979)
b. *Collision Course* (1989)
c. *Real Men* (1987)
d. *Herbie Goes Bananas* (1980)

GAME 79 Q7 ANSWER c
Before the 2005 remake starring Jim Carrey and Téa Leoni, I appeared in 1977's *Fun with Dick and Jane* starring George Segal and Jane Fonda. Directed by Canadian filmmaker Ted Kotcheff, the movie also featured the talents of actor-comedian Richard "Dick" Gautier, actor Allan Miller, and announcer-comedian Ed McMahon.

GAME 2

6. Which member of The Monkees appeared in the 2007 *Halloween* remake?

a. Mike Nesmith

b. Peter Tork

c. Davy Jones

d. Micky Dolenz

GAME 2 Q5 ANSWER b
Laurie earned an Oscar nomination as the fanatical mother of shy, telekinetic Carrie White in this film. Meanwhile, Jessica Tandy played a domineering mother in *The Birds;* Mia Farrow played a dominated mother in *Rosemary's Baby;* and Lee Remick played a doomed mother in the first version of *The Omen*—not the 2006 remake.

GAME 22

6. Which Boston-based movie won an Oscar for Best Picture?

a. *Mystic River* (2003)

b. *The Departed* (2006)

c. *The Verdict* (1982)

d. *Good Will Hunting* (1997)

GAME 22 Q5 ANSWER a
One of 1979's biggest box office hits, this romantic comedy, directed by Blake Edwards, shot Dudley Moore and Bo Derek to stardom. It also made Derek, whose beaded cornrow braids became widely copied, an instant sex symbol. The film popularized Maurice Ravel's classical "Boléro," which was deemed the perfect background music when making love.

GAME 42

6. After which classic author is Al Pacino named in *The Devil's Advocate*?

a. Christopher Marlowe

b. John Donne

c. Robert Burns

d. John Milton

GAME 42 Q5 ANSWER b
Jones won an Oscar for her role as the young French girl who saw visions of the Blessed Virgin Mary. The film was adapted from the 1942 novel by Franz Werfel. When the sultry actress Linda Darnell was cast as the Virgin Mary, Werfel was incensed. To appease him, Darnell's role was uncredited and she was shot in bright light and barely recognizable.

GAME 62

6. In which flick does a young Haley Joel Osment see dead people?

a. *Signs* (2002)

b. *The Haunting* (1963)

c. *The Sixth Sense* (1999)

d. *The Others* (2001)

GAME 62 Q5 ANSWER c
This scene not only made the art of pottery seem sexy, it also reignited the popularity of the Righteous Brothers' song "Unchained Melody." A hit in 1965, its use in one of the film's most memorable moments caused the song to reappear on the Billboard charts in 1990. In 2004, it reached #365 on *Rolling Stone's* "The 500 Greatest Songs of All Time."

GAME 19

7. In which sci-fi film does an alien drive across the country?

a. *Total Recall* (1990)

b. *Starman* (1984)

c. *E.T.* (1982)

d. *Coneheads* (1993)

GAME 19 Q6 ANSWER d
These eight-legged creepy crawlers were originally designed by Swiss surrealist painter H.R. Giger for 1979's *Alien*. When director James Cameron filmed the sequel, he used nine different people to make the facehugger thrash about in one of the film's chilling scenes. One person was assigned to each leg, with the last person in charge of the tail.

GAME 39

7. In *The Hot Chick* (2002), who switches bodies with Rob Schneider?

a. Mandy Moore

b. Jessica Biel

c. Rachel McAdams

d. Brittany Murphy

GAME 39 Q6 ANSWER c
LaFawnduh Lucas is Kip's chatroom love interest and eventual wife. Aaron Ruell, who plays Kip, actually had braces put on his teeth for this role! This movie has one of the longest credited casts since the names of all 181 student extras are listed. Following the closing credits is the movie's final scene—Kip and LaFawnduh's wedding.

GAME 59

7. Who plays Willie Stark in the 2006 remake of *All the King's Men*?

a. Kevin Bacon

b. Jack Nicholson

c. Tim Robbins

d. Sean Penn

GAME 59 Q6 ANSWER c
Having acted opposite him in 1965's *Inside Daisy Clover* and a year later in *This Property Is Condemned*, Natalie Wood's appearance as herself in *The Candidate* marked the third and final time she appeared in a film with Redford. The film also has cameos from real-life politicians Hubert Humphrey and George McGovern among others.

GAME 79

7. In which movie starring Jane Fonda do I appear?

a. *Klute* (1971)

b. *Nine to Five* (1980)

c. *Fun with Dick and Jane* (1977)

d. *The Electric Horseman* (1979)

GAME 79 Q6 ANSWER a
Actually shot in Austin, Texas, *Waiting for Guffman* makes much of the fact that Blaine, Missouri, is the "Stool Capital of the World." Meanwhile, the 1980 comedy *How to Beat the High Co$t of Living* was shot on location in Eugene, Oregon (which is where the story was set). As for Shaker Heights, Ohio, I am proud to say I grew up there.

GAME 2

7. Where was horror movie villain Dr. Hannibal Lecter born?

a. France

b. Italy

c. Lithuania

d. Canada

GAME 2 Q6 ANSWER d
Dolenz, whose first acting role was as Corky in the 1950s TV show *Circus Boy*, has a tasty cameo in this film as a grizzly gun shop owner who sells a handgun to Dr. Sam Loomis (Malcolm McDowell). Over a decade earlier, Dolenz was joined by fellow Monkees Peter Tork and Davy Jones in another cameo appearance for *The Brady Bunch Movie* (1995).

GAME 22

7. Which classic film is set in New Orleans?

a. *A Streetcar Named Desire* (1951)

b. *Cat on a Hot Tin Roof* (1958)

c. *On the Waterfront* (1954)

d. *The Great Gatsby* (1949)

GAME 22 Q6 ANSWER b
All four movies received Oscar nominations for Best Picture, but *The Departed* was the only one to win it. Martin Scorsese directed the crime drama, which centers around the Irish mafia and includes such noted actors as Jack Nicholson and Leonardo DiCaprio. The film earned a total of four Oscars, including Best Director—Scorsese's first.

GAME 42

7. Which actor has *not* portrayed Jesus Christ on film?

a. James Caviezel

b. Jeffrey Hunter

c. Charlton Heston

d. Willem Dafoe

GAME 42 Q6 ANSWER d
Pacino is Lucifer himself—and portrayed as the head of a powerful Manhattan law firm in this 1997 film. His character is named after the author of *Paradise Lost*, an epic poem about man's fall from God's grace. The film contains allusions to the poem, including Pacino's quote of one of its famous lines, "Better to reign in Hell, than serve in Heaven."

GAME 62

7. Who plays a ghost in the 1937 comedy *Topper*?

a. Jimmy Stewart

b. Cary Grant

c. William Powell

d. Ray Milland

GAME 62 Q6 ANSWER c
By age four, Osment had already been cast as Tom Hanks' son in *Forrest Gump* (1994). Five years later, the part of Cole Sear in *The Sixth Sense* would land him a Best Supporting Actor nomination at the 2000 Academy Awards. Though confident Osment would win, Michael Caine ended up taking the Oscar for his role in *The Cider House Rules* (1999).

GAME 19

6. Which sci-fi action flick features crab-like creatures called facehuggers?

a. *The Road Warrior* (1981)

b. *Star Trek III* (1984)

c. *Predator* (1987)

d. *Aliens* (1986)

GAME 19 Q5 ANSWER b
In this outrageous spoof of 1977's *Star Wars*, Moranis delivers a hilarious parody of Darth Vader, complete with oversized helmet, menacing voice, and heavy breathing. No stranger to sci-fi, the actor has also appeared in *Ghostbusters* (1984), *Little Shop of Horrors* (1986), and *Honey, I Shrunk the Kids* (1989). He retired from the film industry in 1997.

GAME 39

6. Who is the woman that Kip meets online in *Napoleon Dynamite* (2004)?

a. LaToya

b. Jessika

c. LaFawnduh

d. Summer

GAME 39 Q5 ANSWER c
In this 1989 sci-fi comedy, buddies Bill (Alex Winter) and Ted (Keanu Reeves) are two slacker "dudes" who travel through time to get info for their history report. Initially, a 1969 Chevy was supposed to be the time machine, but because a car had been used for time travel in *Back to the Future* (1985), a phone booth was used instead.

GAME 59

6. Who has a cameo in Robert Redford's 1972 film *The Candidate*?

a. Barbra Streisand

b. Jane Fonda

c. Natalie Wood

d. Gladys Cooper

GAME 59 Q5 ANSWER d
In this original version of the film, Korean war hero Raymond Shaw (played by Laurence Harvey) had been brainwashed by Manchurian captors. Whenever he is shown a Queen of Diamonds playing card, his mind becomes open to all suggestions. In a bit of visual foreshadowing, a Queen of Diamonds is displayed on-screen during the film's opening credits.

GAME 79

6. Where does the 1996 film *Waiting for Guffman* take place?

a. Blaine, Missouri

b. Austin, Texas

c. Eugene, Oregon

d. Shaker Heights, Ohio

GAME 79 Q5 ANSWER c
Though she isn't in this 1980 film, Gilda Radner—my fellow Second City Improv alumnus—was part of the *Saturday Night Live* cast when I was guest host of the show in 1978. She did appear with me in the 1980 film *First Family* (1980), which was written and directed by Buck Henry.

GAME 2

8. Which film features two actors from TV's *Desperate Housewives*?

a. *Saw* (2004)

b. *The Devil's Rejects* (2005)

c. *Hostel II* (2007)

d. *House of Wax* (2005)

GAME 2 Q7 ANSWER c
In *Hannibal Rising* (2007), Lecter's family is killed in Lithuania at the end of World War II. By the end of that film, Lecter murders people in France, Lithuania, and Canada. Midway through 2001's *Hannibal*—the sequel to *The Silence of the Lambs* (1991)—Dr. Lecter kills a police inspector in the Italian city of Florence before returning to America.

GAME 22

8. Which film's outdoor scenes were shot on the Hawaiian Islands?

a. *King Kong* (2005)

b. *Apocalypse Now* (1979)

c. *Out of Africa* (1985)

d. *Jurassic Park* (1993)

GAME 22 Q7 ANSWER a
In this film adaptation of Tennessee Williams' play, Stanley Kowalski (Marlon Brando) and his wife Stella (Kim Hunter) live in an apartment near the city's French Quarter. Directed by Elia Kazan, the film earned twelve Oscar nominations (including ones for Brando and Kazan) and won four. It ranks #47 on American Film Institute's "Top 100 Movies."

GAME 42

8. Which horror film is based on a novel by Ira Levin?

a. *The Exorcist* (1973)

b. *The Ninth Gate* (1999)

c. *The Devil's Advocate* (1997)

d. *Rosemary's Baby* (1968)

GAME 42 Q7 ANSWER c
Although Heston appeared in many biblical films, including *The Ten Commandments* (1956) and *Ben-Hur* (1959), he never played Christ. The role of Jesus was played by James Caviezel in Mel Gibson's *The Passion of the Christ* (2004); by Jeffrey Hunter in *King of Kings* (1961); and by Willem Dafoe in *The Last Temptation of Christ* (1988).

GAME 62

8. Who stars as a sexy Irish ghost in 1988's *High Spirits*?

a. Michelle Pfeiffer

b. Uma Thurman

c. Kim Basinger

d. Daryl Hannah

GAME 62 Q7 ANSWER b
Grant plays one half of a married couple that returns from the dead to reinvigorate the life of stodgy bank president Cosmo Topper. In 1985, the film became the first motion picture to be "colorized," despite much controversy about the practice. Though many disagreed with the process, Grant was reported to be very pleased by the color version.

GAME 19

5. Who plays Dark Helmet in the 1987 film *Spaceballs*?

a. Mel Brooks
b. Rick Moranis
c. Kevin Costner
d. Dom DeLuise

GAME 19 Q4 ANSWER d
A big fan of the original book by Dougla[s] Adams', Johnny Depp jumped at th[e] chance to play the part of Zaphod Bee[-] blebrox. Bill Murray and Will Ferrell wer[e] also considered to fill the famous alien'[s] shoes. The role, however, ended up go[-] ing to Sam Rockwell, who has said h[e] based his performance on Bill Clinton, George W. Bush, and Elvis Presley.

GAME 39

5. What is used as a time machine in *Bill & Ted's Excellent Adventure*?

a. VW bus
b. Cardboard box
c. Phone booth
d. Bathtub

GAME 39 Q4 ANSWER b
In this R-rated film, the Canadian actress plays a porn star turned "girl next door" who falls in love with a straight-lace[d] high school senior played by Emil[e] Hirsch. Because Hirsch was a minor dur[-] ing production, a stunt double was use[d] for his nude scenes. He also had a la[p] dance scene, during which several pil[-] lows separated him from the dancer.

GAME 59

5. Which card can "brainwash" in 1962's *The Manchurian Candidate*?

a. Ace of Spades
b. King of Hearts
c. Jack of Clubs
d. Queen of Diamonds

GAME 59 Q4 ANSWER b
Mixing conservative politics with acous[-] tic guitar folk songs in the tradition of Bob Dylan, the sudden and swift popu[-] larity of Bob Roberts in the film is simila[r] to the rise of George W. Bush to a Re[-] publican presidency eight years later. Noted writer and political critic Gore Vi[-] dal appears in the film as Democratic senator Brickley Paiste.

GAME 79

5. Who did *not* appear with me in *How to Beat the High Co$t of Living*?

a. Jane Curtin
b. Susan Saint James
c. Gilda Radner
d. Jessica Lange

GAME 79 Q4 ANSWER b
American Wedding was the third film in the successful teen-comedy *American Pie* trilogy. It was directed by Jesse Dy[-] lan (son to singer/songwriter Bob Dylan), who would later direct *Anchorman* star Will Ferrell in the 2005 comedy *Kicking and Screaming*. Back in 2001, I ap[-] peared in Jesse Dylan's first feature film, *How High*, as Chancellor Huntley.

GAME 2

9. What is lead character Christine Brown's job in *Drag Me to Hell* (2009)?

a. Librarian
b. Bank teller
c. Loan officer
d. Teacher

GAME 2 Q8 ANSWER c
When they appeared in the 2007 sequel to Eli Roth's *Hostel* (2005), actors Richard Burgi and Roger Bart were better known for their roles on TV's *Desperate Housewives*. On that show, Burgi played Teri Hatcher's ex-husband Karl, while Bart's character, George, was troubled pharmacist and paramour to Marcia Cross's character Bree.

GAME 22

9. Which city is the setting for the 1980 film *Urban Cowboy*?

a. Houston
b. Tucson
c. Oklahoma City
d. Denver

GAME 22 Q8 ANSWER d
Kauai and Oahu were the islands of choice for filming this sci-fi thriller, which took place on a fictional island off Costa Rica. Directed by Steven Spielberg and based on the Michael Crichton novel, *Jurassic Park* is regarded as a landmark film in the use of computer-generated graphics and the first to use DTS digital surround sound.

GAME 42

9. Which horror film centers on a demon named Pazuzu?

a. *Bedazzled* (1967)
b. *The Exorcist* (1973)
c. *The Omen* (1976)
d. *Angel Heart* (1987)

GAME 42 Q8 ANSWER d
In this horror-film classic, Mia Farrow starred as Rosemary, the young housewife who was impregnated by Satan. Roman Polanski directed the movie (his first American film) and wrote the screenplay—an adaptation of the novel—for which he received an Oscar nod. Ruth Gordon won the film's only Oscar for her role as the meddling Minnie Castavet.

GAME 62

9. What rapper plays a ghost in the 2001 movie *Bones*?

a. Snoop Dogg
b. Eminem
c. Coolio
d. Ice Cube

GAME 62 Q8 ANSWER d
Hannah had already played a robotic being in *Blade Runner* (1982), a mermaid in *Splash* (1984), and a Cro-Magnon woman in *The Clan of the Cave Bear* (1986) by the time she accepted the role of Mary Plunkett in Neil Jordan's romantic comedy. In addition to her film career, this versatile actress has created and released two board games.

GAME 19

4. Which character is from 2005's *The Hitchhiker's Guide to the Galaxy*?

a. Coco Crisp

b. Bela Oxmyx

c. Stumma Bajulista

d. Zaphod Beeblebrox

GAME 19 Q3 ANSWER a
This prequel to 1979's *Alien* was set on remote Bouvet Island in Antarctica to avoid breaking continuity with the series (in which Earth has no prior knowledge of the creatures). Another inspiration for the location was the "Vela Incident" of 1979, during which a Vela satellite detected two powerful flashes near the island that remain unexplained.

GAME 39

4. Who plays the title role in *The Girl Next Door* (2004)?

a. Jessica Alba

b. Elisha Cuthbert

c. Hilary Duff

d. Christina Applegate

GAME 39 Q3 ANSWER c
This teen classic, which stars Jason Biggs, Chris Klein, and Alyson Hannigan, centers around a group of high school senior guys who make a pact to lose their virginity by graduation. It took four tries for this film to get an R-rating instead of an NC-17. The movie led to two sequels: *American Pie 2* (2001) and *American Wedding* (2003).

GAME 59

4. In what film is Tim Robbins a candidate for the US Senate?

a. *The Hudsucker Proxy* (1994)

b. *Bob Roberts* (1992)

c. *Bull Durham* (1998)

d. *Mystic River* (2003)

GAME 59 Q3 ANSWER c
In this film, *Washington Post* reporter Bob Woodward (played by Robert Redford) has secret meetings with Holbrook as an FBI man who helps Woodward and fellow reporter Carl Bernstein (Dustin Hoffman) uncover details of the Nixon administration's "Watergate" cover-up. Retired FBI agent W. Mark Felt revealed in 2005 that *he* was "Deep Throat."

GAME 79

4. In which of these "American" movies do I appear?

a. *American Buffalo* (1996)

b. *American Wedding* (2003)

c. *American Gigolo* (1980)

d. *American Graffiti* (1973)

GAME 79 Q3 ANSWER c
WALL•E made me part of movie history as the first actor to play a live-action character in a Pixar animated film. I was pleased when the film earned Oscar nominations for Best Original Screenplay, Best Original Song, Best Original Score, Sound Mixing, and Sound Editing, and actually won the Academy Award for Best Animated Feature.

10. In which film does a beat-up Ford Pinto gets lots of screen time?

a. *Cujo* (1983)

b. *Christine* (1983)

c. *Maximum Overdrive* (1986)

d. *The Car* (1977)

GAME 2 Q9 ANSWER c
When Brown (played by Alison Lohman) refuses a loan to an old woman, all hell breaks loose—literally. Directed by Sam Raimi, who first exploded on the movie scene with his cult classic *The Evil Dead* (1981), *Drag Me to Hell* was a breath of fresh air for him while he served as director on the first three *Spider-Man* movies.

10. Which country is the setting for the 2003 hit *Lost in Translation*?

a. Japan

b. Chile

c. Scotland

d. Belgium

GAME 22 Q9 ANSWER a
John Travolta and Debra Winger star in this film that popularized country music, line dancing, and mechanical bull riding. Travolta, who had a mechanical bull installed in his home, became so good at riding it that he didn't need a stunt double. The dances were choreographed by Patrick Swayze's mom (Patsy Swayze) and wife (Lisa Niemi).

10. In the 2007 comedy *Evan Almighty*, what does God tell Evan to build?

a. An ark

b. An airplane

c. A school

d. A roller rink

GAME 42 Q9 ANSWER b
During an archeological dig, Father Merrin (Max von Sydow) discovers the demon's statue. Strange occurrences took place during the movie's filming. A fire destroyed the interior sets of the home (except Regan's bedroom); Linda Blair was injured when her harness broke; and Ellen Burstyn sustained a back injury when she was thrown across the room.

10. What causes the death of the newlyweds in *Beetlejuice*?

a. A plane crash

b. An epidemic

c. A factory explosion

d. An auto accident

GAME 62 Q9 ANSWER a
In the movie, Snoop Dogg plays Jimmy Bones, a neighborhood drug lord murdered by a crooked police officer in 1979. Pam Grier was cast as Bones' love interest as a tip of the hat to the blaxploitation films that inspired this horror film. Though they had never worked together on the big screen, the two had already costarred in numerous music videos.

GAME 19

3. In *Alien vs. Predator* (2004), where do scientists discover a pyramid site?

a. Antarctica
b. Egypt
c. Worcester
d. China

GAME 19 Q2 ANSWER c
Before achieving stardom on the big screen, Freeman was an original cast member of the PBS TV series *The Electric Company* with Bill Cosby. His characters included Easy Reader, Mad Scientist, and Vincent the Vegetable Vampire. Intended as an educational sketch comedy show for kids, the program was created by the producers of *Sesame Street*.

GAME 39

3. Which comedy focuses on friends Jim, Oz, Finch, and Kevin?

a. *Clueless* (1995)
b. *Bring It On* (2000)
c. *American Pie* (1998)
d. *Sixteen Candles* (1084)

GAME 39 Q2 ANSWER a
During production, Penn answered only to "Spicoli," his character's name. (The door of his dressing room also bore that name.) A young Nicolas Cage—nephew of director Francis Ford Coppola of *Godfather* fame—had a bit part in the film and is credited as Nicolas Coppola for the first and only time in his long acting career.

GAME 59

3. Who plays FBI informant "Deep Throat" in *All the President's Men* (1976)?

a. Jack Warden
b. Jason Robards
c. Hal Holbrook
d. Martin Balsam

GAME 59 Q2 ANSWER d
In addition to serving as director, co-producer, and co-writer, Beatty stars in this 1998 film as Senator Jay Billington Bulworth. His disenchantment with politics leads him to hire an unknown killer to assassinate him within two days. Halle Berry's character, Nina, is revealed as the assassin, but she cannot bring herself to kill him.

GAME 79

3. Who is my character in the 2008 Pixar animated feature *WALL•E*?

a. Ron Albertson
b. Willard J. Fredericks
c. Shelby Forthright
d. Ed Harken

GAME 79 Q2 ANSWER b
As Mike LaFontaine in the Christopher Guest comedy *A Mighty Wind*, I got to play a former stand-up comic who manages a folk-music group called The New Main Street Singers. My character's biggest claim to fame before becoming the group's manager was being the star of a short-lived '70s TV show called *Wha' Happened?*

GAME 2

11. Which song is heard at the end of *An American Werewolf in London*?

a. "Blue Moon"

b. "Bad Moon Rising"

c. "Moondance"

d. "Werewolves of London"

GAME 2 Q10 ANSWER a
Cujo is the gentle St. Bernard that turns into a killer beast after being bitten by a rabid bat. Based on the Stephen King novel, this film stars Dee Wallace-Stone as a mom who is trapped in a car with her young son as the rabid dog holds them at bay. A year earlier, Wallace played another mother in Steven Spielberg's *E.T.: The Extra-Terrestrial.*

GAME 22

11. Which movie takes place in Modesto, California?

a. *Traffic* (2000)

b. *American Graffiti* (1973)

c. *Vertigo* (1958)

d. *Million Dollar Baby* (2004)

GAME 22 Q10 ANSWER a
Bill Murray (a lonely actor) and Scarlett Johansson (a bored newlywed) meet by chance and strike up an offbeat relationship in this quirky, critically acclaimed film. Interestingly, in spite of their relationship, the two characters never actually introduce themselves to each other. Director Sofia Coppola won the Oscar for Best Original Screenplay.

GAME 42

11. Which film features Robert De Niro as the devil?

a. *The Mission* (1986)

b. *True Confessions* (1981)

c. *Angel Heart* (1987)

d. *Awakenings* (1990)

GAME 42 Q10 ANSWER a
Preserving the environment is the theme of this film starring Steve Carell and Morgan Freeman. Director Tom Shadyac had the crew "go green" as well, and the film became NBC Universal's first to offset the production's carbon emissions. The crew rode bicycles around the set, planted trees, and donated used set materials to Habitat for Humanity.

GAME 62

11. Reese Witherspoon appears as a spirit in which 2005 film?

a. *Junebug*

b. *The Brothers Grimm*

c. *Just Like Heaven*

d. *The Skeleton Key*

GAME 62 Q10 ANSWER d
The couple, played by Alec Baldwin and Geena Davis, drives off a bridge when a stray dog wanders unexpectedly in front of their car. Initially, Davis was the only actor to commit to this 1988 film. Even Michael Keaton, who plays the film's titular character, refused the part at first. The role would go on to become one of his personal favorites.

GAME 19

2. Who stars as the fighter of an alien force in *Dreamcatcher* (2003)?

a. Nicolas Cage

b. Denzel Washington

c. Morgan Freeman

d. Keanu Reeves

GAME 19 Q1 ANSWER a

David Bowie stars as the thirsty alien in this sci-fi cult thriller. It was his first major film role, though not his first time as an extraterrestrial. Bowie had previously inhabited the persona of Ziggy Stardust, a rock star from outer space, on his 1972 concept album *The Rise and Fall of Ziggy Stardust and the Spiders from Mars*.

GAME 39

2. What is Sean Penn's character in *Fast Times at Ridgemont High* (1982)?

a. Stoned surfer

b. Fast food cook

c. History teacher

d. Nerdy bookworm

GAME 39 Q1 ANSWER b

The "Windy City" on a beautiful spring day is the setting for this John Hughes film starring Matthew Broderick as the cocky high school senior. A box office smash, the movie is ranked on many lists, such as *Entertainment Weekly's* "50 Best High School Movies," where it is ranked #10; and Bravo's "100 Funniest Movies," where it's #54.

GAME 59

2. Who plays Warren Beatty's love interest in the political satire *Bulworth*?

a. Diane Keaton

b. Julie Christie

c. Madonna

d. Halle Berry

GAME 59 Q1 ANSWER d

Based on a real series of television interviews that English talk-show host David Frost conducted with former President Nixon in 1977, *Frost/Nixon* is directed by Ron Howard (who actually voted to re-elect Nixon for a second term in 1972). Frank Langella's portrayal of the famously paranoid Nixon in this film led to a Best Actor Oscar nomination.

GAME 79

2. In which "mockumentary" do I play the character Mike LaFontaine?

a. *Waiting for Guffman* (1996)

b. *A Mighty Wind* (2003)

c. *This Is Spinal Tap* (1984)

d. *Best in Show* (2000)

GAME 79 Q1 ANSWER d

This wacky movie also features appearances by celebrities like John Lennon, Yoko Ono, Andy Warhol, and Richard Pryor. That same year, I connected once again with John and Yoko when they co-hosted TV's *The Mike Douglas Show*. I appeared on the show as a member of the improvisational comedy group the Ace Trucking Company.

12. In which movie does Charles Lee Ray's evil soul live on?

a. *Friday the 13th* (1980)
b. *Fright Night* (1985)
c. *Child's Play* (1988)
d. *Magic* (1978)

Game 2 Q11 ANSWER a
John Landis, who would go on to direct Michael Jackson's classic 1983 "Thriller" music video, used only songs in this 1981 film with the word "moon" in the title. Three versions of "Blue Moon" are featured on the soundtrack—slower versions by Bobby Vinton and Sam Cooke, and a doo-wop version by The Marcels that is played during the end credits.

---

12. Where is the *Grand Hotel* located in the 1932 MGM classic?

a. Paris
b. Milan
c. Moscow
d. Berlin

GAME 22 Q11 ANSWER b
George Lucas directed this nostalgic coming-of-age film that kicked off the careers of such notable actors as Harrison Ford, Ron Howard, Cindy Williams, and Richard Dreyfuss. The other answer choices were all set in various California locations. *Traffic* took place in San Diego; *Vertigo*, in San Francisco; and *Million Dollar Baby*, in LA.

---

12. Who plays God in the 1999 movie *Dogma*?

a. Linda Fiorentino
b. Alanis Morissette
c. Kevin Smith
d. Salma Hayek

GAME 42 Q11 ANSWER c
In this thriller, De Niro plays Louis Cyphre—a name that sounds eerily similar to "Lucifer." Director Alan Parker claimed De Niro's role as the devil was so realistic that Parker would avoid him on set and generally let the actor direct himself. De Niro said his portrayal was an impersonation of his friend and frequent collaborator Martin Scorsese.

---

12. In which film is the ghost of Sigmund Freud a character?

a. *Real Genius* (1985)
b. *Modern Problems* (1981)
c. *Frenzy* (1972)
d. *Lovesick* (1983)

GAME 62 Q11 ANSWER c
Witherspoon's portrayal of a ghost may have been overshadowed by her appearance as country star June Carter Cash in the biographical drama *Walk the Line* that same year. As the wife of music legend Johnny Cash, she performed her own vocals throughout that film. The role was praised and won her numerous awards, including the 2005 Best Actress Oscar.

GAME 19

1. In which film does an alien come to earth seeking a source of water?

a. *The Man Who Fell to Earth* (1976)
b. *Barbarella* (1968)
c. *Predator* (1987)
d. *Soylent Green* (1973)

The answer to this question is on:

page 50, top frame, right side.

GAME 39

1. In which city does *Ferris Bueller's Day Off* (1986) take place?

a. Los Angeles
b. Chicago
c. Philadelphia
d. Boston

The answer to this question is on:

page 50, second frame, right side.

GAME 59

1. Which political drama is *not* an Oliver Stone film?

a. *Nixon* (1995)
b. *JFK* (1991)
c. *W.* (2008)
d. *Frost/Nixon* (2008)

The answer to this question is on:

page 50, third frame, right side.

GAME 79

1. Yes, it's true. I actually appeared in a 1972 comedy movie called:

a. *Goofy Hyena*
b. *Lazy Giraffe*
c. *Super Wolf*
d. *Dynamite Chicken*

The answer to this question is on:

page 50, bottom frame, right side.

GAME 3

Westerns

*Turn to page 55
for the first question.*

Turn to page 55 for the first question.

GAME 2 Q12 ANSWER c
Before dying, Ray—a serial killer known as the "Lake Shore Strangler"—comes to possess a doll known as "Chucky" in this creepy tale. *Magic* is another spooky movie about a seemingly disembodied entity. Directed by Sir Richard Attenborough, this film stars Anthony Hopkins as a troubled ventriloquist whose dummy seems to take over his personality.

GAME 23

Working Women

*Turn to page 55
for the first question.*

GAME 22 Q12 ANSWER d
One of MGM's highest grossing pictures, *Grand Hotel* featured a multi-star cast that included such A-listers as Greta Garbo, Joan Crawford, and John Barrymore. Garbo's famous line "I want to be alone" ranks #30 on the American Film Institute's list of "Top 100 US Movie Quotes." The film won the Best Picture Oscar—the only nomination it received.

GAME 43

Shall We Dance?

*Turn to page 55
for the first question.*

GAME 42 Q12 ANSWER b
Salma Hayek and Linda Fiorentino also appear in this comedy that was written and directed by Kevin Smith. Originally, Morissette was supposed to play the leading role of Bethany, but had to decline due to scheduling conflicts. She took the lesser role of God instead. Morissette also wrote and recorded the song "Still" for the movie.

GAME 63

Costume Dramas

*Turn to page 55
for the first question.*

GAME 62 Q12 ANSWER d
Though Alec Guinness plays Freud in the film, the role was originally intended for Peter Sellers. Freud's theories of the unconscious mind had a major impact on psychiatry in the 20th century and influenced numerous other academic disciplines in the process. He founded the practice of psychoanalysis and included Carl Jung among his followers.

GAME 19

Extraterrestrials, UFOs & Aliens

*Turn to page 52
for the first question.*

GAME 18 Q12 ANSWER d
Singer Peggy Lee provided the voices for Si and Am in *Lady and the Tramp*. She was also the voice for Darling, Lady's owner, and Peg, Tramp's former love. The Siamese cats, which made life extremely difficult for Lady, were named Nip and Tuck in the original script.

GAME 39

Teen Comedies

*Turn to page 52
for the first question.*

GAME 38 Q12 ANSWER d
In 1980, Scorsese's *Raging Bull* lost to actor Robert Redford's *Ordinary People*. A decade later, *GoodFellas* lost to actor Kevin Costner's film *Dances with Wolves*. The award seemed to be his in 2004 for *The Aviator*, but it went to Clint Eastwood's *Million Dollar Baby* instead. Finally, Scorsese won his Oscar in 2007 for *The Departed*.

GAME 59

Political Paranoia

*Turn to page 52
for the first question.*

GAME 58 Q12 ANSWER b
Stewart plays a reporter who is assigned to cover the marriage of a socialite (Katharine Hepburn). Although Stewart won the Best Actor Oscar for the role, he always felt it should have gone to Henry Fonda for *The Grapes of Wrath*. He believed he got the award because he had been overlooked the previous year for *Mr. Smith Goes to Washington*.

GAME 79

All About ME
Fred Willard

*Turn to page 52
for the first question.*

GAME 78 Q12 ANSWER d
While the 2008 remake stars Keanu Reeves as the alien Klaatu, the 1951 version features Michael Rennie in the role. Gort stands guard over the spaceship while Klaatu works to bring peace to Earth. This film is said to be based on the story of Jesus, who was a carpenter. Interestingly, Klaatu's alias when he enters into society is "Mr. Carpenter."

GAME 3

1. Who plays happy-go-lucky Jake in *Silverado* (1985)?

a. Kevin Costner
b. Kevin Kline
c. John Cleese
d. Scott Glenn

The answer to this question is on:

page 57, top frame, right side.

GAME 23

1. In which film does Meryl Streep play a ruthless fashion magazine editor?

a. *Sex and the City* (2008)
b. *Confessions of a Shopaholic* (2009)
c. *The Devil Wears Prada* (2006)
d. *Brüno* (2009)

The answer to this question is on:

page 57, second frame, right side.

GAME 43

1. Which film has a dance instructor named Johnny Castle?

a. *Dirty Dancing* (1987)
b. *Billy Elliot* (2000)
c. *Flashdance* (1983)
d. *Staying Alive* (1983)

The answer to this question is on:

page 57, third frame, right side.

GAME 63

1. Which of the following is an adaptation of a William Thackeray novel?

a. *Doctor Zhivago* (1965)
b. *Tess* (1979)
c. *Mildred Pierce* (1945)
d. *Barry Lyndon* (1975)

The answer to this question is on:

page 57, bottom frame, right side.

GAME 18

12. Si and Am are cats in which animated movie?

a. *The Lion King* (1994)

b. *Beauty and the Beast* (1991)

c. *Mulan* (1998)

d. *Lady and the Tramp* (1955)

GAME 18 Q11 ANSWER b
The original idea for the Oscar nominated *Cars* focused on an electric car in a world full of gas-guzzlers. Instead, the young racecar Lightning McQueen must learn the true meaning of the race (the journey is more important than the finish line) with the help of his friends: Doc the 1951 Hudson Hornet, Sally the Porsche, and Mater the tow truck.

GAME 38

12. Which film gave Martin Scorsese his first Best Director Oscar?

a. *Raging Bull* (1980)

b. *GoodFellas* (1990)

c. *The Aviator* (2004)

d. *The Departed* (2006)

GAME 38 Q11 ANSWER a
The film's fictionalized Tanglers casino was based on the real-life Stardust Resort & Casino, which closed its doors in 2006. *Casino* is narrated both by Robert De Niro and Joe Pesci, in a style reminiscent of Ray Liotta and Lorraine Bracco's shared narration in *GoodFellas*. Watch for cameos by Siegfried & Roy and Frankie Avalon.

GAME 58

12. What is Jimmy Stewart's profession in *The Philadelphia Story* (1940)?

a. Car salesman

b. Tabloid reporter

c. Photographer

d. Magazine publisher

GAME 58 Q11 ANSWER d
This 1999 film starring Heath Ledger and Julia Stiles is loosely based on the Bard's classic play and contains many references to it. For example, the film's Kat and Bianca Stratford are Kate and Bianca in the play. Film character Patrick Verona corresponds to the play's Petruchio of Verona. The play's locale is Padua—the film takes place at Padua High.

GAME 78

12. Which sci-fi film features a ten-foot-tall robot named Gort?

a. *Forbidden Planet* (1956)

b. *The Terminator* (1984)

c. *Total Recall* (1990)

d. *The Day the Earth Stood Still* (1951)

GAME 78 Q11 ANSWER c
Having conquered Nazis, voodoo cults, and protectors of the Holy Grail, it makes sense that Indiana Jones (Harrison Ford) would also deal with aliens. And when you consider the fact that series creator George Lucas made *Star Wars* (1977) and the films' director Steven Spielberg made *Close Encounters of the Third Kind* (1977), it seems inevitable.

2. What is John Wayne's character looking for in *The Searchers* (1956)?

a. His unfaithful wife
b. His kidnapped niece
c. A cache of gold coins
d. A store of rifles

GAME 3 Q1 ANSWER a
Costner's breakout role as the romance-minded Jake was actually the result of his work in 1983's critically acclaimed *Big Chill*. When nearly all of Costner's *Big Chill* scenes ended up on the cutting room floor, director and friend Lawrence Kasdan promised the actor a good role in a future film. That film turned out to be the Western *Silverado*.

---

2. Violet, Dora Lee, and Judy are office workers in which comedy?

a. *Swimming with Sharks* (1994)
b. *Look Who's Talking* (1989)
c. *Office Space* (1999)
d. *9 to 5* (1980)

GAME 23 Q1 ANSWER c
Streep received an Oscar nomination (her fourteenth) for her role as Miranda Priestly in this screen adaptation of Lauren Weisberger's 2003 novel. *Vogue* editor Anna Wintour was believed to have been the inspiration for Streep's much-feared character, so most designers and fashion industry people did not appear in the film for fear of angering her.

---

2. Which movie is about a school of aspiring ballet dancers?

a. *On the Town* (2000)
b. *Flashdance* (1983)
c. *Step Up* (2006)
d. *Center Stage* (2000)

GAME 43 Q1 ANSWER a
Initially, director Emile Ardolino considered Billy Zane for the part of Johnny Castle, but dancing tests yielded disappointing results. Patrick Swayze, on the other hand, was a trained dancer with experience from the Joffrey Ballet. Just as important, he had already acted with the film's female lead, Jennifer Grey, in the 1984 movie *Red Dawn*.

---

2. Who plays the composed Elinor Dashwood in *Sense and Sensibility*?

a. Ashley Judd
b. Winona Ryder
c. Emma Thompson
d. Gwyneth Paltrow

GAME 63 Q1 ANSWER d
Loosely based on Thackeray's 1844 novel *The Luck of Barry Lyndon*, this film was not the commercial success for which Warner Brothers and director Stanley Kubrick had hoped. Nevertheless, *Barry Lyndon* won Academy Awards for Best Art Direction, Best Cinematography, Best Costume Design, and Best Music, and is viewed as one of Kubrick's best works.

GAME 18

11. In which town does Lightning McQueen stop in Pixar's *Cars* (2006)?

a. Axle Valley
b. Radiator Springs
c. Carburetor City
d. Hubcap Lake

GAME 18 Q10 ANSWER d
Although the title of this 1988 film appears as a question, a question mark was not added because it is considered bad luck in the film industry. This was a good idea because the movie eventually won three Academy Awards in 1989 (Best Sound Effects, Best Visual Effects, and Best Film Editing).

GAME 38

11. In Martin Scorsese's 1995 film *Casino*, which casino is run by Sam Rothstein?

a. Tangiers
b. Stardust
c. MGM Grand
d. Golden Nugget

GAME 38 Q10 ANSWER c
In *The Aviator*, Howard Hughes (played by Leonardo DiCaprio in an Oscar-nominated role) is seen trying to round up twenty-six movie cameras in order to shoot the dangerous airplane sequences for his 1932 epic *Hell's Angels*. *Wings* (1927) was directed by William Wellman and it was the first film to win a Best Picture Oscar.

GAME 58

11. *10 Things I Hate About You* is similar to which Shakespearean play?

a. *The Tempest*
b. *Romeo and Juliet*
c. *Othello*
d. *The Taming of the Shrew*

GAME 58 Q10 ANSWER c
Renée Zellweger stars as the thirty-something, single, overweight Bridget Jones. In preparation for the role, Zellweger assumed a British accent, gained twenty-five pounds, and worked at a British publishing company for a month. Her efforts paid off as she received a Best Actress Oscar nomination. (She lost to Halle Berry for *Monster's Ball*.)

GAME 78

11. Which *Indiana Jones* film features an alien UFO?

a. *Temple of Doom* (1984)
b. *Last Crusade* (1989)
c. *Kingdom of the Crystal Skull* (2008)
d. *Raiders of the Lost Ark* (1981)

GAME 78 Q10 ANSWER d
Bearing a resemblance to *Star Wars* actor Mark Hamill, *Laserblast* star Kim Milford plays vengeful teenager Billy Duncan, who finds the alien ray gun and uses it to take revenge on the townsfolk who have always given him trouble. *Laserblast* also features veteran actors Keenan Wynn and Roddy McDowell.

GAME 3

3. Which Western borrows its plot from the non-Western *House of Strangers*?

a. *Cheyenne Autumn* (1964)
b. *High Plains Drifter* (1973)
c. *The Searchers* (1956)
d. *Broken Lance* (1954)

GAME 3 Q2 ANSWER b
Based on Alan Le May's 1956 novel of the same name, *The Searchers* is perhaps most notable for its theme of racism towards Native Americans. Ethan Edwards (John Wayne) spends years searching for the niece who was kidnapped by Comanches as a child. But his goal is not to reunite his now grown-up niece (Natalie Wood) with her family, but to kill her.

GAME 23

3. Who played Michael Keaton's working wife in the 1983 comedy *Mr. Mom*?

a. Carrie Fisher
b. Teri Garr
c. Diane Keaton
d. Kirstie Alley

GAME 23 Q2 ANSWER d
Lily Tomlin, Dolly Parton, and Jane Fonda play the coworkers who devise a plan to get even with their sexist, egotistical boss (Dabney Coleman). This was Dolly Parton's first film. To prepare for the role, she memorized her own lines, as well as those of every other actor in the cast. She also wrote "9 to 5," the movie's Oscar-nominated theme song.

GAME 43

3. In which musical do Fred Astaire and Ginger Rogers dance "Cheek to Cheek"?

a. *Top Hat* (1935)
b. *Shall We Dance* (1937)
c. *Flying Down to Rio* (1933)
d. *The Gay Divorcee* (1934)

GAME 43 Q2 ANSWER d
With its focus on the world of professional dance, *Center Stage* features several real-life ballet dancers in its cast, including Amanda Schull, from the San Francisco Ballet, and Ethan Stiefel, a principal dancer with the American Ballet Theater. Interestingly, Susan May Pratt—who plays a star dancing pupil—had no ballet training prior to being cast.

GAME 63

3. Who was originally cast as Robin in 1938's *The Adventures of Robin Hood*?

a. Clark Gable
b. Ward Bond
c. William Powell
d. James Cagney

GAME 63 Q2 ANSWER c
When Emma Thompson wrote the screenplay for this 1995 film, she did not intend to have a starring role. In fact, she thought that she was too old for the part of Elinor. Then director Ang Lee suggested that Thompson simply make the character older—a strategy that made Elinor's fear of remaining single more credible with modern audiences.

GAME 18

10. In *Who Framed Roger Rabbit*, what does Judge Doom want to turn Toontown into?

a. Parking lot
b. Golf course
c. Condominium complex
d. Freeway

GAME 18 Q9 ANSWER d
Nathan Lane and Ernie Sabella were originally supposed to provide the voices of the hyenas; however, they were better suited for their eventual roles of Timon and Pumbaa. Whoopi Goldberg, Cheech Marin, and Jim Cummings filled the roles of the hyenas to great success.

GAME 38

10. Which movie is Howard Hughes filming at the start of Martin Scorsese's *The Aviator* (2004)?

a. *The Outlaw*
b. *Scarface*
c. *Hell's Angels*
d. *Wings*

GAME 38 Q9 ANSWER a
David Bowie also appeared in this controversial film, while fellow British rock icon Peter Gabriel wrote the film's music. Kristofferson was also in Scorsese's film *Alice Doesn't Live Here Anymore* as Ellen Burstyn's boyfriend. And he appears on his own album cover in *Taxi Driver*, while Mick Jagger can be seen in a poster in that movie as well.

GAME 58

10. In *Bridget Jones's Diary* (2001), where does Bridget work?

a. A newspaper
b. A courthouse
c. A publishing house
d. A school

GAME 58 Q9 ANSWER b
Gable and Colbert both won Oscars for their leading role performances in this film, which was the first to win all five major Academy Awards. It also won for Best Picture, Director (Frank Capra), and Writing. To date, the only other films to achieve this feat are *One Flew Over the Cuckoo's Nest* (1975) and *The Silence of the Lambs* (1991).

GAME 78

10. In *Laserblast* (1978), what do the aliens leave behind?

a. A map
b. A spaceship
c. An alien
d. A ray gun

GAME 78 Q9 ANSWER a
Before it was a popular movie serial in 1939 or even a radio show in 1932, Buck Rogers was first seen by the public in a newspaper comic strip that debuted in 1929. Though remembered more as Buck Rogers, actor Buster Crabbe portrayed *Flash Gordon* a few times before 1939. Both characters have repeat adventures among aliens in outer space.

GAME 3

4. Which film's characters include the outlaw William Munny?

a. *Dances with Wolves* (1990)

b. *True Grit* (1969)

c. *Unforgiven* (1992)

d. *Shane* (1953)

GAME 3 Q3 ANSWER d
Both the 1949 film *House of Strangers* and *Broken Lance* are family dramas in which a businessman runs roughshod over his grown sons. In *Broken Lance*, the father, a ranch owner, is played by Spencer Tracy, and his sons are portrayed by Robert Wagner, Richard Widmark, Hugh O'Brien, and Earl Holliman. This film won an Oscar for Best Story.

GAME 23

4. Which actress appears in the 1997 corporate-office comedy *Clockwatchers*?

a. Jennifer Aniston

b. Cameron Diaz

c. Helen Hunt

d. Lisa Kudrow

GAME 23 Q3 ANSWER b
Garr plays suburban mom Caroline Butler who returns to work when husband Jack suddenly loses his job. She has appeared frequently on television and has starred in many highly successful films, including 1977's *Close Encounters of the Third Kind* and *Oh, God!* For her role as Dustin Hoffman's friend in *Tootsie* (1982), she earned an Oscar nomination.

GAME 43

4. Which movie is about a small town that banned dancing?

a. *The Turning Point* (1977)

b. *Footloose* (1984)

c. *Grease* (1978)

d. *Save the Last Dance* (2001)

GAME 43 Q3 ANSWER a
Ginger Rogers chose to wear a dress adorned with ostrich feathers for the now-famous "Cheek to Cheek" number. When the shoot began, feathers started flying off the lovely costume, interrupting the filming and prompting Astaire to call his costar "Feathers." Only after hours of work by a team of seamstresses was filming able to resume.

GAME 63

4. Who directed *A Passage to India* (1984)?

a. David Lean

b. Franco Zeffirelli

c. Stanley Kubrick

d. Richard Thorpe

GAME 63 Q3 ANSWER d
After his success in the 1935 film *A Midsummer Night's Dream*, Cagney was cast as Robin Hood in Warner Brothers' upcoming movie. But due to contract disputes, he abandoned Warner Brothers, leaving the Merry Men without a leader. Errol Flynn, whose popularity had exploded with the release of 1935's *Captain Blood*, got the part instead.

GAME 18

9. Banzai, Shenzi, and Ed are three villainous _____ in *The Lion King* (1994).

a. Deer
b. Coyotes
c. Pigs
d. Hyenas

GAME 18 Q8 ANSWER a
Woody Allen provides the voice of the neurotic worker ant named Z, who strives to gain individuality within his totalitarian colony. Sylvester Stallone is the voice of Weaver, a strong soldier ant and Z's friend. The writers of *Antz,* the first computer-animated movie with a PG rating, had to edit some of the dialogue to maintain this rating.

GAME 38

9. Which singer-songwriter played Pontius Pilate in Martin Scorsese's *The Last Temptation of Christ* (1988)?

a. Kris Kristofferson
b. David Bowie
c. Mick Jagger
d. Peter Gabriel

GAME 38 Q8 ANSWER d
Martin Scorsese is the only non-Japanese performer featured in this series of vignettes based on director Kurosawa's own dreams. Scorsese acted again a year later alongside Robert De Niro in *Guilty by Suspicion,* producer/director Irwin Winkler's film about the anti-communist Hollywood blacklist that destroyed so many lives in the 1950s.

GAME 58

9. Which romantic movie paired Clark Gable and Claudette Colbert?

a. *I Met Him in Paris* (1937)
b. *It Happened One Night* (1934)
c. *The Man Who Came to Dinner* (1942)
d. *Love on the Run* (1936)

GAME 58 Q8 ANSWER d
The title characters, played by Billy Crystal and Meg Ryan, are based somewhat on the film's director, Rob Reiner, and writer, Nora Ephron. Harry tends to be somber, much like Reiner; while Sally, like Ephron, is a picky eater. Once, after Ephron ordered a very specific meal on a plane, the flight attendant asked if she had ever seen the movie.

GAME 78

9. Which old-time movie serial opens George Lucas's 1970 film *THX-1138*?

a. Buck Rogers
b. Captain Marvel
c. Captain America
d. Flash Gordon

GAME 78 Q8 ANSWER b
Based on the real-life story of horror writer Whitley Strieber, who maintains that he has been visited by extraterrestrials, *Communion* also features strong performances from actresses Lindsay Crouse and Frances Sternhagen. In 1981, Strieber's 1978 debut novel, *The Wolfen,* was turned into a film starring Albert Finney.

GAME 3

5. Which Western features members of four acting families?

a. *The Magnificent Seven* (1960)

b. *The Searchers* (1956)

c. *The Wild Bunch* (1969)

d. *The Long Riders* (1980)

GAME 3 Q4 ANSWER c
Clint Eastwood not only directed and produced *Unforgiven*, but also played main character William Munny, an aging outlaw who decides to do one last job before hanging up his guns forever. Regarded by some critics as the zenith of Eastwood's work, this tribute to the Western genre was only the third Western to win the Academy Award for Best Picture.

GAME 23

5. Who played Tess McGill's backstabbing boss in *Working Girl* (1988)?

a. Glenn Close

b. Susan Sarandon

c. Meryl Streep

d. Sigourney Weaver

GAME 23 Q4 ANSWER d
Kudrow stars with Parker Posey, Alanna Ubach, and Toni Collette in this film about four office temps who work in a place filled with unfriendly full-timers. Best known for her role as the ditzy Phoebe Buffay on the TV series *Friends*, Kudrow was the first of the six "friends" to win an Emmy for the show, and the one with the most nominations.

GAME 43

5. Who stars opposite Sean Patrick Thomas in *Save the Last Dance*?

a. Sarah Jessica Parker

b. Katie Holmes

c. Julia Stiles

d. Rosario Dawson

GAME 43 Q4 ANSWER b
Written by Dean Pitchford, the screenplay of the teen flick *Footloose* is loosely based on real-life events in Elmore City, Oklahoma, where dancing was prohibited for nearly a hundred years. The film centers on teenager Ren McCormack (Kevin Bacon), who moves from Chicago to a small dance-free town and decides to wage war against the antiquated ban.

GAME 63

5. Whom does Judi Dench portray in *Shakespeare in Love* (1998)?

a. Shakespeare's wife

b. The Queen of England

c. Lady Viola's nurse

d. Lady Viola's mother

GAME 63 Q4 ANSWER a
Upset with the critical reviews of *Ryan's Daughter* (1970), David Lean took a fourteen-year break from directing. *A Passage to India* was Lean's first film after the hiatus, but it was also his last. This costume drama won two Academy Awards, including Best Music (Original Score) and Best Supporting Actress for Peggy Ashcroft's portrayal of Mrs. Moore.

GAME 18

8. In the 1998 animated film *Antz*, what attacks the ant colony?

a. Termites

b. Grasshoppers

c. Mosquitoes

d. Cockroaches

GAME 18 Q7 ANSWER d

Finding Nemo is the story of a clown fish named Marlin who is on a desperate adventure to find his lost son, Nemo. Marlin meets Dory, a perpetually optimistic fish who suffers from memory loss, but whose optimism provides an excellent contrast to the pessimistic Marlin. Dory's character was specifically created with Ellen DeGeneres in mind.

GAME 38

8. Which famous person did Martin Scorsese portray in Akira Kurosawa's 1990 film *Dreams*?

a. William Shakespeare

b. Peter Tchaikovsky

c. Geoffrey Chaucer

d. Vincent Van Gogh

GAME 38 Q7 ANSWER d

In his third film with Scorsese (as character Jimmy Doyle) learned to mimic all the saxophone parts he was seen performing in the film. Those parts were actually played by Georgie Auld. De Niro's fellow actor and longtime friend Sean Penn did this same thing for his role as guitarist Emmett Ray in Woody Allen's *Sweet & Lowdown* (1999).

GAME 58

8. Which movie asks if men and women can ever just be friends?

a. *Rumor Has It* (2005)

b. *What Women Want* (2000)

c. *Splash* (1984)

d. *When Harry Met Sally* (1989)

GAME 58 Q7 ANSWER c

This 1999 film is a modern adaptation of George Bernard Shaw's 1913 play, *Pygmalion,* which also served as the basis for the 1956 Broadway musical and 1964 Oscar-winning film *My Fair Lady. She's All That* was filmed at the same high school that was used in *Not Another Teen Movie* (2001) and the TV series *Buffy the Vampire Slayer.*

GAME 78

8. In which film does Christopher Walken meet extraterrestrials?

a. *Click* (2006)

b. *Communion* (1989)

c. *The Dead Zone* (1983)

d. *The Prophecy* (1995)

GAME 78 Q7 ANSWER a

This film stars James Caan as cop Matthew Sykes, who teams up with alien "newcomer" Sam Francisco (Mandy Patinkin) and sets out to solve a murder. The initial success of the film spawned a TV series that aired for one season starting in 1989. This was later followed by five TV-movie sequels called *Alien Nation: Dark Horizon.*

GAME 3

6. What happens at twelve o'clock in the classic Western *High Noon*?

a. A train's arrival

b. A trial

c. A wedding

d. A hanging

GAME 3 Q5 ANSWER d
Director Walter Hill decided to cast four sets of brothers to portray famous brothers of the Old West. James and Stacy Keach play Jesse and Frank James; David, Keith, and Robert Carradine are Cole, Jim, and Bob Younger; Dennis and Randy Quaid take the roles of Ed and Clell Miller; and Christopher and Nicholas Guest are Charley and Robert Ford.

GAME 23

6. In *Perfect Stranger*, who goes undercover as a journalist to catch a killer?

a. Hilary Swank

b. Rose McGowan

c. Halle Berry

d. Kate Beckinsale

GAME 23 Q5 ANSWER d
Weaver played the arrogant Katharine Parker, while Melanie Griffith starred as the savvy but underappreciated secretary. The film received six Oscar nominations, including Best Picture, Best Director (Mike Nichols), Best Actress (Griffith), and two for Supporting Actress (Weaver and Joan Cusack). Carly Simon's "Let the River Run" won for Best Song.

GAME 43

6. Which film's soundtrack features "More Than a Woman"?

a. *Swing Kids* (1993)

b. *Shall We Dance?* (2004)

c. *Mad Hot Ballroom* (2005)

d. *Saturday Night Fever* (1977)

GAME 43 Q5 ANSWER c
Julia Stiles didn't want a double for her dance scenes in *Save the Last Dance* (2001), and insisted on hard-core training to prepare for her role as Sara Johnson. For weeks, Stiles followed a grueling schedule of instruction, and on weekends, she worked on specific dances with choreographers Fatima Robinson (for hip-hop) and Randy Duncan (for ballet).

GAME 63

6. Which costume film is based on a play by George Bernard Shaw?

a. *The Crucible* (1996)

b. *Harvey* (1950)

c. *Gaslight* (1940)

d. *Androcles and the Lion* (1952)

GAME 63 Q5 ANSWER b
This film won a total of seven Academy Awards, including one for Best Supporting Actress for Dench's portrayal of Queen Elizabeth I. That same year, Cate Blanchett, playing the title role in *Elizabeth*, was nominated for Best Actress. This was the only year in which two actresses were nominated for playing the same character in different films.

GAME 18

7. Who is the voice of the forgetful Dory in *Finding Nemo* (2003)?

a. Lisa Kudrow
b. Fran Drescher
c. Julia Louis-Dreyfus
d. Ellen DeGeneres

GAME 18 Q6 ANSWER c
When aliens kidnap all the parents on Earth, genius Jimmy Neutron and his friends set out to rescue them. The movie, which received an Oscar nomination for Best Animated Film, was so popular that it led to three seasons on Nickelodeon of *The Adventures of Jimmy Neutron: Boy Genius* and several made-for-TV movies.

GAME 38

7. In Martin Scorsese's *New York, New York* (1977), Robert De Niro's character is a:

a. Trumpet player
b. Guitarist
c. Piano player
d. Saxophonist

GAME 38 Q6 ANSWER a
Before he made the Rolling Stones concert film *Shine a Light* in 2008, Scorsese used the group's songs "Tell Me" and "Jumpin' Jack Flash" in 1973's *Mean Streets*. "Memo From Turner" was first sung by Rolling Stones frontman Mick Jagger in Nicolas Roeg's 1970 film *Performance* before Scorsese used it and "Gimme Shelter" in *GoodFellas*.

GAME 58

7. Who is transformed into a prom princess in *She's All That* ?

a. Eliza Dushku
b. Gabrielle Union
c. Rachael Leigh Cook
d. Thora Birch

GAME 58 Q6 ANSWER b
Depressed over failed relationships, the two strangers meet online and decide to switch homes (one's in LA, the other's in the English countryside) for the Christmas holiday. The film was written and directed by Nancy Meyers, who also wrote screenplays for such movies as *Baby Boom* (1987), *Something's Gotta Give* (2003), and *It's Complicated* (2009).

GAME 78

7. In which film do the aliens call themselves "newcomers"?

a. *Alien Nation* (1988)
b. *Enemy Mine* (1985)
c. *Contact* (1997)
d. *Spawn* (1997)

GAME 78 Q6 ANSWER d
After appearing first as a Bond girl opposite Sean Connery in *Never Say Never Again* (1983) and then with eccentric actor Mickey Rourke in the erotic drama *9 1/2 Weeks* (1986), Kim Basinger took to lighter fare as the kind-hearted alien Celeste in *My Stepmother Is an Alien*. She later won a Best Supporting Actress Oscar for the 1997 film *L.A. Confidential*.

GAME 3

7. Who made his film debut in Howard Hawks' *Red River*?

a. Marlon Brando
b. John Ireland
c. James Dean
d. Montgomery Clift

GAME 3 Q6 ANSWER a
When *High Noon* was released in 1952, some filmgoers disliked the fact that most of the film offers not action, but dialogue, as ex-Marshal Will Kane (Gary Cooper) tries to recruit men to help him face the vengeful outlaw Frank Miller. The action scene—a shootout between Kane and the Miller gang—takes place in the last few minutes of the movie.

GAME 23

7. Who is Jennifer Lopez's costar in *Maid in Manhattan*?

a. Ben Affleck
b. Michael Vartan
c. Ralph Fiennes
d. Matthew McConaughey

GAME 23 Q6 ANSWER c
Berry costars with Bruce Willis in this 2007 psychological thriller. The movie was supposed to be shot on location in New Orleans; however, Hurricane Katrina made that impossible and the story was rewritten to take place in New York. The writers also provided three different endings to the film, each with a different character as the killer.

GAME 43

7. Which musical includes Donald O'Connor's "Make 'Em Laugh" dance routine?

a. *Swing Time* (1936)
b. *An American in Paris* (1951)
c. *Singin' in the Rain* (1952)
d. *Meet Me in St. Louis* (1944)

GAME 43 Q6 ANSWER d
Composed and performed chiefly by the Bee Gees, the *Saturday Night Fever* soundtrack won the 1978 Grammy Award for Album of the Year, became one of the best-selling soundtracks in the history of film, and breathed new life into the disco era. "More Than a Woman" is just one of the five Bee Gees songs written especially for the movie.

GAME 63

7. In which country does Helena Bonham Carter want *A Room with a View*?

a. England
b. Spain
c. Italy
d. The United States

GAME 63 Q6 ANSWER d
Centering on the persecution of Christians in Ancient Rome, *Androcles and the Lion* was produced by Gabriel Pascal, a long-time friend of playwright George Bernard Shaw. The Hungarian-born filmmaker also produced successful film versions of other Shaw plays, including *Pygmalion* (1938), *Major Barbara* (1941), and *Caesar and Cleopatra* (1945).

GAME 18

6. ____ : *Boy Genius* is an animated movie released in late 2001.

a. *Jamey Jupiter*
b. *Johnny Proton*
c. *Jimmy Neutron*
d. *Joey Electron*

GAME 18 Q5 ANSWER b
This all-time family favorite about a wooden puppet who wants to become a real boy earned an Oscar for its original theme song, "When You Wish Upon a Star." This song also ranked #7 on the 2004 American Film Institute's (AFI's) list of top movie songs of all time. The film itself earned the #2 spot on the AFI list of 10 greatest animated films.

GAME 38

6. Which Rolling Stones song was the first to be used in a Martin Scorsese movie?

a. "Tell Me (You're Coming Back)"
b. "Memo From Turner"
c. "Heart of Stone"
d. "Gimme Shelter"

GAME 38 Q5 ANSWER b
Martin Scorsese was married to Isabella Rossellini—daughter of Swedish actress Ingrid Bergman and Italian neo-realist film director Roberto Rossellini—from 1979 to 1981. While making *New York, New York* (1977), Scorsese had a passionate romance with Liza Minnelli—daughter of Judy Garland and American film director Vincente Minnelli.

GAME 58

6. Who switches homes with Kate Winslet in *The Holiday* (2006)?

a. Alicia Silverstone
b. Cameron Diaz
c. Renée Zellweger
d. Kate Hudson

GAME 58 Q5 ANSWER d
Reese Witherspoon and Josh Lucas star as Melanie and Jake in this romantic comedy about a girl who leaves Alabama, her backwoods roots, and her husband Jake to reinvent herself as a NY fashion designer. The "Down Home Glass" Jake sells is formed after lightning strikes sand on the beach—something he and Melanie discovered as kids.

GAME 78

6. Who plays the title role in *My Stepmother Is an Alien* (1988)?

a. Melanie Griffith
b. Kathleen Turner
c. Jamie Lee Curtis
d. Kim Basinger

GAME 78 Q5 ANSWER d
Based on Stanislaw Lem's 1961 novel, the first *Solaris* was released in 1972 and directed by Andrei Tarkovsky. Steven Soderbergh's remake with star George Clooney came out in 2002, the same year Clooney directed his first film, *Confessions of a Dangerous Mind*. In both films, Solaris is an alien planet that feeds hallucinations to all who approach it.

8. Who portrays gunfighter Jack Wilson in the 1953 classic *Shane*?

a. Robert Mitchum
b. Jack Palance
c. Eli Wallach
d. Charles Bronson

GAME 3

GAME 3 Q7 ANSWER d
Montgomery Clift acted on Broadway for ten years before appearing in the 1948 film *Red River,* in which he plays Matthew Garth, adopted son of Tom Dunson (John Wayne). This classic Western centers on the feud between Garth and Dunson as they drive a massive herd of cattle along the Chisholm Trail, from Dunson's Texas ranch to Kansas.

---

8. In *Office Space*, what's the name of the restaurant where Jennifer Aniston works?

a. Chochkies
b. Buttons
c. Milton's Place
d. Yours Truly

GAME 23

GAME 23 Q7 ANSWER c
Fiennes plays a politician in this 2002 romantic comedy. Lopez's next project was *Gigli* (2003), in which she costarred and began a very public relationship with Ben Affleck that ended in 2004. A few years earlier, Matthew McConaughey starred with her in *The Wedding Planner* (2001), and Michael Vartan was her love interest in *Monster-in-Law* (2005).

---

8. Whose rapid-fire footwork appears in the 1936 musical *Born to Dance*?

a. Jane Powell's
b. Ann Miller's
c. Ruby Keeler's
d. Eleanor Powell's

GAME 43

GAME 43 Q7 ANSWER c
In addition to sharing song-and-dance routines with Gene Kelly and Debbie Reynolds, Donald O'Connor showcased his athletic and comedic skills in the solo "Make 'Em Laugh" number. The high-energy choreography—which featured walking up walls, pratfalls, and back flips—made this the best-remembered scene of O'Connor's career.

---

8. Which of the following films depicts Guinevere as a Celtic warrior?

a. *King Arthur* (2004)
b. *Camelot* (1967)
c. *Excaliber* (1981)
d. *First Knight* (1995)

GAME 63

GAME 63 Q7 ANSWER c
Based on the E.M. Forster novel of the same name, this 1985 film begins in an Italian *pensione*, where Miss Lucy Honeychurch (Bonham Carter) and chaperone Charlotte Bartlett (Maggie Smith) are enjoying a very proper holiday. After Lucy is kissed by the free-thinking George Emerson (Julian Sands), her life becomes a little less conventional.

GAME 18

5. Which Disney classic features the line, "A lie keeps growing and growing"?

a. *Dumbo* (1941)

b. *Pinocchio* (1940)

c. *Peter Pan* (1953)

d. *The Jungle Book* (1967)

GAME 18 Q4 ANSWER b

Larry King provided his voice for two episodes of *The Simpsons* in which he played himself. However, Doris, the ugly stepsister and barmaid in *Shrek 2*, is the first original character for which King lent his voice. The British release of this movie replaced King with another actor, although King still received the credit.

GAME 38

5. Which movie actress did Martin Scorsese marry in 1979?

a. Liza Minnelli

b. Isabella Rossellini

c. Ileanna Douglas

d. Ellen Burstyn

GAME 38 Q4 ANSWER c

Albert Brooks plays the part of a political campaign worker who vies with Robert De Niro for Cybill Shepherd's attention. Scorsese likes giving serious roles to comedians in his movies: Jerry Lewis and Sandra Bernhard both appeared in 1982's *The King of Comedy*, while both Alan King and Don Rickles played old gangsters in *Casino* (1995).

GAME 58

5. In *Sweet Home Alabama* (2002), what does Jake sell in his shop?

a. Jewelry

b. Antiques

c. Candles

d. Glass

GAME 58 Q4 ANSWER a

Hepburn plays the chauffeur's daughter who is infatuated with a wealthy playboy (William Holden), but finds true love with his workaholic brother (Humphrey Bogart). Bogart openly disliked Holden—who was having an affair with Hepburn at the time. He wanted his wife Lauren Bacall cast as Sabrina, and resented Hepburn, saying she lacked acting skills.

GAME 78

5. Who directed George Clooney in the 2002 remake of *Solaris*?

a. George Clooney

b. Andrei Tarkovsky

c. James Cameron

d. Steven Soderbergh

GAME 78 Q4 ANSWER c

In *Modern Romance*, Brooks plays Robert Cole, a film editor who is trying to save an awful science-fiction movie starring George Kennedy before its release. The sci-fi film's clueless director (played by director James L. Brooks) is more fixated on the look of the spaceship (which he fears looks too much like the one in *Alien*) than the movie itself.

9. Who plays dual roles in the 1965 comedy-Western *Cat Ballou*?

a. Jane Fonda

b. Dwayne Hickman

c. Lee Marvin

d. Michael Callan

GAME 3 Q8 ANSWER b
Before appearing in *Shane,* Jack Palance had been a coal miner, a member of the US Air Force, and a professional boxer, but he had never ridden a horse. Director George Stevens therefore had to be creative to get the shots he wanted for the film. A famous scene in which Palance mounts his horse is actually a film of a dismount played in reverse.

9. Which type of baked goods is actress Keri Russell's specialty in *Waitress* (2007)?

a. Pies

b. Brownies

c. Cream puffs

d. Donuts

GAME 23 Q8 ANSWER a
In this 1999 film about a group of fed-up office workers, Chochkies was a nearby restaurant where the servers were encouraged to wear as many buttons on their suspenders as possible—as a sign of employee spirit. The place was actually modeled after the TGI Friday's restaurant chain, where the servers wear the same type of uniform.

9. Which dance movie is set against the backdrop of a coal mining town?

a. *Billy Elliot* (2000)

b. *Nine* (*2009*)

c. *Our Town* (1940)

d. *Coal Miner's Daughter* (1980)

GAME 43 Q8 ANSWER d
Eleanor Powell began dancing professionally at the age of eleven, working first on stage and later in films. Best known for her stunning machine-gun tap dancing—Fred Astaire once remarked, "She really knocked out a tap dance in a class by herself"—Powell appeared in a string of money-making MGM musicals in the '30s and '40s.

9. Who plays the title role in Franco Zeffirelli's 1990 version of *Hamlet*?

a. Jude Law

b. Kevin Costner

c. Mel Gibson

d. Timothy Dalton

GAME 63 Q8 ANSWER a
In this unique version of the classic tale, Guinevere is a Celtic warrior who fights alongside Arthur and his men during battle. Actress Keira Knightley, nineteen years old at the time, chose the role because she thought it would be interesting to portray the legendary queen as a ruthless, leather-clad fighter rather than a damsel in distress.

GAME 18

4. The voice of Doris in 2004's *Shrek 2* is provided by which unlikely person?

a. Bill Clinton

b. Larry King

c. Joan Rivers

d. Jessica Simpson

GAME 18 Q3 ANSWER c
Walt Disney's Imagineers have an inside joke known as the "Hidden Mickey,"— an image of Mickey Mouse hidden in the Disney's attractions. Sharp-eyed viewers will notice the cookies that spunky Merryweather magically creates in *Sleeping Beauty* are in the shape of mouse ears. These cookies are among the earliest Hidden Mickeys.

GAME 38

4. Which stand-up comedian appeared in Martin Scorsese's film *Taxi Driver* (1976)?

a. Jerry Lewis

b. Alan King

c. Albert Brooks

d. Don Rickles

GAME 38 Q3 ANSWER b
Just like Alfred Hitchcock before him, Martin Scorsese has done cameos in many of his films. In *Gangs of New York*, he appeared as an aristocrat, and he voiced the part of an ambulance dispatcher in *Bringing Out the Dead*. He even played a TV director standing alongside Tony Randall in *The King of Comedy*.

GAME 58

4. Who has the title role in the original *Sabrina* (1954)?

a. Audrey Hepburn

b. Marilyn Monroe

c. Grace Kelly

d. Barbara Stanwyck

GAME 58 Q3 ANSWER a
This Farrelly Brothers blockbuster comedy, starring Cameron Diaz and Ben Stiller, was the famous quarterback's second film appearance; the first was in *Reggie's Prayer* (1996). Although NFL star Steve Young was the original choice to play Mary's former lover, he refused the role because he was a practicing Mormon and objected to the film's content.

GAME 78

4. In which Albert Brooks comedy does he edit a sci-fi movie?

a. *Real Life* (1979)

b. *Lost in America* (1985)

c. *Modern Romance* (1981)

d. *The Muse* (1999)

GAME 78 Q3 ANSWER d
After the family-friendly fun of *Star Wars* and the benign aliens in *Close Encounters of the Third Kind* in 1977, the savage horrors of *Alien* were a shocking change of pace for moviegoers. John Hurt's character, Kane, is killed when an alien that has been implanted in his stomach bursts through his chest.

10. Which Western features memorable music by Elmer Bernstein?

a. *Bandolero!* (1968)

b. *High Noon* (1952)

c. *The Alamo* (1960)

d. *The Magnificent Seven* (1960)

GAME 3 Q9 ANSWER c
Lee Marvin drew critical attention when he played both the silver-nosed killer Tim Strawn and the drunken gunfighter Kid Shelleen, who is hired (in vain) to defeat Strawn. As a result, Marvin won not only the 1965 Oscar for Best Actor in a Leading Role, but also—to his delight—acting roles that were more varied and sympathetic than ever before.

---

10. In which movie does Sandra Bullock play a subway toll-booth operator?

a. *Miss Congeniality* (2000)

b. *While You Were Sleeping* (1995)

c. *The Net* (1995)

d. *Infamous* (2006)

GAME 23 Q9 ANSWER a
Russell plays Jenna—a waitress at Joe's Pie Diner whose specialty is creating unusual pies that she names after people or events in her life. The movie was written and directed by Adrienne Shelly, who also costarred in the film. Tragically, less than three months before the film's premiere, Shelly was murdered by an intruder during a home invasion.

---

10. Which MGM musical features Gene Kelly and Judy Garland?

a. *Easter Parade* (1948)

b. *Summer Stock* (1950)

c. *On the Town* (1949)

d. *Meet Me in St. Louis* (1944)

GAME 43 Q9 ANSWER a
Set during a miners' strike in the UK, *Billy Elliot* is the story of an eleven-year-old boy who pursues his dream of becoming a ballet dancer despite opposition from his working class father. The screenplay is partially based on the experiences of Royal Ballet dancer Philip Marsden, who rose from a mining background to achieve professional success.

---

10. Who made her film debut in the 1957 costume drama *Saint Joan*?

a. Ingrid Bergman

b. Jean Seberg

c. Natalie Wood

d. Audrey Hepburn

GAME 63 Q9 ANSWER c
Italian-born director Franco Zeffirelli claims that he cast Mel Gibson as Hamlet after watching the *Lethal Weapon* scene in which Gibson's character contemplates suicide. Because Gibson is so well known in the action film genre, the Italian-born director decided to make Hamlet less dark and brooding, and more of a self-confident fighter.

GAME 18

3. What is the name of the blue fairy in *Sleeping Beauty* (1959)?

a. Glinda

b. Flora

c. Merryweather

d. Fauna

GAME 18 Q2 ANSWER b

Director Chris Wedge provides the voice for Scrat, which is a combination of a squirrel and a rat. Scrat was originally set to appear only in the movie's opening sequence. However, test audiences loved the neurotic character so much that he received more scenes in this movie and its sequels, *The Meltdown* (2006) and *Dawn of the Dinosaurs* (2009).

GAME 38

3. In which of his films does Martin Scorsese make an appearance as a photographer?

a. *Gangs of New York* (2002)

b. *The Age of Innocence* (1993)

c. *Bringing Out the Dead* (1999)

d. *The King of Comedy* (1982)

GAME 38 Q2 ANSWER c

Aside from a brief home movie color sequence midway through the film, *Raging Bull* is a black-and-white movie. All you film buffs should note that *The Color of Money* is a sequel to the 1961 black-and-white film *The Hustler*, while *Cape Fear* is a remake of the original black-and-white film from 1962.

GAME 58

3. Which noted athlete appears in *There's Something About Mary* (1998)?

a. Brett Favre

b. Derek Jeter

c. Steve Young

d. Tiger Woods

GAME 58 Q2 ANSWER d

William Thacker (Hugh Grant) first meets famous film star Anna Scott (Julia Roberts) when she walks into his bookstore. The screenwriter of this 1999 film, Richard Curtis, who also wrote *Four Weddings and a Funeral,* claims that he and Grant had a "writer/actor marriage made in heaven," so Grant was his one and only choice for the film.

GAME 78

3. Which actor is the first to be killed in *Alien* (1979)?

a. Harry Dean Stanton

b. Tom Skerritt

c. Veronica Cartwright

d. John Hurt

GAME 78 Q2 ANSWER b

After Orson Welles caused nationwide panic with his 1938 radio version of the 1898 H.G. Wells novel *The War of the Worlds,* the prospect of Martian attacks became an obsession of sci-fi fans. In addition to *Invaders from Mars,* 1953 also saw producer George Pal release a film of *The War of the Worlds,* which won a Best Special Effects Oscar.

GAME 3

11. What film is *not* part of John Ford's trilogy on the US Cavalry?

a. *My Darling Clementine* (1946)

b. *Fort Apache* (1948)

c. *She Wore a Yellow Ribbon* (1949)

d. *Rio Grande* (1950)

GAME 3 Q10 ANSWER d
Elmer Bernstein composed both the film's score, which was nominated for an Academy Award, and its main theme, which was known to millions of '60s television viewers as the Marlboro cigarette theme. Bernstein also created music for the films *The Ten Commandments* (1956), *The Great Escape* (1963), *To Kill a Mockingbird* (1962), and *Ghostbusters* (1984).

GAME 23

11. Who played the gum-smacking secretary in the 1993 film *The Firm*?

a. Julia Roberts

b. Jeanne Tripplehorne

c. Holly Hunter

d. Demi Moore

GAME 23 Q10 ANSWER b
Her role in this romantic comedy was written for Demi Moore; but the part was given to Bullock because she had more in common with the character. In *Miss Congeniality*, Bullock plays a cop who goes undercover at a beauty pageant. In *The Net*, she is a software programmer, and in *Infamous*, she plays Harper Lee—author of *To Kill a Mockingbird*.

GAME 43

11. Which country produced the film *Strictly Ballroom*?

a. Great Britain

b. Canada

c. Australia

d. India

GAME 43 Q10 ANSWER b
Summer Stock paired Kelly and Garland for the third and last time. They had also sung and danced their way through *Me and My Gal* (1942) and *The Pirate* (1948). Strangely, the most famous *Summer Stock* number, "Get Happy," does not feature the unparalled dancing of Kelly, but rather Judy Garland's exuberant performance of the song.

GAME 63

11. For which period piece did Jane Campion win the Best Screenplay Oscar?

a. *The Portrait of a Lady* (1996)

b. *Little Women* (1994)

c. *Girl With a Pearl Earring* (2003)

d. *The Piano* (1993)

GAME 63 Q10 ANSWER b
Director Otto Preminger chose eighteen-year-old Jean Seberg from among thousands of hopefuls. When the film was not a critical success, Preminger disagreed with those who blamed Seberg's inexperience. Instead, he held himself responsible, explaining that he had not fully understood the George Bernard Shaw play on which the movie was based.

GAME 18

2. In the film *Ice Age* (2002), a creature called Scrat constantly protects his:

a. Scooter

b. Acorn

c. Hair

d. Trumpet

GAME 18 Q1 ANSWER d

Andreas Deja, the supervising animator for *Aladdin,* based his design for the villain Jafar on a previous Disney villain—Maleficent from *Sleeping Beauty.* The first animated movie to gross over $200 million at the box office, *Aladdin* also received two Oscars, including Best Original Song for "A Whole New World" written by Alan Menken and Tim Rice.

GAME 38

2. Which of these Martin Scorsese films was shot in black and white?

a. *The Aviator* (2004)

b. *The Color of Money* (1986)

c. *Raging Bull* (1980)

d. *Cape Fear* (1991)

GAME 38 Q1 ANSWER b

Portraying a shady character named "Sport," Keitel made an impact with audiences as the man responsible for keeping the twelve-and-a-half-year-old Iris (played by Jodie Foster in an Oscar-nominated role) trapped in a life of child prostitution. Keitel made his film debut in Scorsese's first feature film *Who's That Knocking at My Door* (1967).

GAME 58

2. What type of store does Hugh Grant's character own in *Notting Hill* ?

a. A pet store

b. An antique store

c. A toy store

d. A bookstore

GAME 58 Q1 ANSWER b

Tom Hanks plays lonely widower Sam Baldwin in this Nora Ephron film, and Meg Ryan has the role of Annie Reed. Reminiscent of the 1957 romantic classic *An Affair to Remember,* their meeting place is atop the Empire State Building. Before Ryan was cast, the role had been offered to a number of actresses including Julia Roberts and Jodie Foster.

GAME 78

2. Where do humans battle Martians in 1953's *Invaders from Mars* ?

a. In space

b. Underground

c. On Mars

d. At sea

GAME 78 Q1 ANSWER a

When he first started to shoot the film in 1965, Stanley Kubrick intended for US astronaut David Bowman (Keir Dullea) to make contact with the aliens' monolith near the planet Saturn. However, the meeting took place near Jupiter in the finished 1968 film. The famous black monolith represents the aliens' presence (though they are never seen).

GAME 3	**12.** Where do the title characters flee in *Butch Cassidy and the Sundance Kid*? **a.** Chile **b.** Paraguay **c.** Bolivia **d.** Brazil	**GAME 3 Q11 ANSWER a** Besides sharing the theme of the US Cavalry, *Fort Apache, She Wore a Yellow Ribbon,* and *Rio Grande* share American icon John Wayne. Director John Ford and actor John Wayne were friends and colleagues for over fifty years, and produced not just great Westerns, but also classics such as *They Were Expendable* (1945) and *The Quiet Man* (1952).
GAME 23	**12.** Who plays a very busy mother in the 2003 comedy *Cheaper by the Dozen*? **a.** Uma Thurman **b.** Jennifer Connelly **c.** Shelley Long **d.** Bonnie Hunt	**GAME 23 Q11 ANSWER c** For her role as Tammy Hemphill, secretary to private investigator Eddie Lomax (Gary Busey), Hunter received an Oscar nomination for Best Supporting Actress. As a point of interest, she appears on screen for a very short time—a total of five minutes and fifty-nine seconds! It is one of the shortest performances ever nominated for an Oscar.
GAME 43	**12.** Who stars opposite Gene Kelly in *An American in Paris* (1951)? **a.** Ginger Rogers **b.** Cyd Charisse **c.** Leslie Caron **d.** Rita Hayworth	**GAME 43 Q11 ANSWER c** *Strictly Ballroom* (1992) both mocks and celebrates the world of competitive ballroom dancing by telling the tale of two young misfits who strive to win the Australian Pan Pacific Championships. Highly praised at the 1992 Cannes Film Festival, the movie was sought after by distributors from around the world and sold to eighty-six countries.
GAME 63	**12.** Who seeks to seduce Uma Thurman in *Dangerous Liaisons* (1988)? **a.** Keanu Reeves **b.** Tom Cruise **c.** John Malkovich **d.** Daniel Day-Lewis	**GAME 63 Q11 ANSWER d** Jane Campion not only wrote the screenplay for this critically acclaimed film, but also directed it. In fact, Campion is one of only a handful of women ever nominated for the Academy Award for Best Director. Other women who won recognition for their work on *The Piano* include Holly Hunter (Best Actress) and Anna Paquin (Best Supporting Actress).

GAME 18

1. Which animated film features the characters Jasmine, Jafar, and Iago?

a. *An American Tail* (1986)

b. *The Little Mermaid* (1989)

c. *The Rescuers* (1977)

d. *Aladdin* (1992)

The answer to this question is on:

page 76, top frame, right side.

GAME 38

1. In which Martin Scorsese film does Harvey Keitel portray a pimp?

a. *Mean Streets* (1973)

b. *Taxi Driver* (1976)

c. *Alice Doesn't Live Here Anymore* (1974)

d. *Casino* (1995)

The answer to this question is on:

page 76, second frame, right side.

GAME 58

1. On which holiday do Sam and Annie meet in 1993's *Sleepless in Seattle*?

a. Christmas

b. Valentine's Day

c. Halloween

d. New Year's Eve

The answer to this question is on:

page 76, third frame, right side.

GAME 78

1. Near which planet do the aliens wait in *2001: A Space Odyssey*?

a. Jupiter

b. Mars

c. Saturn

d. Pluto

The answer to this question is on:

page 76, bottom frame, right side.

GAME 4

GRAB BAG

*Turn to page 81
for the first question.*

GAME 3 Q12 ANSWER c

In this award-winning 1969 film, the two infamous bank robbers—played by Paul Newman and Robert Redford—are at first handicapped when they reach Bolivia because they cannot speak Spanish. Fortunately, companion Etta Place (played by Katharine Ross) is able to teach them all the words they must know to successfully commit bank heists.

GAME 24

GRAB BAG

*Turn to page 81
for the first question.*

GAME 23 Q12 ANSWER d

In this film, Hunt and Steve Martin play Kate and Tom Baker, the parents of twelve kids. (In real life, neither Hunt nor Martin has any children.) The movie has the same name as the 1948 biography of Frank and Lillian Gilbreth and their twelve children, but that's as far as the similarities go. A sequel, *Cheaper by the Dozen 2,* came out in 2005.

GAME 44

GRAB BAG

*Turn to page 81
for the first question.*

GAME 43 Q12 ANSWER c

Gene Kelly first saw Leslie Caron performing in a Paris ballet troupe, and cast the eighteen-year-old dancer in the role of French orphan Lise Bouvier. Audiences were charmed, and over the next few years, Caron won starring roles in successful movies such as *Lili* (1953), *Daddy Long Legs* (1955), and the Academy Award-winning *Gigi* (1958).

GAME 64

GRAB BAG

*Turn to page 81
for the first question.*

GAME 63 Q12 ANSWER c

Malkovich's portrayal of the wily Vicomte Sébastien de Valmont divided the critics. Some felt that he turned in a strong performance, while others observed that he lacked the charm necessary to make Valmont believable. Costars Glenn Close and Michelle Pfeiffer received Academy Award nominations for their work in the film, but Malkovich did not.

GAME 18

Animated Features

Turn to page 78
for the first question.

Turn to page 78 for the first question.

GAME 17 Q12 ANSWER c

Before starting a successful career in films, Burt Lancaster worked as a circus acrobat along with childhood friend Nick Cravat. The 1950 adventure film *The Flame and the Arrow* is one of nine films that feature both Lancaster and Cravat, with Cravat often playing a mute character to hide the heavy Brooklyn accent that he was never able to lose.

GAME 38

Martin Scorsese

Turn to page 78
for the first question.

Turn to page 78 for the first question.

GAME 37 Q12 ANSWER a

Although no members of the *Stand by Me* cast received Academy Award nominations, reviewers noted the young actors' outstanding performances in this film about kids growing up in the fictional town of Castle Rock, Oregon. The movie was further praised for avoiding the saccharine sweet ending that is typical of so many coming-of-age movies.

GAME 58

Romantic Comedies

Turn to page 78
for the first question.

Turn to page 78 for the first question.

GAME 57 Q12 ANSWER a

Starring Emilio Estevez as Billy the Kid, *Young Guns* has been called the most historically accurate of all the films that have portrayed this nineteenth-century outlaw. The movie was also quite successful. In fact, *Young Guns* did so well at the box office that in 1990, Morgan Creek Productions released a sequel, *Young Guns II.*

GAME 78

More Extraterrestrials, UFOs & Aliens

Turn to page 78
for the first question.

Turn to page 78 for the first question.

GAME 77 Q12 ANSWER c

Jackson was already known as a cult splatter film director in his native New Zealand before making this unsettling drama. Based on the infamous Parker-Hulme murder, the movie earned a Best Screenplay nomination at the Oscars and also marked the big screen debut of both Melanie Lynskey and Kate Winslet, who won her role over 175 other girls.

GAME 4

1. Who uttered the famous line, "Look Ma, I'm on top of the world"?

a. Humphrey Bogart
b. Jimmy Cagney
c. Adam Sandler
d. Robert Redford

The answer to this question is on:

**page 83,
top frame,
right side.**

GAME 24

1. What activity is the focus of *Iron Monkey*?

a. Martial arts
b. Sculpting
c. Marathon running
d. Competitive cooking

The answer to this question is on:

**page 83,
second frame,
right side.**

GAME 44

1. Who is the only actor to appear in all four *Airport* films?

a. George Kennedy
b. Charlton Heston
c. Joseph Cotten
d. Clark Gable

The answer to this question is on:

**page 83,
third frame,
right side.**

GAME 64

1. Which film is loosely based on the life of choreographer Bob Fosse?

a. *The Turning Point* (1977)
b. *Dancing with Time* (2007)
c. *All That Jazz* (1979)
d. *Shall We Dance* (2004)

The answer to this question is on:

**page 83,
bottom frame,
right side.**

GAME 17

12. Which of Burt Lancaster's friends is his costar in *The Flame and the Arrow*?

a. Rock Hudson

b. Kirk Douglas

c. Nick Cravat

d. Dana Andrews

GAME 17 Q11 ANSWER d
In *Scaramouche*, Stewart Granger plays Andre Moreau, a man intent on revenge against the Marquis de Maynes (Mel Ferrer). Moreau takes fencing lessons while working with an acting troupe, and the final clash between him and the Marquis (one of the longest duels in film history) ranges throughout a theater, from the balcony to the seats to the stage.

GAME 37

12. Which young actor does *not* appear in the 1986 film *Stand by Me*?

a. Christian Slater

b. River Phoenix

c. Wil Wheaton

d. Kiefer Sutherland

GAME 37 Q11 ANSWER c
Eleven-year-old Keisha Castle-Hughes had no previous acting experience when she was cast in *The Whale Rider*. In 2004, she became the youngest person—and the first Polynesian—ever nominated for Best Actress in a Leading Role. Although she didn't win the Oscar, since then, the young actress has won parts in several films.

GAME 57

12. Which figure of the American West is depicted in 1988's *Young Guns*?

a. Billy the Kid

b. George Custer

c. Jesse James

d. Wyatt Earp

GAME 57 Q11 ANSWER d
Director Sam Peckinpah considered Richard Boone, Robert Mitchum, Lee Marvin, Burt Lancaster, and several other well-known actors when casting the lead role in *The Wild Bunch*. Lee Marvin actually accepted the job, but when he was offered a bigger paycheck for *Paint Your Wagon*, he pulled out, and William Holden was cast as Pike Bishop.

GAME 77

12. Which film was directed by *The Lord of the Rings'* Peter Jackson?

a. *Last Tycoon* (1976)

b. *Eating Raoul* (1982)

c. *Heavenly Creatures* (1994)

d. *Romper Stomper* (1992)

GAME 77 Q11 ANSWER a
This 1984 cult flick features Emilio Estevez in one of his earliest roles. He soon established himself as one of Hollywood's "Brat Pack" by appearing in such movies as *The Breakfast Club* (1985) and *St. Elmo's Fire* (1985) alongside members Judd Nelson and Ally Sheedy. As a director, his works include *The War at Home* (1996) and *Bobby* (2006).

GAME 4

2. Who plays the title character in the 1954 movie *The Barefoot Contessa*?

a. Rita Hayworth

b. Ava Gardner

c. Marilyn Monroe

d. Lana Turner

GAME 4 Q1 ANSWER b

These are Cagney's concluding words in the 1949 thriller *White Heat*. Cagney, who is best known for the gangster roles he played in the '30s and '40s, portrays Cody Jarrett in this film. He screams this line at the top of his lungs before the fuel tank he is standing on explodes into a ball of fire. Talk about going out with a bang!

GAME 24

2. Which film stars Robert Redford as a security expert?

a. *Sneakers* (1992)

b. *The Last Castle* (2001)

c. *Brubaker* (1980)

d. *Three Days of the Condor* (1975)

GAME 24 Q1 ANSWER a

In 2001, Miramax released this 1993 Hong Kong film in the US. To the dismay of Hong Kong moviegoers, numerous changes were made for the US version. Several comedic sequences, especially those in fight scenes, were removed; subtitles were edited to tone down the story's political context; and scenes were cut to reduce the level of violence.

GAME 44

2. What name does Stanley Kowalski scream in *A Streetcar Named Desire*?

a. Judy

b. Blanche

c. Stella

d. Audrey

GAME 44 Q1 ANSWER a

Along with his recurring role in this '70s disaster movie series, Kennedy is also well known for his Academy Award performance as Dragline in 1967's *Cool Hand Luke* opposite Paul Newman. Later in his career, the actor found success playing Captain Ed Hocken, boss to Leslie Neilsen's Sergeant Frank Drebin, in the 1988 comedy *The Naked Gun*.

GAME 64

2. Who plays the title role in the 1995 remake of *Sabrina*?

a. Julia Roberts

b. Julia Ormond

c. Winona Ryder

d. Gwyneth Paltrow

GAME 64 Q1 ANSWER c

Choreographer/dancer Bob Fosse co-wrote and directed this semi-autobiographical fantasy, starring Roy Scheider as the chain-smoking, womanizing, workaholic Joe Gideon, whose overstressed body is heading towards collapse. Yet the film is fascinating and funny, and every dance scene features Bob Fosse's brilliant choreography.

GAME 17

11. Where does the climactic duel take place in 1952's *Scaramouche*?

a. In a castle
b. In a brothel
c. On a ship
d. In a theater

GAME 17 Q10 ANSWER a
Cutthroat Island paired Geena Davis (as female pirate Morgan Adams) with Matthew Modine (as Morgan's educated slave). Unfortunately for Davis, Modine, and, producer/director Renny Harlin, the film cost about $115 million to produce, but grossed only $10 million in the US. This spelled the end of Harlin's company, Carolco Pictures.

GAME 37

11. For which film did Keisha Castle-Hughes receive an Oscar nomination?

a. *Dreamcatcher* (2003)
b. *In America* (2003)
c. *Whale Rider* (2003)
d. *Big Fish* (2003)

GAME 37 Q10 ANSWER d
Because Samantha Baker's (Molly Ringwald's) sister is getting married the next day, Sam's family has forgotten her sixteenth birthday. Even worse, both sets of grandparents are staying at the Baker home for the upcoming event, and one set has brought along a peculiar foreign exchange student whom Sam is supposed to bring to her school dance.

GAME 57

11. Who plays the leader of an aging outlaw gang in 1969's *The Wild Bunch*?

a. Lee Marvin
b. Marlon Brando
c. Robert Mitchum
d. William Holden

GAME 57 Q10 ANSWER a
In Mel Brooks' satire *Blazing Saddles,* Madeline Kahn's character, Lili Von Shtupp, is a parody of Dietrich's character, Frenchy, in the 1939 Western *Destry Rides Again.* Because the word "shtupp" has a vulgar meaning in Yiddish, when *Blazing Saddles* is broadcast on television, the last name of the saloon singer is often changed to "Shhhh."

GAME 77

11. What happens to those who look into the Chevy's trunk in *Repo Man*?

a. They disintegrate
b. They freeze
c. They start dancing
d. They melt

GAME 77 Q10 ANSWER d
Written by Oliver Stone and directed by Brian De Palma, this crime epic has become a touchstone of the gangster film genre. De Palma is, however, responsible for more than just one classic gangster flick, having directed the Prohibition-era true story *The Untouchables* (1987) and 1993's *Carlito's Way*, which reteamed him with *Scarface* star Al Pacino.

3. Which character hails from Skull Island?

a. Captain Nemo
b. King Kong
c. Captain Hook
d. Long John Silver

GAME 4 Q2 ANSWER b
Ava Gardner stars as Maria Vargas in this movie about a peasant dancer who rises from poverty in her native Spain to become an international movie star and marry into royalty. The title of this movie is telling in that, although she achieves great wealth and fame, Maria actually prefers walking barefoot in the dirt rather than wearing shoes.

3. What gruesome secret is hidden in *The Fog* (1980)?

a. Nuclear plant radiation
b. Ghostly sailors
c. Demons from Earth's core
d. Alien invaders

GAME 24 Q2 ANSWER a
A fast-paced comedy/thriller about cryptography and computers, blackmail and betrayal, this film boasts an all-star cast. Robert Redford's fellow "sneakers" (high-tech wizards) include Sidney Poitier, Dan Aykroyd, River Phoenix, and David Strathairn. The movie also features the talents of Mary McDonell, Ben Kingsley, and James Earl Jones.

3. Which automobile model "costars" in 1983's *Christine*?

a. Chevrolet Bel Air
b. Plymouth Fury
c. Ford Mustang
d. Mercury Sable

GAME 44 Q2 ANSWER c
This 1951 film won an unprecedented three acting Oscars. Karl Malden took the Best Supporting Actor Oscar; Kim Hunter brought home the Best Supporting Actress award; and Vivien Leigh won the Best Actress honor. Marlon Brando was nominated for his role as Stanley Kowalski, but lost to Humphrey Bogart, who won for *The African Queen* (1951).

3. In which movie does a blind man fall in love with the girl next door?

a. *Wait Until Dark* (1967)
b. *Butterflies Are Free* (1972)
c. *Ice Castles* (1978)
d. *Blind Date* (1985)

GAME 64 Q2 ANSWER b
The role of Sabrina Fairchild—played by Audrey Hepburn in the 1954 film—did not immediately go to Ormond. Demi Moore, Gwyneth Paltrow, and Winona Ryder were all considered before Ormond was cast. Unfortunately, *Sabrina* was not a box office success, probably because it suffered from comparisons to the original star-studded film.

GAME 17

10. Who stars in the 1995 pirate film *Cutthroat Island*?

a. Geena Davis
b. Robin Wright
c. Jodie Foster
d. Demi Moore

GAME 17 Q9 ANSWER b
The 1985 fantasy-action film *Ladyhawke* stars Rutger Hauer and Michelle Pfeiffer as lovers doomed to separate lives by a curse that causes him to become a black wolf at night, and her to become a hawk by day. Matthew Broderick and Leo McKern are the escaped thief and monk who become unlikely partners in a scheme to break the evil spell.

GAME 37

10. Who contributes to Samantha's misery in *Sixteen Candles* (1984)?

a. A cruel principal
b. A cheating boyfriend
c. A vindictive cheerleader
d. Annoying grandparents

GAME 37 Q9 ANSWER b
Director Peter Bogdanovich decided to shoot *The Last Picture Show* in black and white after discussing the project with friend and mentor Orson Welles. This made it the first mainstream black-and-white film produced since the early '60s. The almost documentary-like realism of the movie won Robert Surtees an Academy Award for Best Cinematography.

GAME 57

10. Which Western includes a parody of a Marlene Dietrich character?

a. *Blazing Saddles* (1974)
b. *The Frisco Kid* (1979)
c. *Cat Ballou* (1965)
d. *Son of Paleface* (1952)

GAME 57 Q9 ANSWER c
By 1962, most movies—Westerns included—were being made in color, but *The Man Who Shot Liberty Valance* was filmed in black and white on a Paramount sound stage. Some film historians claim that the studio was trying to cut costs, but others maintain that director John Ford deliberately chose black and white to evoke a sense of nostalgia.

GAME 77

10. In 1983's *Scarface*, what is Tony Montana's first job in America?

a. Bouncer
b. Parking lot attendant
c. Housepainter
d. Dishwasher

GAME 77 Q9 ANSWER b
One of the most successful independent films ever made, this terrifying horror film was director Tobe Hooper's first feature-length release. Hooper soon added to his accomplishments in the genre by directing an Emmy-nominated television adaptation of Stephen King's *Salem's Lot* in 1979, as well as the Steven Spielberg-produced *Poltergeist* in 1982.

GAME 4

4. John Cho and Kal Penn are on a quest for burgers in *Harold and Kumar Go to:*

a. *McDonald's*
b. *Burger King*
c. *White Castle*
d. *In-N-Out Burger*

GAME 4 Q3 ANSWER b
Skull Island is where explorers captured the giant gorilla. In the 1933 film, the human inhabitants of the island were of West African descent; but their barbaric portrayal caused heated controversy. In the 2005 remake, the island inhabitants belonged to a unique race. To appear as no one else on earth, they were sprayed a unique brown color.

GAME 24

4. In what film does Peter O'Toole say, "I'm not an actor. I'm a movie star"?

a. *The Final Curtain* (2006)
b. *Network* (1976)
c. *The Stunt Man* (1980)
d. *My Favorite Year* (1982)

GAME 24 Q3 ANSWER b
John Carpenter wrote and directed this horror film, but wasn't pleased with the first cut. After Carpenter added new scenes and reshot a third of the footage to make the action more understandable and more frightening, *The Fog* was recut and released to the public. Although it received only mixed reviews, the movie was a success in the box office.

GAME 44

4. Which movie features the song "Can You Feel the Love Tonight?"

a. *Aladdin* (1992)
b. *Mulan* (1998)
c. *Pocahontas* (1995)
d. *The Lion King* (1994)

GAME 44 Q3 ANSWER b
Although Stephen King describes Christine as a four-door 1958 Fury in his identically titled 1983 novel, the filmmakers of this movie adaptation were forced to change the car to a two-door coupe when they discovered that Plymouth had only begun adding rear doors to that model in 1959. The car's inaccurate red and white color, however, was kept.

GAME 64

4. Which Alfred Hitchcock movie was filmed in and around San Francisco?

a. *Spellbound* (1945)
b. *Rear Window* (1954)
c. *Vertigo* (1958)
d. *The Birds* (1963)

GAME 64 Q3 ANSWER b
Based on a Leonard Gershe play, the film stars Edward Albert (actor Eddie Albert's son) as Don Baker, a blind man trying to live on his own, and Goldie Hahn as Jill Tanner, Don's free-thinking neighbor. *Butterflies Are Free* was a success, with much of the credit going to Hahn, who was praised for being "funny and touching, a delight throughout."

GAME 17

9. What animal form does Rutger Hauer's character take in *Ladyhawke*?

a. A stag
b. A wolf
c. A leopard
d. A flying horse

GAME 17 Q8 ANSWER d
Based on Sir Walter Scott's novel of the same name, this film stars Robert Taylor as Ivanhoe, Elizabeth Taylor as Rebecca, and Joan Fontaine as Rowena. Grossing $6.2 million, *Ivanhoe* was MGM's highest earning film of 1952, and became the first in an unofficial swashbuckling trilogy directed by Richard Thorpe and starring Robert Taylor.

GAME 37

9. Which coming-of-age movie was shot in black and white?

a. *To Sir, With Love* (1967)
b. *The Last Picture Show* (1971)
c. *American Graffiti* (1973)
d. *Diner* (1982)

GAME 37 Q8 ANSWER d
Louisa May Alcott's novel *Little Women* has inspired over a dozen films—as well as several plays and one opera—and has showcased an impressive number of young actresses. In addition to featuring Kirsten Dunst, the 1994 film version cast Winona Ryder as Jo March, Trini Alvarado as Meg, Samantha Mathis as the older Amy, and Claire Danes as Beth.

GAME 57

9. Which of these Westerns was shot in black and white?

a. *The Horse Soldiers* (1959)
b. *The Alamo* (1960)
c. *The Man Who Shot Liberty Valance* (1962)
d. *The Comancheros* (1961)

GAME 57 Q8 ANSWER b
Tom Chaney was played by Jeff Corey, an actor whose initial career was halted in 1951, when he refused to supply names to the House on Un-American Activities Committee. While Corey was blacklisted, he became a respected acting teacher whose students included James Dean, Jane Fonda, and Jack Nicholson. Corey resumed his film work in 1962.

GAME 77

9. Which character appears in 1974's *The Texas Chainsaw Massacre*?

a. Jason
b. Leatherface
c. Freddy Krueger
d. Chucky

GAME 77 Q8 ANSWER c
Having previously worked together in Cecil B. DeMille's *The Ten Commandments* (1956), Charlton Heston and Edward G. Robinson costar in this dystopian tale based on Harry Harrison's 1966 novel *Make Room! Make Room!* The film also features the last big screen appearance of Robinson, who succumbed to cancer twelve days after shooting had ended.

GAME 4

5. Who sang "There's No Business Like Show Business" in the 1954 movie of the same name?

a. Lucille Ball
b. Ethel Merman
c. Betty Grable
d. Rosalind Russell

GAME 4 Q4 ANSWER c
Kal Penn, who plays Kumar, is a vegetarian, so special "veggie "White Castle burgers had to be made for him during the filming. Upon the movie's release, White Castle distributed "Harold and Kumar" collectible cups in appreciation for all of the free advertising it received. It was the first time an R-rated movie was advertised on a fast-food container.

GAME 24

5. Which urban drama has Sal's Famous Pizzeria at the center of its action?

a. *Do the Right Thing* (1989)
b. *Blackboard Jungle* (1955)
c. *Boyz n the Hood* (1991)
d. *Stand and Deliver* (1988)

GAME 24 Q4 ANSWER d
Set in the age of live television, *My Favorite Year* tells the story of a washed-up movie star (O'Toole) who is ill prepared for his guest shot on a popular comedy-variety show. O'Toole's knock-out performance—which includes both clever dialogue and physical comedy—won him a 1982 Academy Award nomination for Best Actor in a Leading Role.

GAME 44

5. Which film stars Humphrey Bogart as a salty riverboat captain?

a. *Caine Mutiny* (1954)
b. *Key Largo* (1948)
c. *The Big Sleep* (1946)
d. *The African Queen* (1951)

GAME 44 Q4 ANSWER d
Featuring original songs by Elton John and Tim Rice and a score by Hans Zimmer, the accompanying album to this Disney musical became the top-selling soundtrack of 1994. While three of their compositions were nominated for Best Original Song, this song by John and Rice won them the Oscar. Zimmer also earned the Oscar for Best Original Score.

GAME 64

5. In which film does H.G. Wells travel through time to catch Jack the Ripper?

a. *Time After Time* (1979)
b. *The Time Machine* (1960)
c. *Somewhere in Time* (1980)
d. *Timestalkers* (1987)

GAME 64 Q4 ANSWER c
Filmed from September to December 1957, *Vertigo* includes extensive footage of the San Francisco Bay Area. Mission San Juan Bautista, Mission Dolores, Coit Tower, Fort Point, and the California Palace of the Legion of Honor are just a few of the sights that appear in the film and are routinely visited by knowledgeable Alfred Hitchcock fans.

GAME 17

8. Which tale of knights and ladies features two "Taylors" in leading roles?

a. *The Golden Blade* (1952)

b. *Cyrano de Bergerac* (1950)

c. *The Three Musketeers* (1948)

d. *Ivanhoe* (1952)

GAME 17 Q7 ANSWER a
In this inventive spin on the Zorro legend, Hopkins portrays the "original" Zorro (whose real name is Diego de la Vega) and Antonio Banderas plays the young man whom Diego trains to become his successor. This 1998 swashbuckler was a critical and box office success in the US, and was also well received in Wales, Hopkins' home country.

GAME 37

8. Who plays young Amy March in the 1994 version of *Little Women*?

a. Julia Stiles

b. Scarlett Johansson

c. Natalie Portman

d. Kirsten Dunst

GAME 37 Q7 ANSWER a
Dustin Hoffman's breakthrough role was that of Benjamin Braddock, the college grad who is reluctant to adopt his parents' artificial lifestyle. Hoffman and co-stars Anne Bancroft and Katharine Ross all received Oscar nominations for their performances, but *The Graduate* garnered only one Academy Award—that for Best Director Mike Nichols.

GAME 57

8. Which heartless killer is the subject of the search in 1969's *True Grit*?

a. Frank Miller

b. Tom Chaney

c. Tim Strawn

d. Jack Wilson

GAME 57 Q7 ANSWER d
With music by Jay Livingston and lyrics by Ray Evans, "Buttons and Bows" (sung by Bob Hope in *The Paleface*) won the Academy Award for Best Song in 1948. While Hope's version of the song first brought it to public attention, it was a recording by Dinah Shore that made it the most popular song of 1948 and kept it #1 on the charts for ten weeks.

GAME 77

8. Which movie concludes with the shocking revelation, "It's people!"

a. *THX 1138* (1971)

b. *Westworld* (1973)

c. *Soylent Green* (1973)

d. *The Running Man* (1987)

GAME 77 Q7 ANSWER c
Known for its audience participation, this unmistakable cult classic is the longest-running theatrical release in film history, having never been taken out of the cinemas since its release. A fixture on the midnight movie scene, it marks the film debut of Tim Curry as Dr. Frank N. Furter—a role he originally played on stage in *The Rocky Horror Show*.

6. The thumbless Howard Payne is the villain in which action movie?

a. *Speed* (1994)

b. *The Rock* (1996)

c. *Die Hard* (1988)

d. *Air Force One* (1997)

GAME 4

GAME 4 Q5 ANSWER b

Known for her ability to belt out a song, Merman was also very competitive. Her marriage to Ernest Borgnine lasted only 32 days because, according to Borgnine (who was in TV's hit show *McHale's Navy*), he got more fan attention than she did during their honeymoon. In Merman's autobiography, she dedicated a chapter to their marriage—one blank page.

---

6. What was Marion Crane doing when she saw Norman Bates for the last time?

a. Buying a used car

b. Gazing out the window

c. Taking a shower

d. Eating a sandwich

GAME 24

GAME 24 Q5 ANSWER a

Spike Lee's hit movie *Do the Right Thing* was filmed entirely on Stuyvesant Avenue in the Bedford-Stuyvesant area of Brooklyn, New York. Sal's Famous Pizzeria was specially constructed for the shoot, and to give the impression of a stifling heat wave, the street's color scheme was changed through liberal use of orange and red paint.

---

6. Who plays convict Andy Dufresne in *The Shawshank Redemption*?

a. Kevin Costner

b. Tim Robbins

c. Clint Eastwood

d. Tom Hanks

GAME 44

GAME 44 Q5 ANSWER d

Though he had been nominated twice before, Bogart won his first and only Oscar for his role as Charlie Allnut in this John Huston film. Of the cast and crew who traveled to Africa, Bogey and Huston were the only two people to avoid illness. The actor attributed their immunity to a steady diet of baked beans, canned asparagus, and Scotch whiskey.

---

6. Which movie's casting practices led to a controversy at Wellesley College?

a. *Animal House* (1978)

b. *Mona Lisa Smile* (2003)

c. *Legally Blonde* (2001)

d. *The Paper Chase* (1973)

GAME 64

GAME 64 Q5 ANSWER a

Starring Malcom McDowell as H.G. Wells, David Warner as Jack the Ripper, and Mary Steenburgen as bank employee Amy Robbins, this film not only explores the magic of time travel, but also cleverly contrasts Victorian England and contemporary America. McDowell and Steenburgen fell in love both in the film and in real life, and eventually married.

GAME 17

7. Who portrays an aging Diego de la Vega in *The Mask of Zorro* (1998)?

a. Anthony Hopkins
b. Sean Connery
c. George Hamilton
d. Frank Langella

GAME 17 Q6 ANSWER c
A prolific writer, William Goldman has written screenplays for over two dozen movies, including *Butch Cassidy and the Sundance Kid* (1969), *The Stepford Wives* (1975), *Marathon Man* (1976), *All the President's Men* (1976), and *Misery* (1990). *Marathon Man* and *The Princess Bride* were based on novels also written by the talented William Goldman.

GAME 37

7. What word of advice is whispered to Dustin Hoffman in 1967's *The Graduate*?

a. "Plastics"
b. "Sugar-free"
c. "Computers"
d. "Exercise"

GAME 37 Q6 ANSWER d
The romantic comedy *Mystic Pizza* gave Damon his first film role—and just a single line of dialogue. *Mystic Pizza* better displayed the acting talents of stars Annabeth Gish, Julia Roberts, and Lili Taylor, all of whom received critical praise. In fact, Roger Ebert predicted that the film might someday be known for the young actresses it showcased.

GAME 57

7. Which song won an Oscar after it was featured in 1948's *The Paleface*?

a. "Man with the Harmonica"
b. "In the Summer Time"
c. "Thanks for the Memory"
d. "Buttons and Bows"

GAME 57 Q6 ANSWER a
Harold Robbins' best-selling novel *The Carpetbaggers* includes the story of Nevada Smith, an older cowboy who gains wealth as an actor in Western movies. The film *Nevada Smith*, which was written as a prequel to Robbins' book, stars Steve McQueen as the young Smith—a man determined to avenge the murder of his white father and Indian mother.

GAME 77

7. Which character is murdered in 1975's *The Rocky Horror Picture Show*?

a. Magenta
b. Riff Raff
c. Rocky Horror
d. Brad Majors

GAME 77 Q6 ANSWER d
After his experience acting in this Rob Reiner-directed mock musical documentary, actor Christopher Guest went on to direct a number of his own successful "mockumentaries." Featuring a loose repertory group of comedic performers, these highly improvisational films include 1996's *Waiting for Guffman*, 2000's *Best in Show*, and 2003's *A Mighty Wind*.

GAME 4

7. Which movie is set at Kellerman's Mountain House?

a. *My Cousin Vinny* (1992)

b. *Dirty Dancing* (1987)

c. *Terms of Endearment* (1983)

d. *The Sound of Music* (1965)

GAME 4 Q6 ANSWER a
Dennis Hopper plays a disgruntled retired cop, who plants a bomb on an LA bus that is set to explode if the speed of the bus goes below 50 mph. Sandra Bullock and Keanu Reeves also star in this movie, which took twelve buses to film, including one just for the high-speed scenes, another for the "jump" sequence, and two for getting blown up.

GAME 24

7. Which Disney film features the song "I'd Like to Be You for a Day"?

a. *The Parent Trap* (1961)

b. *Freaky Friday* (1976)

c. *Midnight Madness* (1980)

d. *Never a Dull Moment* (1968)

GAME 24 Q6 ANSWER c
The iconic composition that plays during the *Psycho* (1960) shower scene almost never existed. Director Alfred Hitchcock wanted all Bates Motel scenes to play without music, but agreed to try the murder scene with music at the composer's unrelenting request. Hitchcock agreed that the music intensified the scene, and the composer received a raise.

GAME 44

7. The 2002 film *Blue Crush* features which sport?

a. Gymnastics

b. Bobsledding

c. Surfing

d. Cycling

GAME 44 Q6 ANSWER b
Hanks' commitment to *Forrest Gump* (1994) forced him to turn down the role of the banker-turned-prisoner in this 1994 adaptation of the Stephen King short story. It became one of Robbins' best-known acting performances. Robbins is also the director of such films as *Bob Roberts* (1992) and *Dead Man Walking* (1995).

GAME 64

7. Who has *not* portrayed the Tom Clancy character Jack Ryan?

a. Alec Baldwin

b. Harrison Ford

c. Ben Affleck

d. Sean Connery

GAME 64 Q6 ANSWER b
The casting call for Wellesley students asked for women who were "not too tan." When students complained that the casting directors were discriminating against black women, the producers explained that the extras had to reflect the Wellesley student body of 1953. This led to a campus-wide protest called "Too Tan for Mona Lisa Smile."

GAME 17

6. Who wrote the screenplay for *The Princess Bride*?

a. Lawrence Kasdan

b. George Lucas

c. William Goldman

d. Delia Ephron

GAME 17 Q5 ANSWER b
The son of actors Errol Flynn and Lili Damita, Sean Leslie Flynn tried his hand at several careers. After a number of years as a film actor, both in the US and abroad, Flynn became a big game hunter, a game warden, a singer, and finally, a successful photojournalist. In 1970, he disappeared while on assignment for *Time* magazine in Cambodia.

GAME 37

6. What big-name actor has a very small part in 1988's *Mystic Pizza*?

a. Ben Affleck

b. Leonardo DiCaprio

c. Ethan Hawke

d. Matt Damon

GAME 37 Q5 ANSWER c
Complementing the nostalgic mood of the film, "The Summer Knows" was composed by Michel Legrand. The score of *Summer of '42*—also by Legrand—contains many variations of the theme, but few other songs. For that reason, when the film's Oscar-winning soundtrack was released, it also included music that was not related to the film.

GAME 57

6. Which film is based on a character in the 1961 novel *The Carpetbaggers*?

a. *Nevada Smith* (1966)

b. *Johnny Yuma* (1967)

c. *Will Penny* (1968)

d. *Young Billy Young* (1969)

GAME 57 Q5 ANSWER b
Because A *Fistful of Dollars* was one of the first so-called Spaghetti Westerns to be released in the United States, several members of the film's cast and crew adopted stage names that sounded more American. For instance, Italian actor Gian Maria Volontè was credited in the US as Johnny Wels, and composer Ennio Morricone used the name Dan Savio.

GAME 77

6. Which monument is comically miniaturized in 1984's *This Is Spinal Tap*?

a. Taj Mahal

b. Roman Coliseum

c. Leaning Tower of Pisa

d. Stonehenge

GAME 77 Q5 ANSWER a
Astin made his first big screen appearance in this Richard Donner adventure-comedy at the age of thirteen. The actor's success continued in such movies as *Toy Soldiers* (1991), *Encino Man* (1992), and *Rudy* (1993). After a series of smaller roles, he found worldwide fame as Samwise Gamgee in Peter Jackson's popular *Lord of the Rings* trilogy.

GAME 4

8. Where do Bandit and Snowman pick up the cases of beer in *Smokey and the Bandit*?

a. Mobile

b. Amarillo

c. Texarkana

d. Wichita

GAME 4 Q7 ANSWER b
Jennifer Grey and Patrick Swayze star as the young couple that finds love at a Catskills resort during the 1960s. The movie takes place in the summer, but was filmed in October when the leaves had started to turn colors—so they had to be painted green. In the scene at the lake, there are no close-ups because the actors' lips were blue from the cold.

GAME 24

8. Who plays driven TV producer Jane Craig in 1987's *Broadcast News*?

a. Joan Cusack

b. Lois Chiles

c. Holly Hunter

d. Debra Winger

GAME 24 Q7 ANSWER b
Freaky Friday's title song is sung by Barbara Harris and Jodie Foster, who play mother and daughter in this 1976 film. Disney remade the film twice, once in 1995 for television and then as a feature film in 2003. Originally, Disney asked Jodie Foster to play the mother in the 2003 remake, but the actress declined and the role went to Jamie Lee Curtis.

GAME 44

8. Who plays Daphne in 2002's live-action film *Scooby-Doo*?

a. Sarah Michelle Gellar

b. Renée Zellweger

c. Jennifer Love Hewitt

d. Lisa Kudrow

GAME 44 Q7 ANSWER c
Most of the movie's action takes place on the Hawaiian island of Oahu and features many real-life resident surfers—to lend authenticity to the footage. While she did learn to surf for the film, star Kate Bosworth's head was digitally superimposed onto shots of a world-class female surfer for the more dangerous waves.

GAME 64

8. Which children's movie features the song "I've Got a Golden Ticket"?

a. *Willy Wonka & the Chocolate Factory* (1971)

b. *Annie* (1982)

c. *Pete's Dragon* (1977)

d. *Mary Poppins* (1964)

GAME 64 Q7 ANSWER d
Alec Baldwin portrays Jack Ryan in *The Hunt for Red October* (1990); Harrison Ford plays him in *Patriot Games* (1992) and *Clear and Present Danger* (1994); and Ben Affleck won the role in the 2002 movie *The Sum of All Fears*. To date, Sean Connery has not played Ryan, but he does appear in *Red October* as Soviet submarine captain Marko Ramius.

GAME 17

5. What son-of-a-swashbuckler starred in 1964's *The Son of Captain Blood*?

a. Douglas Fairbanks, Jr.

b. Sean Flynn

c. Cornel Wilde, Jr.

d. William Lancaster

GAME 17 Q4 ANSWER c
The fictional character D'Artagnan first appeared in Alexander Dumas' nineteenth-century work *The Three Musketeers*. D'Artagnan is not one of the title characters, but is the friend of Athos, Porthos, and Aramis. This "fourth Musketeer" has also been portrayed by Douglas Fairbanks (1921 and 1929), Cornel Wilde (1979), and Chris O'Donnell (1993).

GAME 37

5. Which film features the theme song "The Summer Knows"?

a. *A Summer Place* (1959)

b. *Summer Storm* (2006)

c. *Summer of '42* (1971)

d. *Greengage Summer* (1961)

GAME 37 Q4 ANSWER b
Featuring David Moscow as thirteen-year-old Josh Baskin and Tom Hanks as his grownup counterpart, the coming-of-age fantasy *Big* was enthusiastically received by critics and moviegoers alike. Moscow's performance was praised, and Hanks was nominated for Best Actor in a Leading Role. The film also drew a nomination for Best Original Screenplay.

GAME 57

5. In which movie is Clint Eastwood caught between two feuding families?

a. *Pale Rider* (1985)

b. *A Fistful of Dollars* (1964)

c. *Joe Kidd* (1972)

d. *Hang 'Em High* (1968)

GAME 57 Q4 ANSWER c
With its craggy red buttes and endless sage flats, Monument Valley provided the perfect setting for dozens of Westerns, including seven directed by John Ford. The first film that Ford shot here was *My Darling Clementine* (1946) and the last was *Cheyenne Autumn* (1964). John Wayne once referred to the area as the place "where God put the West."

GAME 77

5. Which *Lord of the Rings* star made his film debut in *The Goonies* (1985)?

a. Sean Astin

b. Elijah Wood

c. Orlando Bloom

d. Viggo Mortensen

GAME 77 Q4 ANSWER d
This film is one of many low-budget works by legendary B-moviemaker Roger Corman. As a producer, he is known for giving numerous future Oscar-winning directors and actors a break in the industry. Lovingly nicknamed "The Corman Film School," these motion picture icons include Francis Ford Coppola, Jack Nicholson, and Martin Scorsese.

GAME 4

9. In *The Terminal*, Tom Hanks plays a would-be immigrant stranded at which airport?

a. O'Hare

b. LAX

c. JFK

d. Dallas/Ft. Worth

GAME 4 Q8 ANSWER c
Their mission is to drive a truckload of beer illegally across state lines—from Texas to Georgia—within 28 hours. Burt Reynolds and Sally Field costar in this 1977 action-comedy, which was the highest grossing film for the year after *Star Wars*. The stars' eight-year relationship ended when Fields turned down Reynolds' marriage proposal.

GAME 24

9. In which film do Sandra Bullock and Nicole Kidman play sister witches?

a. *Practical Magic* (1998)

b. *The Witches* (1990)

c. *The Craft* (1996)

d. *Hocus Pocus* (1993)

GAME 24 Q8 ANSWER c
The role of the feisty Jane Craig was written for actress Debra Winger, who had impressed director James L. Brooks when they worked together on 1983's *Terms of Endearment*. When Winger dropped out due to pregnancy, Hunter won the part and, eventually, a nomination for Best Actress in a Leading Role. (Cher won the award for *Moonstruck*.)

GAME 44

9. Which 1997 film features Cyrus the Virus, Diamond Dog, and Johnny 23?

a. *Grosse Pointe Blank*

b. *L.A. Confidential*

c. *Con Air*

d. *Starship Troopers*

GAME 44 Q8 ANSWER a
Gellar first rose to prominence through the role of Buffy Summers on the highly acclaimed TV series *Buffy the Vampire Slayer*. She soon launched her film career by appearing in 1997's *I Know What You Did Last Summer* and 1999's *Cruel Intentions*. An actual couple off screen, she and her *Scooby-Doo* costar Freddie Prinze, Jr. were married in 2002.

GAME 64

9. Which 1946 movie is set in the fictional city of Bedford Falls?

a. *The Yearling*

b. *It's a Wonderful Life*

c. *Best Years of Our Lives*

d. *Duel in the Sun*

GAME 64 Q8 ANSWER a
Leslie Bricusse and Anthony Newley wrote the Academy Award-nominated lyrics and score for this rags-to-riches musical. Perhaps the best-known song created for the movie is "The Candy Man," which, after being recorded by Sammy Davis, Jr., hit #1 on the charts in 1972, and has been used in other movies as well as in television sitcoms.

GAME 17

4. What character has been played by Gene Kelly, Don Ameche, and Michael York?

a. The Scarlet Pimpernel
b. The Count of Monte Cristo
c. D'Artagnan
d. Zorro

GAME 17 Q3 ANSWER b
Also known as *Douglas Fairbanks in Robin Hood*, this film had a budget of $1 million (which was high for the time) and was the first movie to have a Hollywood premiere. Held at Grauman's Egyptian Theatre, the premiere was open to anyone who could pay the admission price of $5. Those who missed the opening could later see the film for a dollar.

GAME 37

4. What makes character Josh Baskin grow up overnight in *Big* (1988)?

a. A prayer
b. A fortune-telling machine
c. A magic potion
d. A mysterious stranger

GAME 37 Q3 ANSWER a
Director John Hughes first chose Emilio Estevez to play the *Breakfast Club's* working-class troublemaker, but when Hughes couldn't cast the role of popular athlete Andrew Clark, Estevez took that part instead. Nicolas Cage and John Cusack were also considered to portray John Bender, but the role finally went to Brat Packer Judd Nelson.

GAME 57

4. What area of the United States is featured in seven John Ford Westerns?

a. Cody, Wyoming
b. Grand Canyon, Arizona
c. Monument Valley, Utah
d. Jackson Hole, Wyoming

GAME 57 Q3 ANSWER b
Richard Boone appeared in over fifty films and was best known for his work in Westerns. Although he played a moral gunslinger in the TV show *Have Gun, Will Travel*, in movies, Boone usually portrayed a villain. Westerns must have seemed like a good fit to the actor as he was descended from Squire Boone, brother of pioneer Daniel Boone.

GAME 77

4. Which film features unpopular school administrator Principal Togar?

a. *Valley Girl* (1983)
b. *The Breakfast Club* (1985)
c. *Dazed and Confused* (1993)
d. *Rock N' Roll High School* (1979)

GAME 77 Q3 ANSWER c
Originally released as a shocking cautionary tale to warn teenagers about the dangers of marijuana use, this film was rediscovered in the '70s and embraced as a midnight movie cult comedy. Still inspiring laughter, it was turned into an off-Broadway musical satire in 2004, which was then adapted into an Emmy Award-winning television movie in 2005.

GAME 4

10. Which movie has the line, "That's a real badge. I'm a real cop. And this is a real gun"?

a. *Lethal Weapon* (1987)

b. *Cobra* (1986)

c. *Die Hard* (1988)

d. *Sudden Impact* (1983)

GAME 4 Q9 ANSWER c
This movie may be based on the true story of Mehran Nasseri, an Iranian refugee who got stuck at Charles de Gaulle Airport in Paris when his passport and papers were stolen. He was arrested and released, but chose to stay in the departure lounge of Terminal One where he lived for eighteen years until he was hospitalized for an undisclosed ailment.

GAME 24

10. Who sang the theme song for the 1952 Western *High Noon*?

a. Frankie Lane

b. Gene Autry

c. Hank Williams

d. Tex Ritter

GAME 24 Q9 ANSWER a
When director Griffin Dune was asked why two such different looking people were cast as sisters, he said that according to his research, witch siblings frequently look dissimilar. Interestingly, when he cast two actresses to play the daughters of Bullock's character, Sally, he chose one child who looked like Bullock and one who looked like Kidman.

GAME 44

10. Who does Halle Berry play in the James Bond flick *Die Another Day*?

a. Whammy

b. Hex

c. Jinx

d. Bane

GAME 44 Q9 ANSWER c
In this 1997 Simon West-directed action film, John Malkovich plays Cyrus "the Virus" Grissom, a cold-hearted criminal who spearheads a plan to take control of a plane during a prison transfer. The part is a far cry from his Oscar-nominated debut as blind war hero Mr. Will in the 1984 period drama *Places in the Heart* opposite Sally Field.

GAME 64

10. What does Tom Hanks "befriend" in the 2000 film *Cast Away*?

a. A GI Joe action figure

b. A coconut

c. A volleyball

d. A stuffed dog

GAME 64 Q9 ANSWER b
RKO created the city of Bedford Falls on the RKO ranch in Encino, California. The set covered four acres, had a main street that stretched three hundred yards, included seventy-five buildings, and featured twenty full-grown oak trees. Months before filming began, cats, dogs, and pigeons were added to make the city seem more realistic.

GAME 17

3. In which 1920s film does Douglas Fairbanks slide down a tapestry?

a. *The Three Musketeers* (1921)

b. *Robin Hood* (1922)

c. *The Thief of Bagdad* (1924)

d. *The Black Pirate* (1926)

GAME 17 Q2 ANSWER d
Disneyland's Pirates of the Caribbean was the last ride designed by Walt Disney himself. It opened in 1967. In 1973, another version of the attraction opened in Florida's Magic Kingdom. In 2006, to coincide with the release of the second *Pirates* film, Walt Disney Imagineering made movie-inspired alterations to both attractions.

GAME 37

3. In what school film does rebel John Bender describe his violent father?

a. *The Breakfast Club* (1985)

b. *Sixteen Candles* (1984)

c. *Heathers* (1988)

d. *The Karate Kid* (1984)

GAME 37 Q2 ANSWER b
In this coming-of-age film, four working-class teens—called "cutters" after the stonecutters who once worked in Bloomington's quarries—find themselves clashing with Indiana University students. *Breaking Away,* which marked the debut of actor Daniel Stern, was filmed entirely on location, with many scenes being shot on the Indiana U campus.

GAME 57

3. Who plays villain Cicero Grimes in the 1967 movie *Hombre*?

a. Bruce Dern

b. Richard Boone

c. Martin Balsam

d. Eli Wallach

GAME 57 Q2 ANSWER a
Because the *Rio Bravo* cast included two singers—Rick Nelson and Dean Martin—director Howard Hawks decided to feature three songs in the soundtrack. Besides Nelson's performance of "Cindy," the movie has Dean Martin singing "My Rifle, My Pony, and Me" and "Rio Bravo," both of which were written by Dimitri Tiomkin and Paul Francis Webster.

GAME 77

3. *Tell Your Children* is the original title of which movie?

a. *Happiness* (1998)

b. *Freaks* (1932)

c. *Reefer Madness* (1936)

d. *Ghost World* (2001)

GAME 77 Q2 ANSWER d
In addition to being a musical superstar, Bowie has played a number of memorable roles on the silver screen—appearing as an alien in *The Man Who Fell to Earth* (1976), a vampire in *The Hunger* (1983), and inventor Nichola Tesla in *The Prestige* (2006). He was even considered for the role of the Joker in Tim Burton's 1989 superhero film *Batman.*

GAME 4

11. What place does Indiana Jones visit that is infested with poisonous snakes?

a. Well of Souls
b. Pyramid at Giza
c. Lascaux Cave
d. Temple of Doom

GAME 4 Q10 ANSWER a
At the core of this intense action-comedy is the loyal yet hilarious partnership-turned-friendship between Martin Riggs (a suicidal rookie cop played by Mel Gibson) and Sergeant Roger Murtaugh (a veteran officer played by Danny Glover). The movie was so successful, it resulted in three sequels. Bruce Willis was also considered for the role of Riggs.

GAME 24

11. Who plays homesteader Marian Starrett in 1953's *Shane*?

a. Jean Arthur
b. Vera Miles
c. Maureen O'Hara
d. Claire Trevor

GAME 24 Q10 ANSWER d
"The Ballad of High Noon"—which is sometimes referred to as "Do Not Forsake Me, Oh My Darlin'"—was composed by Dimitri Tiomkin with lyrics by Ned Washington. Country singer and actor Tex Ritter sang "High Noon" over the movie's opening credits and at the 1952 Oscar ceremony, where the popular ballad won the award for Best Original Song.

GAME 44

11. Who costars with Jet Li in *Kiss of the Dragon* (2001)?

a. Reese Witherspoon
b. Sandra Bullock
c. Bridget Fonda
d. Kate Hudson

GAME 44 Q10 ANSWER c
Berry achieved critical success playing actress and singer Dorothy Dandridge—the first African-American woman to be nominated for a Best Actress Oscar—in the 1999 HBO movie *Introducing Dorothy Dandridge*. Coincidentally, Berry became the first African-American woman to *win* the Best Actress Oscar, for her performance in 2001's *Monster's Ball*.

GAME 64

11. Whose film debut was as a frustrated mother in *Miracle on 34th Street*?

a. Lucille Ball
b. Thelma Ritter
c. Elsa Lanchester
d. Selma Diamond

GAME 64 Q10 ANSWER c
In the film, Wilson the volleyball is the only companion of castaway Chuck Noland (Tom Hanks) during the four long years he is stranded on a uninhabited island. When *Cast Away* was released, Wilson Sporting Goods launched a joint promotion of the film and even manufactured a special "Mr. Wilson" volleyball featuring a painted face.

GAME 17

2. What inspired *Pirates of the Caribbean: Curse of the Black Pearl* (2003)?

a. A true story

b. A children's book

c. A British legend

d. An amusement park ride

GAME 17 Q1 ANSWER a

Captain Blood provided Basil Rathbone with a relatively small part, but gave Errol Flynn his first starring role—one that made him an overnight sensation. Portraying doctor-turned-bucaneer Peter Blood, Flynn was able to display vibrant energy, natural physical prowess, good looks, and great charm, if not finely honed acting skills.

GAME 37

2. Where does the action take place in 1979's *Breaking Away*?

a. Boston, Massachusetts

b. Bloomington, Indiana

c. Cleveland, Ohio

d. Mystic, Connecticut

GAME 37 Q1 ANSWER c

Duddy Kravitz gave Dreyfuss his first leading role. Although Dreyfuss's portrayal of a Jewish kid making his way in the world would win him critical acclaim, initially, the young actor was not pleased with his performance. Fearing that no one would hire him once the film was released, Dreyfuss jumped at the chance to play Matt Hooper in 1975's *Jaws*.

GAME 57

2. In which film does Rick Nelson sing "Get Along Home, Cindy"?

a. *Rio Bravo* (1959)

b. *Flaming Star* (1960)

c. *Cimarron* (1960)

d. *One-Eyed Jacks* (1961)

GAME 57 Q1 ANSWER d

Based on the story of the 1881 gunfight at the O.K. Corral, this film features an ensemble cast that also includes Henry Fonda as Wyatt Earp, Ward Bond as Morgan Earp, Walter Brennan as Old Man Clanton, and Cathy Downs in the title role of Clementine. Although the movie deviates quite a bit from actual history, it is considered a classic Western.

GAME 77

2. Who plays Jareth the Goblin King in 1986's *Labyrinth*?

a. Jeff Goldblum

b. Christian Bale

c. Tim Curry

d. David Bowie

GAME 77 Q1 ANSWER a

Though it took director David Lynch five years to complete this surrealistic feature film, it was an immediate success with his fellow filmmakers. Directors John Waters, Stanley Kubrick, and George Lucas openly praised the movie. Lucas even offered Lynch the chance to direct the *Star Wars* sequel *Return of the Jedi* (1983), which he turned down.

GAME 4

12. For which movie did Marlon Brando win his first Oscar?

a. *Last Tango in Paris* (1972)

b. *On the Waterfront* (1954)

c. *A Streetcar Named Desire* (1951)

d. *Apocalypse Now* (1979)

GAME 4 Q11 ANSWER a
This is the tomb in *Raiders of the Lost Ark* (1981) that contained the lost Ark of the Covenant. For this scene, the crew gathered as many snakes as it could, but there were simply not enough. So director Steven Spielberg had several hoses cut into various lengths to use as filler. Looking at the scene closely, you can tell the real snakes from the fake.

GAME 24

12. Which film did Sydney Pollack both act in and direct?

a. *Eyes Wide Shut* (1999)

b. *Tootsie* (1982)

c. *Out of Africa* (1985)

d. *Havana* (1990)

GAME 24 Q11 ANSWER a
Director George Stevens first considered Katharine Hepburn for the role, but then cast Jean Arthur—even though she was in her fifties and much older than her male costars. This was Arthur's final film, her only color film, and her greatest box office hit. In later years, the actress taught drama at Vassar and the North Carolina School of the Arts.

GAME 44

12. Who are Agent Smith's two cohorts in *The Matrix* (1999)?

a. Jones and Brown

b. Cooper and McMahon

c. Miller and Dietz

d. Johnson and Clarke

GAME 44 Q11 ANSWER c
Fonda comes from a family of respected actors that includes her grandfather Henry Fonda, her father Peter Fonda, and her aunt Jane Fonda. She made her first appearance on the big screen at the tender age of five, in her father's classic film *Easy Rider* (1969). Her adult career includes roles in such movies as *Singles* (1992) and *Jackie Brown* (1997).

GAME 64

12. Which *Jerry Maguire* character is referred to as an "ambassador of Kwan"?

a. Jerry Maguire

b. Rod Tidwell

c. Dorothy Boyd

d. Marcee Tidwell

GAME 64 Q11 ANSWER b
Thelma Ritter worked in stock theater and radio before her foray into films. Although she was not credited for her role in the 1947 Christmas movie, she made a big impact playing a shopper who is unable to find the toy she wants at Macy's, and is told that the item is available at Gimbels. Eventually, Ritter would earn six Academy Award nominations.

GAME 17

1. In which swashbuckler film do Basil Rathbone and Errol Flynn cross swords?

a. *Captain Blood* (1935)

b. *The Corsican Brothers* (1941)

c. *Beau Geste* (1939)

d. *The Prince and the Pauper* (1937)

The answer to this question is on:

page 102, top frame, right side.

GAME 37

1. Who plays the title role in 1974's *The Apprenticeship of Duddy Kravitz*?

a. Al Pacino

b. Dustin Hoffman

c. Richard Dreyfuss

d. Mandy Patinkin

The answer to this question is on:

page 102, second frame, right side.

GAME 57

1. In which Western does Victor Mature play Doc Holliday?

a. *High Noon* (1952)

b. *Stagecoach* (1939)

c. *The Wild Bunch* (1969)

d. *My Darling Clementine* (1946)

The answer to this question is on:

page 102, third frame, right side.

GAME 77

1. Which film features a strangely deformed baby?

a. *Eraserhead* (1977)

b. *Raising Arizona* (1987)

c. *Blue Velvet* (1986)

d. *Pink Flamingos* (1972)

The answer to this question is on:

page 102, bottom frame, right side.

GAME 5

Love Stories

*Turn to page 107
for the first question.*

Turn to page 107
for the first question.

GAME 4 Q12 ANSWER b

In this film classic, which won eight Oscars, including Best Picture and Best Director, Brando earned the Best Actor award for his role as a longshoreman who stands up to a corrupt union boss. During his career, Brando was nominated for eight Best Actor Oscars and won two. The second was for his role as Vito Corleone in *The Godfather* (1972).

GAME 25

Prequels and Sequels

*Turn to page 107
for the first question.*

Turn to page 107
for the first question.

GAME 24 Q12 ANSWER b

It was actor Dustin Hoffman who thought that Sydney Pollack should take the role of George Fields, Michael Dorsey's agent, in addition to directing *Tootsie*. Both Hoffman and Pollack were nominated for Academy Awards that year (Hoffman for best actor and Pollack for best director), but *Gandhi* made a nearly clean sweep of the Oscars.

GAME 45

Cinema at Sea

*Turn to page 107
for the first question.*

Turn to page 107
for the first question.

GAME 44 Q12 ANSWER a

Nigerian-born Hugo Weaving plays the brutal Agent Smith in this sci-fi favorite by the Wachowskis. Weaving has become a fixture in many big-budget franchise films, reprising his role in the *Matrix* sequels, appearing as the half-elf Elrond in *The Lord of the Rings* trilogy, and providing the voice of Megatron in the *Transformers* series.

GAME 65

More Locations, Locations, Locations

*Turn to page 107
for the first question.*

Turn to page 107
for the first question.

GAME 64 Q12 ANSWER a

This 1996 comedy-drama is packed with memorable quotes and catchy coined words, most of which have been attributed to screenwriter Cameron Crowe. Character Rod Tidwell's "You are my ambassador of Kwan [love and respect]" and "Show me the money!" are among the phrases that keep the film fresh in the minds of movie lovers.

GAME 17

Swashbucklers

Turn to page 104
for the first question.

GAME 16 Q12 ANSWER c
Steve Buscemi plays Mr. Pink in this ultra-violent film about a botched diamond heist. The gang, whose members are known only by their "color" code names, include such actors as Harvey Keitel, Tim Roth, and Michael Madsen. *Reservoir Dogs* marked the directorial debut of Tarantino, who also wrote the script and starred in the film.

GAME 37

Coming of Age

Turn to page 104
for the first question.

GAME 36 Q12 ANSWER c
Clint Eastwood not only returned to play Police Inspector "Dirty" Harry Callahan in this fourth installment of the *Dirty Harry* franchise, he also directed the film. Though this line is often mistakenly attributed to the first movie (1971's *Dirty Harry*), Eastwood first utters the famous words in the diner-robbery scene of this 1983 crime drama.

GAME 57

More Westerns

Turn to page 104
for the first question.

GAME 56 Q12 ANSWER b
Written by Steve Martin, Lorne Michaels, and Randy Newman, this 1986 comedy was originally titled *The Three Caballeros* and was going to team Martin with Dan Aykroyd and John Belushi. Ultimately, though, Chevy Chase was cast as Dusty Bottoms and Martin Short took the role of Ned Nederlander, while Steve Martin played Lucky Day.

GAME 77

Cult Classics

Turn to page 104
for the first question.

GAME 76 Q12 ANSWER a
Although some moviegoers thought that Taiwan-born Ang Lee was a strange choice to direct an adaptation of a Jane Austen book, *Sense and Sensibility* received critical acclaim not only for Lee's direction, but also for the screenplay written by British actress-comedienne Emma Thompson. It was Lee's idea to cast Thompson as Elinor Dashwood.

GAME 5

1. Who starred opposite Natalie Wood in *Splendor in the Grass*?

a. Anthony Perkins

b. Warren Beatty

c. James Franciscus

d. Robert Redford

The answer to this question is on:

page 109, top frame, right side.

GAME 25

1. *Texasville* (1990) was the long-awaited sequel to which film?

a. *The Last Boy Scout*

b. *Last Tango in Paris*

c. *The Last Unicorn*

d. *The Last Picture Show*

The answer to this question is on:

page 109, second frame, right side.

GAME 45

1. What habit reveals Captain Queeg's anxiety in *The Caine Mutiny* (1954)?

a. Clearing his throat

b. Playing with ball bearings

c. Eating jelly beans

d. Fingering his brass buttons

The answer to this question is on:

page 109, third frame, right side.

GAME 65

1. What is the setting for Alfred Hitchcock's *To Catch a Thief* (1955)?

a. Beverly Hills

b. French Riviera

c. Greek Islands

d. Italian Riviera

The answer to this question is on:

page 109, bottom frame, right side.

GAME 16

12. In which Quentin Tarantino film will you find the character Mr. Pink?

a. *Pulp Fiction* (1994)

b. *Jackie Brown* (1997)

c. *Reservoir Dogs* (1992)

d. *Kill Bill: Vol. 1* (2003)

GAME 16 Q11 ANSWER c
In this 1983 comedy, Chevy Chase takes his family on a cross-country road trip from Chicago to the fictional LA theme park. The film is based on a story written by John Hughes (who also wrote the screenplay) that appeared in *National Lampoon* magazine. The story was based on one of Hughes' own ill-fated family vacations when he was a kid.

GAME 36

12. In which movie would you hear the classic line, "Go ahead, make my day"?

a. *Dirty Harry* (1971)

b. *Magnum Force* (1973)

c. *Sudden Impact* (1983)

d. *Tightrope* (1984)

GAME 36 Q11 ANSWER b
Julie Newmar and Eartha Kitt played the Batman villain on TV's *Batman;* Lee Meriwether purred through the role in 1966's *Batman: The Movie;* Michelle Pfeiffer cracked her whip in 1992's *Batman Returns;* while Berry donned the signature feline ears in 2004's *Catwoman.* Only Pfieffer's film, however, included Catwoman's actual alter ego, Selina Kyle.

GAME 56

12. Who does *not* play one of the *Three Amigos*?

a. Steve Martin

b. Dan Aykroyd

c. Chevy Chase

d. Martin Short

GAME 56 Q11 ANSWER a
William Wyler's drama about returning World War II servicemen garnered awards in all the major categories in which it had received nominations. For his portrayal of Homer Parish, real-life veteran Harold Russell actually won *two* Oscars—an award for Best Supporting Actor, and an honorary award "for bringing hope and courage to his fellow veterans."

GAME 76

12. Which costume drama was directed by Ang Lee?

a. *Sense and Sensibility* (1995)

b. *Jane Eyre* (1996)

c. *Anna Karenina* (1997)

d. *Vanity Fair* (1998)

GAME 76 Q11 ANSWER c
Although Nevil Shute's novel *On the Beach* described the scientist as a thirty-something bachelor named John Osborne, in the movie, he is a sixty-year-old bachelor named Julian Osborne. Astaire won rave reviews for playing a man who, knowing that the end of the world is near, decides to race in the Grand Prix—even though he's never raced before.

GAME 5

2. In the 1980 romantic fantasy *Somewhere in Time,* who is Christopher Reeve's costar?

a. Genevieve Bujold

b. Jane Seymour

c. Ann-Margret

d. Jacqueline Bisset

GAME 5 Q1 ANSWER b
Although Wood and Beatty didn't appear to get along during the filming of this 1961 movie, it was rumored that they were having an affair—which led to the end of Wood's marriage to actor Robert Wagner. *Splendor in the Grass* was the first Hollywood movie to show a French kiss; no one under sixteen was permitted in theaters to watch the film.

GAME 25

2. The 1954 movie *Long John Silver* is the sequel to what adventure story?

a. *Blackbeard*

b. *Kidnapped*

c. *Treasure Island*

d. *Peter Pan*

GAME 25 Q1 ANSWER d
Filmed in black and white, *The Last Picture Show* (1971) is the only film to date to be nominated for four acting Oscars solely for supporting roles. Ben Johnson, Jeff Bridges, Cloris Leachman, and Ellen Burstyn were all nominated (Johnson and Leachman won the awards). The film was also nominated for Best Picture and Best Director—Peter Bogdonovich.

GAME 45

2. Who plays Fletcher Christian in 1935's version of *Mutiny on the Bounty*?

a. Errol Flynn

b. Clark Gable

c. Marlon Brando

d. Mel Gibson

GAME 45 Q1 ANSWER b
When Captain Queeg's (Humphrey Bogart's) men become convinced that he is mentally unfit for command, his habit of nervously rolling steel ball bearings in a shaking hand seems to confirm their opinion. Of course, Lieutenant Keefer's (Fred MacMurray's) amateur analysis of Queeg's mental state does a good deal more to push the officers towards mutiny.

GAME 65

2. Which former federal prison is the site of two Clint Eastwood films?

a. Folsom

b. Attica

c. Alcatraz

d. Leavenworth

GAME 65 Q1 ANSWER b
The landscape of the French Riviera is showcased in this romantic thriller during Grace Kelly's famous car chase, in which she speeds down a winding Monaco road. (In 1982, Kelly was killed in a car accident while driving with her daughter down that same road.) Cary Grant came out of his two-year retirement to costar in the film.

GAME 16

11. Where is the Griswold Family headed in *National Lampoon's Vacation*?

a. Water World
b. World of Fun
c. Walley World
d. Candy Land

GAME 16 Q10 ANSWER c

For her work on this film, which is based on a true story, Roberts became the first actress to receive an unprecedented salary of over $20 million. She also received a Best Actress Oscar nomination for her role as a prostitute in the 1990 "fairy tale" *Pretty Woman,* and a Best Supporting Actress nod as a southern belle in *Steel Magnolias* (1989).

GAME 36

11. Which comic book character has been played by Halle Berry?

a. Supergirl
b. Catwoman
c. Elektra
d. Batgirl

GAME 36 Q10 ANSWER d

Christie gives a dual performance as wife Linda Montag and neighbor Clarisse in this, director François Truffaut's only, English-language film. Her breakthrough performance, however, had already come one year prior with the role of Diana Scott in John Schlesinger's Oscar-nominated *Darling* (1965), for which she won an Academy Award for Best Actress.

GAME 56

11. Which film received seven Oscars at the 1946 Academy Awards?

a. *The Best Years of Our Lives*
b. *Brief Encounter*
c. *It's a Wonderful Life*
d. *Notorious*

GAME 56 Q10 ANSWER d

Based on Fanny Flagg's best-selling novel *Fried Green Tomatoes at the Whistle Stop Café,* this movie was shot in the nearly deserted town of Juliette, Georgia, where a former hardware store was redesigned as the café. After the film's release, tourists started streaming into Juliette and the make-believe café was turned into a functioning restaurant.

GAME 76

11. Which dancer-actor plays an Australian scientist in *On the Beach*?

a. James Cagney
b. Gene Kelly
c. Fred Astaire
d. Donald O'Connor

GAME 76 Q10 ANSWER b

Humphrey Bogart plays boat captain Charlie Allnut and Katharine Hepburn portrays missionary Rose Sayer in this story of two people who escape from danger by taking a small boat down an African river during World War I. At first, the two characters use formal titles when they speak to each other, but after a while, they become "Charlie" and "Rosie."

GAME 5

3. Which movie features a love connection at the Empire State Building on Valentine's Day?

a. *Pretty Woman* (1990)

b. *Sleepless in Seattle* (1993)

c. *Love Actually* (2003)

d. *Hannah and Her Sisters* (1986)

GAME 5 Q2 ANSWER b
Each actress who auditioned for the role of Elise was asked if she had ever been in love. Jane Seymour was the only one who answered no. Director Jeannot Szwarc did not allow Reeve to see the beautiful portrait of Elise until they filmed the scene in which his character sees it for the first time. Szwarc wanted Reeve to have a genuine reaction to it.

GAME 25

3. *The Scorpion King* (2002) is a prequel to which film?

a. *The Sixth Sense*

b. *Mission to Mars*

c. *Stargate*

d. *The Mummy Returns*

GAME 25 Q2 ANSWER c
Treasure Island (1950) was Disney's first live-action movie. It starred Robert Newton as Long John Silver, the iconic pirate captain. It is believed that the modern association of the phrase "Arrrgh!" with pirates originated from Newton's performance in this film. Newton reprised his role in *Long John Silver*, the non-Disney produced sequel.

GAME 45

3. Which lovely leading lady is terrorized by Billy Zane in *Dead Calm*?

a. Sandra Bullock

b. Gwyneth Paltrow

c. Jennifer Grey

d. Nicole Kidman

GAME 45 Q2 ANSWER b
Errol Flynn, Marlon Brando, and Mel Gibson each had a turn playing first mate Fletcher Christian—Flynn in 1933, Brando in 1962, and Gibson in 1984. But in 1935, the handsome Clark Gable shaved off his trademark moustache to assume the role of the fair-minded Christian, and in doing so, helped solidify his place among the leading actors of the time.

GAME 65

3. Where does the 1954 romance *Three Coins in the Fountain* take place?

a. Italy

b. France

c. Spain

d. Ireland

GAME 65 Q2 ANSWER c
Also known as "The Rock," Alcatraz is located on an island off the coast of San Francisco. In addition to serving as the location of Eastwood's films *The Enforcer* (1976) and *Escape from Alcatraz* (1979), it is the setting for a number of other notable films, including *Birdman of Alcatraz* (1962), *The Rock* (1996), and *Murder in the First* (1995).

GAME 16

10. For which film did Julia Roberts win a Best Actress Oscar?

a. *Pretty Woman* (1990)

b. *Steel Magnolias* (1989)

c. *Erin Brockovich* (2000)

d. *Sleeping with the Enemy* (1991)

GAME 16 Q9 ANSWER b
All four of these directors were Oscar nominees for their 1939 films: Frank Capra for *Mr. Smith Goes to Washington;* John Ford for *Stagecoach;* and William Wyler for *Wuthering Heights.* Although Victor Fleming didn't win for *The Wizard of Oz,* he won for his other nominated film that year, *Gone With the Wind.*

GAME 36

10. Who plays the fireman's wife in the 1966 film *Fahrenheit 451*?

a. Diana Rigg

b. Rita Tushingham

c. Vanessa Redgrave

d. Julie Christie

GAME 36 Q9 ANSWER c
Fans of this classic should thank Walt Disney. The success of his 1937 animated feature *Snow White and the Seven Dwarfs* proved that children's stories could make lucrative films, prompting MGM Studios to buy the rights to Frank L. Baum's novel *The Wonderful Wizard of Oz.* Coincidentally, Disney would make the 1985 sequel, *Return to Oz.*

GAME 56

10. Which women's friendship film features the Whistle Stop Café?

a. *Steel Magnolias* (1989)

b. *Boys on the Side* (1995)

c. *Thelma and Louise* (1991)

d. *Fried Green Tomatoes* (1991)

GAME 56 Q9 ANSWER a
A faithful reproduction of Thornton Wilder's Pulitzer Prize-winning play of the same name, *Our Town* tells the story of average people living in a small New England town in the early part of the twentieth century. Martha Scott repeated her stage role as Emily Webb, delivering a performance that earned her a Best Actress Oscar nomination.

GAME 76

10. What is Bogart's nickname for Hepburn in 1951's *The African Queen*?

a. Queenie

b. Rosie

c. Katie

d. Stretch

GAME 76 Q9 ANSWER d
Although the film received mixed reviews, it was so popular with moviegoers that it lead to widespread use of the word "whisperer" to describe anyone who is unusually talented at communicating with or helping animals or people. For instance, the TV show *Ghost Whisperer* concerns a psychic who communicates with the spirits of the dead.

GAME 5

4. In which movie are Sam Wheat and Molly Jensen the loving couple?

a. *Ghost* (1990)

b. *Always* (1989)

c. *The Way We Were* (1973)

d. *The English Patient* (1996)

GAME 5 Q3 ANSWER b
Tom Hanks and Meg Ryan are on screen together for only about two minutes in this romantic film. For the scene on the Empire State Building, the crew built a fake observation deck with an enormous photo of the NYC skyline in the background. To accommodate all of the film equipment, they had to make the reconstructed deck larger than the real thing.

GAME 25

4. The sequel to *Conan the Barbarian* (1982) is *Conan the _____* (1984).

a. Defeater

b. Destroyer

c. Mercenary

d. Conqueror

GAME 25 Q3 ANSWER d
The Scorpion King takes place 5,000 years prior to *The Mummy Returns* (2001). It stars World Wrestling Federation favorite Dwayne "The Rock" Johnson in the title role. Although Johnson tried to avoid using The Rock's signature moves in his portrayal of the Scorpion King, he *did* include "The People's Eyebrow" as a shout out to his wrestling fans.

GAME 45

4. Which animal is featured in the 1955 film *It Came from Beneath the Sea*?

a. An octopus

b. A whale

c. A shark

d. A squid

GAME 45 Q3 ANSWER d
Australian actress Nicole Kidman had appeared in both movies and television series before the 1989 thriller *Dead Calm*, but it was the part of Rae Ingram in this film that grabbed the attention of moviegoers and critics. Shortly after, she would land leading roles in *Days of Thunder* (1990), *Billy Bathgate* (1991), and *Far and Away* (1992).

GAME 65

4. Where does Adam Sandler find romance in *Punch-Drunk Love* (2002)?

a. Taiwan

b. Easter Island

c. Bali

d. Hawaii

GAME 65 Q3 ANSWER a
Rome's famous Trevi Fountain is the centerpiece of this romantic film about three American roommates looking for romance in Italy. Among this Best Picture nominee's stellar cast are Dorothy McGuire, Jean Peters, Clifton Webb, and Louie Jourdan. The movie's title song, written by Jule Styne and Sammy Cahn, won the Oscar for Best Song.

GAME 16

9. Who directed *The Wizard of Oz* (1939)?

a. Frank Capra
b. Victor Fleming
c. John Ford
d. William Wyler

GAME 16 Q8 ANSWER c
Auric Goldfinger intends to increase the worth of his own gold by devaluing the gold owned by the US in this third film of the James Bond series. He plans to contaminate the gold by setting off a nuclear bomb within the depository. Filming was not allowed in the real Fort Knox, so set designer Ken Adams had to recreate it from photographs.

GAME 36

9. Which film features farm hands Hunk, Hickory, and Zeke?

a. *The Grapes of Wrath* (1940)
b. *Charlotte's Web* (1973)
c. *The Wizard of Oz* (1939)
d. *Gone With the Wind* (1939)

GAME 36 Q8 ANSWER b
Marlon Brando based his performance as Don Vito in 1972's *The Godfather* on New York City crime lord Frank Costello. The actor wanted the character to look like a bulldog, and stuffed his cheeks with cotton to achieve the effect for his audition. He won an Oscar for the role, but refused it in protest of the industry's treatment of Native Americans.

GAME 56

9. Which film is set in the fictional town of Grover's Corners?

a. *Our Town* (1940)
b. *Mr. Deeds Goes to Town* (1936)
c. *Picnic* (1955)
d. *State Fair* (1945)

GAME 56 Q8 ANSWER b
Based on the Pulitzer Prize-winning book of the same name, *A Beautiful Mind* tells the story of John Nash, an American economist and mathematician who won the 1994 Nobel Prize in Economics despite a nearly lifelong struggle with paranoid schizophrenia. Russell Crowe's portrayal of the troubled genius won him critical acclaim and an Oscar nomination.

GAME 76

9. Which movie did Robert Redford both star in and direct?

a. *Sneakers* (1992)
b. *Out of Africa* (1985)
c. *Spy Game* (2001)
d. *The Horse Whisperer* (1998)

GAME 76 Q8 ANSWER b
A number of names came up when it was time to cast the role of parapsychologist Egon Spengler. Chevy Chase, Michael Keaton, Christopher Lloyd, and several other actors were considered, but eventually, Harold Ramis—one of the writers of the *Ghostbusters* screenplay—took the part, reasoning that since he had created the character, he knew him best.

GAME 5

5. Who stars opposite Humphrey Bogart in the 1942 romantic classic *Casablanca*?

a. Elizabeth Taylor

b. Audrey Hepburn

c. Lana Turner

d. Ingrid Bergman

GAME 5 Q4 ANSWER a
Demi Moore and Patrick Swayze star as the ill-fated lovers in this romantic flick. The role of Sam was originally offered to Bruce Willis (Moore's then husband), who turned it down because he didn't think the film would work. Initially, director Jerry Zucker was against the idea of Swayze for the part, but during the audition, Swayze won him over.

GAME 25

5. *Nevada Smith* (1966), starring Steve McQueen, is a prequel to which film?

a. *Peyton Place*

b. *The Carpetbaggers*

c. *Splendor in the Grass*

d. *Rebel Without a Cause*

GAME 25 Q4 ANSWER b
There are many similarities between Arnold Schwarzenegger and Conan, the character he portrays in both films. Both grew up in small villages, both found fame due to their physicality, and both had reputations as womanizers. Conan eventually became a king, which can be compared to Schwarzenegger's being elected Governor of California in 2003.

GAME 45

5. What was Disney's first science-fiction film?

a. *Space Buddies*

b. *Deep Blue Sea*

c. *20,000 Leagues Under the Sea*

d. *Tron*

GAME 45 Q4 ANSWER a
Because of a small budget, special effects creator Ray Harryhausen could animate only six legs of the giant octopus, and had to remove the other two, causing Harryhausen to call his creature a "hextapus." Even without a full complement of appendages, the octopus was able to destroy the Golden Gate Bridge and several other San Francisco landmarks.

GAME 65

5. Which movie was filmed primarily inside the Bellagio in Las Vegas?

a. *Casino* (1995)

b. *Swingers* (1996)

c. *Ocean's Eleven* (2001)

d. *Rounders* (1998)

GAME 65 Q4 ANSWER d
Sandler plays depressed businessman Barry Egan, who follows Lena Leonard (portrayed by Emily Watson) to Hawaii in hopes of starting a relationship. A quirky romantic comedy-drama directed by Paul Thomas Anderson, the film was a departure from the comedies that had made Sandler a star. He received positive reviews for his performance.

GAME 16

8. In *Goldfinger*, what does the villain plan to do to the gold in Fort Knox?

a. Melt it down
b. Steal it
c. Contaminate it
d. Turn it into coins

GAME 16 Q7 ANSWER b
Winters plays the prostitute mother of a blind girl who finds love with a black man during the growing civil rights movement. It was her second Oscar. Her first, also for a supporting role, was for *The Diary of Anne Frank* (1959). Winters also received Oscar nominations for her work in 1951's *A Place in the Sun* and 1972's *The Poseidon Adventure*.

GAME 36

8. Which movie character owns the Genco importing company?

a. Gordon Gecko
b. Vito Corleone
c. Waring Hudsucker
d. Max Zorin

GAME 36 Q7 ANSWER a
Adam Sandler plays the aimless layabout Sonny in this heartfelt comedy. The former Saturday Night Live star met future wife Jackie Titone—who had been cast as a waitress in a bar—while filming the movie. They worked together again on the 2000 flick *Little Nicky*, as well as the animated *Eight Crazy Nights* (2002). They eventually married in 2003.

GAME 56

8. What does Russell Crowe play in the 2001 movie *A Beautiful Mind*?

a. A reporter
b. A math genius
c. A police detective
d. An artist

GAME 56 Q7 ANSWER d
British actor John Rhys-Davies plays Jones' good friend Sallah in both *Raiders of the Lost Ark* (1981) and *Indiana Jones and the Last Crusade* (1989). Sallah was originally supposed to be a thin, short Bedouin, but when director Steven Spielberg saw Rhys-Davies in the 1980 miniseries *Shogun*, he changed the role to fit the more substantial actor.

GAME 76

8. Who plays Dr. Egon Spengler in 1984's *Ghostbusters*?

a. Bill Murray
b. Harold Ramis
c. Dan Aykroyd
d. Ernie Hudson

GAME 76 Q7 ANSWER c
Hanna R. Paul plays young Jenny Curran and Robin Wright plays a more mature Jenny in 1994's *Forrest Gump*. Forrest is taken with Jenny the second he sees her, and always insists that they belong together, like peas and carrots. Not until Jenny contracts an untreatable health disorder, though, is she willing to share her life with Forrest.

GAME 5

6. Who is the object of affection in the 1970 movie *Love Story*?

a. Ali MacGraw

b. Diane Keaton

c. Susan Saint James

d. Mia Farrow

GAME 5 Q5 ANSWER d
The on-screen chemistry between Bogart and Bergmen was extraordinary, yet this was the only movie they made together. (They also had very little off-screen contact.) Because Bogart was noticeably shorter than his costar, he was directed to stand on boxes, sit on pillows, and slouch down during a number of their scenes together.

GAME 25

6. *The Return of Jafar* is the 1994 sequel to which Disney film?

a. *Aladdin*

b. *Snow White and the Seven Dwarfs*

c. *The Fox and the Hound*

d. *Beauty and the Beast*

GAME 25 Q5 ANSWER b
Based on a Harold Robbins novel, this 1964 film is loosely centered on the life of Howard Hughes. Due to its mature theme and racy content, *The Carpetbaggers* was originally advertised as being "for adults only." When restored for DVD release in 2003, it received a new MPAA rating of PG, signifying how drastically standards have changed over time.

GAME 45

6. Who plays the title role in the 1955 film *Mr. Roberts*?

a. John Wayne

b. Cary Grant

c. Jack Lemmon

d. Henry Fonda

GAME 45 Q5 ANSWER c
Based on a novel by Jules Verne, *20,000 Leagues Under the Sea* (1954) was also the first sci-fi film to feature major Hollywood stars, including Kirk Douglas as harpooner Ned Land, and James Mason as Captain Nemo, commander of the *Nautilus* submarine. This is one of the many reasons *20,000 Leagues* is considered a classic in the sci-fi genre.

GAME 65

6. Which city is the setting for the 1953 film classic *From Here to Eternity*?

a. San Francisco

b. Honolulu

c. Long Beach

d. Fort Lauderdale

GAME 65 Q5 ANSWER c
This remake of the 1960 Rat Pack film about a Vegas heist also features hotels like The Mirage and MGM Grand. Its all-star cast includes such A-listers as George Clooney, Don Cheadle, and Brad Pitt. Amazingly, Cheadle removed his name from the credits when he was told that it couldn't appear before Clooney's, despite the cast being alphabetized.

GAME 16

7. Who won the Best Supporting Actress Oscar for *A Patch of Blue* (1965)?

a. Ruth Gordon
b. Shelley Winters
c. Patricia Neal
d. Anne Bancroft

GAME 16 Q6 ANSWER a
Fields' image was on the first stamp (15-cent) in the Performing Arts and Artists series, which was released over several years beginning in 1980. It was, however, the 29-cent Elvis Presley stamp—issued on Elvis's fifty-eighth birthday (January 8, 1993)—that holds the record for the most commemorative stamps ever sold. Elvis is still "The King."

GAME 36

7. Which movie features a character named Sonny Koufax?

a. *Big Daddy* (1999)
b. *She's All That* (1999)
c. *The Wedding Singer* (1998)
d. *Snake Eyes* (1998)

GAME 36 Q6 ANSWER c
Cato Fong first appears as Inspector Clouseau's servant in 1964's *A Shot in the Dark*, the second film in the *Pink Panther* series. Based on the Bruce Lee role of Kato from TV's *The Green Hornet*, the character's name is spelled with a "K" in this film, but would be spelled with a "C" in all subsequent sequels of the Clouseau movie franchise.

GAME 56

7. Which screen hero has a loyal friend named Sallah?

a. Sinbad
b. James Bond
c. Luke Skywalker
d. Indiana Jones

GAME 56 Q6 ANSWER b
At one point, screenwriter Tom Mankiewicz contemplated turning Bond's love interest, the psychic Solitaire, into a black woman so that they could cast Diana Ross in the role. Ultimately, though, the film's producers decided not to stray from author Ian Fleming's description of Solitaire, and Jane Seymour joined the long list of movie Bond girls.

GAME 76

7. Whose life does character Jenny Curran pop in and out of over the years?

a. Edward Lewis
b. Benjamin Braddock
c. Forrest Gump
d. Arthur Bach

GAME 76 Q6 ANSWER d
The role of factory worker Paula Pokrifski was offered to several people before it was won by Debra Winger. Sigourney Weaver, Angelica Huston, and Jennifer Jason Leigh were all considered, as were Rebecca De Mornay and Meg Ryan. Because she disliked the 1982 movie, Winger—who is known to be difficult—refused to do any publicity for it.

GAME 5	**7. Which Brooke Shields' film involves an obsessive love between two teens?** **a.** *Valley Girl* (1983) **b.** *Endless Love* (1981) **c.** *Running Wild* (1992) **d.** *Pretty Baby* (1978)	**GAME 5 Q6 ANSWER a** Ali MacGraw and Ryan O'Neal earned Oscar nominations for their performances in this film. The most famous line in the movie, "Love means never having to say you're sorry," was actually misspoken by O'Neal. It was supposed to be, "Love means not ever having to say you're sorry."

GAME 25	**7. *The Road Warrior* (1981) is the sequel to which movie?** **a.** *Time Bandits* **b.** *Mad Max* **c.** *Dune* **d.** *The Beastmaster*	**GAME 25 Q6 ANSWER a** *Aladdin* was the most successful film of 1992 and the first animated film to gross more than $200 million—it earned more than $217 million in the US and over $504 million worldwide. Aladdin initially resembled Michael J. Fox, but in an effort to have the character appeal to more women, the producer had him redesigned to look more like Tom Cruise.

GAME 45	**7. What is the *Albatross* in the 1996 fact-based film *White Squall*?** **a.** Floating hospital **b.** Floating church **c.** Floating prep school **d.** Floating post office	**GAME 45 Q6 ANSWER d** Although movie lovers cannot imagine *Mr. Roberts* without Henry Fonda, he was not Warner Brothers' first choice for the lead. Believing that Fonda was no longer a box office draw, producers considered Marlon Brando and William Holden. But director John Ford insisted on Fonda, who went on to deliver one of his career-making performances.

GAME 65	**7. Which John Huston film was shot on location in Puerto Vallarta, Mexico?** **a.** *The Misfits* (1961) **b.** *Prizzi's Honor* (1985) **c.** *The Night of the Iguana* (1964) **d.** *The Unforgiven* (1960)	**GAME 65 Q6 ANSWER b** Based on James Jones' 1952 novel of the same name, *From Here to Eternity* follows the lives of four soldiers stationed in Hawaii prior to the Japanese attack on Pearl Harbor. Nominated for thirteen Oscars, the film won eight, including Best Picture, Director (Fred Zinnemann), Supporting Actor (Frank Sinatra), and Supporting Actress (Donna Reed).

GAME 16

6. Who is the first male actor to appear on a US postage stamp?

a. W.C. Fields
b. Elvis Presley
c. Jimmy Stewart
d. James Dean

GAME 16 Q5 ANSWER b

Sorvino plays crime family kingpin Paul Cicero in this Martin Scorsese film. Robert De Niro is the "Don" of the Corleone crime family in *The Godfather: Part II* (1974), while Jack Nicholson heads up an Irish mafia crew in *The Departed* (2006). In the 2007 film *Eastern Promises*, Armin Mueller-Stahl plays a Russian mob boss.

GAME 36

6. Which sidekick frequently launches surprise attacks on his boss?

a. Robin
b. Oddjob
c. Cato
d. Felix Leiter

GAME 36 Q5 ANSWER b

In preparation for the role of self-centered rancher Hud Bannon, Newman spent weeks on an actual Texas cattle ranch to achieve the callused hands and bona fide walk of a cowboy. The film garnered seven Academy Award nominations, including an Oscar nod for Best Actor in a Leading Role for Newman's performance (the third of his career).

GAME 56

6. In which 007 thriller does Jane Seymour appear as a "Bond girl"?

a. *Goldfinger* (1964)
b. *Live and Let Die* (1973)
c. *Moonraker* (1979)
d. *Octopussy* (1983)

GAME 56 Q5 ANSWER d

Although Stephen King is perhaps best known as an author of horror fiction (his first published book was *Carrie*) many King-based movies explore other genres. *Stand By Me*, which had its origins in the story *The Body*, is a coming-of-age movie; *Dolores Claiborne* is a psychological thriller; and *The Green Mile* is a drama with fantasy elements.

GAME 76

6. Who is literally carried away by Richard Gere in *An Officer and a Gentleman*?

a. Jennifer Jason Leigh
b. Sigourney Weaver
c. Sally Field
d. Debra Winger

GAME 76 Q5 ANSWER a

When scientist Jan Benes develops a blood clot in his brain, a team of doctors is miniaturized and injected into his body to fix the problem. This popular science fiction film inspired a television series and more than a few parodies, including a 1980 *Saturday Night Live* skit in which miniaturized dentists attempt to fix Anwar Sadat's teeth.

GAME 5

8. Which ungainly actor came to prominence with his performance in _Marty_ (1955)?

a. Raymond Burr
b. Ernest Borgnine
c. Jack Palance
d. Karl Malden

GAME 5 Q7 ANSWER b
Shields was just fourteen years old when she landed the role of Jade. Although this film has been described by movie critics as one of the worst of its time, it debuted such rising stars as Tom Cruise, James Spader, Ian Ziering, and Jamie Gertz. It also received an Oscar nomination for Lionel Richie's "Endless Love" as Best Original Song.

GAME 25

8. Which cast member from _American Graffiti_ (1973) was not in the sequel?

a. Candy Clark
b. Paul LeMat
c. Harrison Ford
d. Richard Dreyfuss

GAME 25 Q7 ANSWER b
Mad Max (1979) is the film that turned Mel Gibson into an international star. Gibson had attended the audition with a friend, but did not plan to audition himself (he had been in a fight the night before and his face was badly bruised). The producers, however, liked his "look" and asked him to come back and audition. He did and landed the part.

GAME 45

8. Which at-sea film enjoyed new popularity because of _Sleepless in Seattle_?

a. _An Affair to Remember_ (1957)
b. _A Night to Remember_ (1958)
c. _The Poseidon Adventure_ (1972)
d. _The Sea Hawk_ (1940)

GAME 45 Q7 ANSWER c
The real-life _Albatross_, a schooner, was built in 1920 to serve as a North Sea pilot boat. By the time it became a school for boys in 1959, the ship had been refitted several times, making it top-heavy. The 1966 film _White Squall_ recounts the _Albatross's_ last journey under the command of instructor Christopher B. Sheldon, played by Jeff Bridges.

GAME 65

8. Which film is well known for being shot in the city of Chicago?

a. _Dirty Harry_ (1971)
b. _West Side Story_ (1961)
c. _Pretty Baby_ (1978)
d. _The Blues Brothers_ (1980)

GAME 65 Q7 ANSWER c
Based on Tennessee Williams' 1961 play, this film, starring Richard Burton and Ava Gardner, is credited with turning the unknown Puerta Vallarta into a famous vacation spot. During filming, Elizabeth Taylor's visits to Richard Burton attracted the paparazzi, whose headlines of the pair's public affair brought much attention to the Mexican site.

GAME 16

5. Who plays the head mob boss in Martin Scorsese's *Goodfellas* (1990)?

a. Robert De Niro
b. Paul Sorvino
c. Jack Nicholson
d. Armin Mueller-Stahl

GAME 16 Q4 ANSWER c
Fields starred in all these films, but *My Little Chickadee* was the only one that the two comedians did together. Apparently, the pair fought over everything—billing, casting, work ethics—and after the project, West refused to work with Fields again. However, both appeared on the album cover of The Beatles' *Sgt. Pepper's Lonely Hearts Club Band*.

GAME 36

5. Which film stars Paul Newman as an unscrupulous cattle rancher?

a. *Hombre* (1967)
b. *Hud* (1963)
c. *Quintet* (1979)
d. *Cool Hand Luke* (1967)

GAME 36 Q4 ANSWER d
Though Hoffman portrays this Prohibition-era crook, every one of these actors has on-screen experience as a real-life member of the mafia. Beatty plays the infamous Bugsy Siegel in *Bugsy* (1991); De Niro plays gangster Jimmy Conway in *Goodfellas* (1990); and Pacino plays low-level mobster Benjamin "Lefty" Ruggiero in 1997's *Donnie Brasco*.

GAME 56

5. Which film is *not* based on a work by Stephen King?

a. *Stand By Me* (1986)
b. *The Green Mile* (1999)
c. *Dolores Claiborne* (1995)
d. *Cemetery Man* (1994)

GAME 56 Q4 ANSWER c
The film's title role was first offered to Bruce Lee's real-life son, actor Brandon Lee, but he turned it down and chose instead to star in the movie *The Crow*. Tragically, during the last few weeks of *The Crow's* production, Brandon was killed by a gun loaded with dummy cartridges. Both *Dragon* and *The Crow* were dedicated to his memory.

GAME 76

5. In which film are the characters shrunk to microscopic size?

a. *Fantastic Voyage* (1966)
b. *The Power* (1968)
c. *The Illustrated Man* (1969)
d. *The Omega Man* (1971)

GAME 76 Q4 ANSWER b
Glory tells the story of the 54th Massachusetts Volunteer Infantry—one of the first units of the US Army to be composed of black men. This Civil War movie is packed with strong performances, but Denzel Washington's portrayal of Trip, a bitter ex-slave who is fighting for his people's freedom, earned the actor his first Academy Award.

GAME 5

9. A blind white woman falls in love with a black man in which film?

a. *Blackboard Jungle* (1955)

b. *Lolita* (1962)

c. *The Slender Thread* (1965)

d. *A Patch of Blue* (1965)

GAME 5 Q8 ANSWER b
This touching Oscar-winning film centers around a lonely butcher's romance with an equally lonely schoolteacher. Supposedly, the film's producers expected it to lose money, so they financed it as a tax write-off. Instead, the movie, which cost $340,000 to make, earned $3 million at the box office. This made it one of the most profitable movies of all time.

GAME 25

9. Which sequel won an Oscar for Best Picture?

a. *The Empire Strikes Back* (1980)

b. *Batman Returns* (1992)

c. *The Godfather: Part II* (1974)

d. *A Very Brady Sequel* (1996)

GAME 25 Q8 ANSWER d
Although most of the original cast appeared in *More American Graffiti* (1978), Dreyfuss, who had just won the Oscar for his role in *The Goodbye Girl* (1977), was not available. Unlike *American Graffiti*, which met with critical acclaim, financial achievement, and multiple Oscar nominations, the sequel achieved only minor box office success.

GAME 45

9. Which at-sea film involves a skipper named Quint?

a. *Orca* (1977)

b. *Jaws* (1975)

c. *Moby Dick* (1956)

d. *The Abyss* (1989)

GAME 45 Q8 ANSWER a
Inspired by *An Affair to Remember*, the 1993 film *Sleepless in Seattle* made numerous references to the 1957 tearjerker, played the film's theme song, and even included clips of famous scenes featuring stars Cary Grant and Deborah Kerr. As a result, a whole new generation was introduced to *An Affair* nearly forty years after its release.

GAME 65

9. Just where *are* the boys in the 1960 movie *Where the Boys Are*?

a. Acapulco

b. Manhattan

c. Los Angeles

d. Fort Lauderdale

GAME 65 Q8 ANSWER d
Starring John Belushi and Dan Akyroyd, this comedy features many "Windy City" locations, including Wrigley Field, the Richard J. Daley Center, and the South Shore Country Club. As for the other answer choices, *Dirty Harry* is set in San Francisco; *Pretty Baby* takes place in a New Orleans red-light district; and *West Side Story* is set in Manhattan.

GAME 16

4. Which classic comedy paired W.C. Fields and Mae West?

a. *The Bank Dick* (1940)
b. *Fatal Glass of Beer* (1933)
c. *My Little Chickadee* (1940)
d. *International House* (1933)

GAME 16   Q3   ANSWER c
He plays "Popeye" Doyle, a character based on real narcotics detective Eddie Egan, in this William Friedkin-directed film. One highlight of this box office smash is an intense chase scene that was filmed on the streets of New York. The movie won five Oscars, including Best Director, Actor, and Picture (the first original R-rated film to do so).

GAME 36

4. Who plays gangster Dutch Schultz in the film *Billy Bathgate* (1991)?

a. Robert De Niro
b. Warren Beatty
c. Al Pacino
d. Dustin Hoffman

GAME 36   Q3   ANSWER b
Humphrey Bogart utters that and many other memorable lines as nightclub owner Rick Blaine in 1942's *Casablanca*. Adding to the film's long list of famous quotes, Bogart improvised "Here's looking at you, kid" while filming a flashback scene. The filmmakers loved the expression so much, they had him use it in other key moments throughout the movie.

GAME 56

4. Who plays Bruce Lee in *Dragon: The Bruce Lee Story* (1993)?

a. Brandon Lee
b. Christopher Lee
c. Jason Scott Lee
d. Tommy Lee Jones

GAME 56   Q3   ANSWER d
In the pre-CGI world of 1933, it was necessary for artists Marcel Delgado and Willis O'Brien to build four models of the full "beast." They also constructed a huge bust of Kong, two versions of the gorilla's right hand and arm, and one of his leg and foot. Great care was taken to streamline Kong so that he would not look comical or awkward.

GAME 76

4. Which film won Denzel Washington an Oscar for best supporting actor?

a. *Cry Freedom* (1987)
b. *Glory* (1989)
c. *The Pelican Brief* (1993)
d. *Training Day* (2001)

GAME 76   Q3   ANSWER c
Played by Henry Fonda in the 1955 Oscar-nominated film, Mister Roberts is the chief of a cargo ship who yearns for transfer to combat duty, and ends up paying the ultimate price for realizing his dream. The cast also includes James Cagney, William Powell, Ward Bond, and Jack Lemmon, who earned an Academy Award for his portrayal of Ensign Pulver.

10. Cher played a lovestruck widow in which 1987 film?

a. *Street Smart*

b. *Moonstruck*

c. *The Princess Bride*

d. *A Room with a View*

GAME 5   Q9   ANSWER d

Elizabeth Hartman and Sidney Poitier star as the lovers in this controversial film. Although it went against what the film stood for, scenes of the couple kissing were edited out for showings in the southern states. In the movie, Hartman wore dark glasses that she was unable to see through and that made her appear to be blind.

10. *Monsters Unleashed* is the subtitle of the 2004 film sequel to:

a. *X-Men*

b. *Spider-Man*

c. *Scooby-Doo*

d. *The Mummy*

GAME 25   Q9   ANSWER c

The first sequel to win a Best Picture Oscar, *The Godfather: Part II* is actually a sequel *and* a prequel to *The Godfather* (1972), telling the story of the Corleone Family before and after the events of the original film. With eleven Oscar nominations, the film won six, including Best Director (Coppola) and Best Supporting Actor (Robert De Niro).

10. What was the initial name of Sparrow's ship in *Pirates of the Caribbean*?

a. *Wicked Wench*

b. *Interceptor*

c. *Flying Dutchman*

d. *Sparrow's Nest*

GAME 45   Q9   ANSWER b

Quint, commander of the *Orca*, is played by Robert Shaw, who won acclaim for his portrayal of the vengeance-driven captain. Director Steven Spielberg had first offered the role to Sterling Harden and Lee Marvin, but when neither actor was interested, producers David Brown and Richard D. Zanuck suggested Shaw, an English actor and novelist.

10. Where is the prison located in *The Shawshank Redemption*?

a. Indiana

b. Massachussets

c. Maine

d. Ohio

GAME 65   Q9   ANSWER d

Based on Glendon Swarthout's novel of the same name, this coming-of-age film is about four college girls (Dolores Hart, Paula Prentiss, Yvette Mimieux, and Connie Francis) who head to Fort Lauderdale on their spring break. Directed at teens, this film was one of the first to delve into the then-taboo topic of sexuality among college students.

GAME 16

3. In which movie does Gene Hackman play a NYC police detective?

a. *Mississippi Burning* (1988)

b. *No Way Out* (1987)

c. *The French Connection* (1971)

d. *The Conversation* (1988)

GAME 16 Q2 ANSWER a
They help evil Ursula foil Prince Eric's romantic plans in the Disney animated film. The other pairs are from TV series. Beavis and Butt-head are the socially inept teens in the series of the same name. The evil wizard Gargamel and his cat Azrael are characters in *The Smurfs*. Boris and Natasha are the bad guys in the *Rocky and Bullwinkle* series.

GAME 36

3. Which movie character admits, "I'm no good at being noble"?

a. Rhett Butler

b. Rick Blaine

c. Atticus Finch

d. Terry Malloy

GAME 36 Q2 ANSWER b
David Mamet's 1982 play of the same name won a Tony for Best Play and the Pulitzer Prize for Drama before being adapted for the big screen. Each of the film's stars—Al Pacino, Jack Lemmon, Kevin Spacey, Alan Arkin, Alec Baldwin, and Ed Harris—has won or been nominated for an Oscar; and Pacino's performance nabbed him another nomination.

GAME 56

3. What movie ends with the words, "It was beauty killed the beast"?

a. *The Wolf Man* (1941)

b. *Phantom of the Opera* (1925)

c. *Frankenstein* (1931)

d. *King Kong* (1933)

GAME 56 Q2 ANSWER a
English actor Ronald Colman won critical acclaim and an Oscar nomination for his role as an officer whose wartime experiences cause him to lose his memory and rely on the kindness of strangers. Fortunately, a showgirl (Greer Garson) is ready to care for him—until an accident makes him remember his former life, but forget his new one.

GAME 76

3. Which title character dies at the end of the film?

a. Zorba the Greek

b. Robinson Crusoe

c. Mister Roberts

d. Mad Max

GAME 76 Q2 ANSWER a
Written by Sonny Bono and recorded by husband-and-wife singing team Sonny and Cher, "I Got You Babe" was a #1 hit single in 1965, and was soon adopted as the duo's signature song. When it played time and time again in the 1993 comedy *Groundhog Day*, "I Got You Babe" made a modest comeback and even rose to #66 on the UK charts.

GAME 5

11. In which movie does John Cusack hold up a boom box that blares "In Your Eyes"?

a. *Say Anything* (1989)

b. *Sixteen Candles* (1984)

c. *High Fidelity* (2000)

d. *America's Sweethearts* (2001)

GAME 5 Q10 ANSWER b
Cher earned an Oscar for her role in this warmhearted romantic comedy as Loretta Castorini—a widowed bookkeeper who lives in Brooklyn with her "very" Italian family (and who is torn between her mild-mannered fiancé and his estranged passionate brother). *Moonstruck* was also nominated for Best Picture but lost to the historic epic *The Last Emperor*.

GAME 25

11. Which 2007 film is a prequel to *The Silence of the Lambs* (1991)?

a. *Dance of the Dead*

b. *Hannibal Rising*

c. *Infernal Affairs*

d. *Hannibal*

GAME 25 Q10 ANSWER c
Based on the Hanna-Barbera cartoon TV series, *Scooby-Doo* (2002) and its sequel are live-action films, starring Freddie Prinze Jr. (Fred), Sarah Michelle Gellar (Daphne), Linda Cardellini (Velma), and Matthew Lillard (Shaggy). Scooby-Doo—the comically nervous, talking Great Dane—was computer-generated and voiced by Neil Fanning.

GAME 45

11. What leads eight people to leave a big ship for a tiny boat in *Lifeboat*?

a. Iceberg

b. Ballroom fire

c. Torpedo attack

d. Aerial attack

GAME 45 Q10 ANSWER a
Jack Sparrow (Johnny Depp) commanded the *Wicked Wench* in this 2003 film until an order was given to burn and sink it. When a pact with Davy Jones resulted in the ship's resurrection, it was renamed *The Black Pearl*. *Wicked Wench* is also the name of the ship at Disneyland's Pirates of the Caribbean attraction.

GAME 65

11. Which movie turned Lancaster County, PA, into a popular tourist site?

a. *Witness* (1985)

b. *Driving Miss Daisy* (1989)

c. *Field of Dreams* (1989)

d. *Fried Green Tomatoes* (1991)

GAME 65 Q10 ANSWER c
The fictional Shawshank Prison is located in Maine—the site of many works by Stephen King, whose 1981 novella *Rita Hayworth and the Shawshank Redemption* is the basis for this 1994 multiple Oscar-nominated film. Actual filming of the movie, however, took place in Ohio at the Reformatory in Mansfield, with actual inmates used as movie extras.

GAME 16

2. Who are Ursula's vile pair of helpers in *The Little Mermaid* (1989)?

a. Flotsam/Jetsam

b. Beavis/Butt-head

c. Gargamel/Azrael

d. Boris/Natasha

GAME 16 Q1 ANSWER d

Ivanhoe is based on the 1819 novel of the same name by Sir Walter Scott. *The Taming of the Shrew* is based on the Shakespearean play; *Who's Afraid of Virginia Woolf* is adapted from the play by Edward Albee; and *Doctor Faustus* is based on Christopher Marlowe's *The Tragical History of Doctor Faustus*. Elizabeth Taylor appeared in all four films.

GAME 36

2. Which 1992 movie deals with unsavory real estate agents?

a. *The Player*

b. *Glengarry Glen Ross*

c. *Howards End*

d. *The Crying Game*

GAME 36 Q1 ANSWER d

A play on the English words "cruel" and "devil," Cruella's name is slightly different in other languages. In Italian, she is called "Crudelia De Mon" (substituting "demon" for "devil"). The French call her "Cruella D'Enfer," which literally means "Cruella of Hell." Her surname remains the same in Spanish, but refers to the Spanish word for "vile."

GAME 56

2. In which film does Ronald Colman play a shellshocked World War I soldier?

a. *Random Harvest* (1942)

b. *Arrowsmith* (1931)

c. *The Light That Failed* (1939)

d. *A Double Life* (1947)

GAME 56 Q1 ANSWER c

Several better-known actresses were considered for the role of Vivian Ward, but all—including Michele Pfeiffer, Meg Ryan, Mary Steenburgen, and Daryl Hannah—turned it down. Finally, the part went to relative newcomer Julia Roberts, whose performance earned her widespread praise as well as an Oscar nomination for Best Actress.

GAME 76

2. What song greets Bill Murray's character each morning in *Groundhog Day*?

a. "I Got You Babe"

b. "A Day in the Life"

c. "Time After Time"

d. "All You Need Is Love"

GAME 76 Q1 ANSWER d

When her performance in 1948's *Johnny Belinda* earned an Academy Award for Best Actress in a Leading Role, Jane Wyman became the first actress in a "talkie" to receive an Oscar without speaking any dialogue. At the awards ceremony, Wyman remarked, "I accept this, very gratefully, for keeping my mouth shut once. I think I'll do it again."

GAME 5

12. Cary Elwes and Robin Wright Penn star as lovers in which Rob Reiner film?

a. *A Knight's Tale* (2001)

b. *The Princess Bride* (1987)

c. *When Harry Met Sally* (1989)

d. *The Story of Us* (1999)

GAME 5 Q11 ANSWER a
In this classic scene, Lloyd Dobler (Cusack) plays the song while standing under his girl's window. When director Cameron Crowe had asked songwriter Peter Gabriel's permission to use the song, he also sent a cut of the movie to help persuade him. Gabriel agreed to the song usage, but didn't like that the character overdosed. Turns out he was sent the wrong film—*Wired!*

GAME 25

12. Which film is the sequel to *Romancing the Stone* (1984)?

a. *Thief of Baghdad*

b. *Pearl of Death*

c. *The Jewel of the Nile*

d. *The Dark Crystal*

GAME 25 Q11 ANSWER b
Based on the 2006 Thomas Harris novel, this film tells the story of Lecter's past (including the reason for his evolution into cannibalism). There are two other *Silence of the Lambs* prequel films—*Manhunter* (1986) and the 2002 release *Red Dragon*, which took the title of the Thomas Harris 1981 novel from which both of these films were adapted.

GAME 45

12. Who stars with Gregory Peck in 1951's *Captain Horatio Hornblower*?

a. Elizabeth Taylor

b. Virginia Mayo

c. Lana Turner

d. Grace Kelly

GAME 45 Q11 ANSWER c
Torpedoes were about the only thing that *didn't* plague the cast of this 1944 Alfred Hitchcock movie. During filming, Hume Cronyn suffered two cracked ribs and nearly drowned, Tallulah Bankhead developed pneumonia twice, and Mary Anderson also became seriously ill. In fact, several days of production were lost due to illness and accidents.

GAME 65

12. In which city does the 1973 hit movie *The Sting* take place?

a. Philadelphia

b. Chicago

c. Detroit

d. New York

GAME 65 Q11 ANSWER a
Shot on location in Lancaster and the surrounding areas, this movie starring Harrison Ford is about a young Amish boy who witnesses a murder. As a point of interest, no actual Amish people were used as extras in the film (they don't like having their pictures taken), but they did offer their services on the set as carpenters and electricians.

GAME 16

1. Which of the following movies is *not* based on a play?

a. *Doctor Faustus* (1967)

b. *The Taming of the Shrew* (1967)

c. *Who's Afraid of Virginia Woolf?* (1966)

d. *Ivanhoe* (1952)

The answer to this question is on:

page 128, top frame, right side.

GAME 36

1. Which Disney villain wears furs and smokes incessantly?

a. Captain Hook

b. Jafar

c. Queen of Hearts

d. Cruella De Vil

The answer to this question is on:

page 128, second frame, right side.

GAME 56

1. Which film earned Julia Roberts an Oscar nomination?

a. *Flatliners* (1989)

b. *Dying Young* (1991)

c. *Pretty Woman* (1990)

d. *The Pelican Brief* (1993)

The answer to this question is on:

page 128, third frame, right side.

GAME 76

1. Who was the first actress to win an Oscar for playing a deaf character?

a. Dorothy McGuire

b. Patty Duke

c. Marlee Matlin

d. Jane Wyman

The answer to this question is on:

page 128, bottom frame, right side.

GAME 6

The Classics

*Turn to page 133
for the first question.*

Turn to page 133 for the first question.

GAME 26

Spies and Assassins

*Turn to page 133
for the first question.*

GAME 46

Literature and
the Movies

*Turn to page 133
for the first question.*

GAME 66

More Directors

*Turn to page 133
for the first question.*

GAME 5 Q12 ANSWER b
William Goldman wrote the book upon which this film is based as well as the screenplay. He was on set during the filming of the "fire swamp" scene in which Buttercup (Penn's character) wears a dress that catches on fire. Goldman was so immersed in the action that he yelled, "Her dress is on fire!" even though he knew it was in the script.

GAME 25 Q12 ANSWER c
Kathleen Turner, Michael Douglas, and Danny DeVito all reprised their roles in this 1985 sequel, which did almost as well at the box office as *Romancing the Stone,* although critics felt it lacked *Romancing's* charm. In 1989, the three actors reunited once again when they starred in the dark comedy *The War of the Roses,* which DeVito directed.

GAME 45 Q12 ANSWER b
British critics voiced their objections when Missouri-born Virginia Mayo was cast as the English-born Lady Barbara Wellesley. (Peck's personal choice for the part was British actress Margaret Leighton.) But since Peck did not affect an English accent when playing Royal Navy officer Horatio Hornblower, Mayo did not seem at all out of place.

GAME 65 Q12 ANSWER b
Paul Newman and Robert Redford star as professional con men who pull off an intricate sting operation on a Chicago crime boss played by Robert Shaw. Of its ten Oscar nods, *The Sting* won eight, including Best Picture and Best Director for George Roy Hill, who had worked with Newman and Redford earlier on 1969's *Butch Cassidy and the Sundance Kid.*

GAME 16

GRAB BAG

Turn to page 130 for the first question.

GAME 15 Q12 ANSWER b
This tale stars Gene Hackman as volatile Coach Dale and Dennis Hopper as a former star player turned town drunk—a role for which he earned an Oscar nomination. The story is loosely based on the true story of the Milan Indians—1954 Indiana State Champs. In 2008, the American Film Institute ranked *Hoosiers* as the #4 best film in the sports genre.

GAME 36

GRAB BAG

Turn to page 130 for the first question.

GAME 35 Q12 ANSWER c
Ferrer was in the 1965 film *The Greatest Story Ever Told*, but not as Jesus. He played Herod, who was instrumental in the death of John the Baptist. Victor Garber played Jesus in the 1973 musical *Godspell*, while Ted Neeley played him that same year in another musical *Jesus Christ Superstar*. Robert Powell had the role in *Jesus of Nazareth* (1977).

GAME 56

GRAB BAG

Turn to page 130 for the first question.

GAME 55 Q12 ANSWER b
This Spanish film was directed by Alejandro Amenábar and stars Javier Bardem, whose work in *No Country for Old Men* (2007) won him a Best Supporting Actor Oscar. Germany's *The Lives of Others* won in 2007, while Argentina's *The Secret in Their Eyes* won the award in 2010. The first film to win in this category was Italy's *La Strada* in 1954.

GAME 76

GRAB BAG

Turn to page 130 for the first question.

GAME 75 Q12 ANSWER a
Michelle Kwan plays herself as a television commentator in this inspiring 2005 ice skating movie. Another film that features many real-life ice skating icons is the 2007 comedy *Blades of Glory* with Will Ferrell and Jon Heder. It has cameos by Sasha Cohen, Nancy Kerrigan, Scott Hamilton, Peggy Fleming, and Dorothy Hamill among others.

GAME 6

1. Which character in *The Maltese Falcon* (1941) is known as "The Fat Man"?

a. Sam Spade

b. Kasper Gutman

c. Joel Cairo

d. Miles Archer

The answer to this question is on:

page 135, top frame, right side.

GAME 26

1. Who is the assassination target in the 1993 film *In the Line of Fire*?

a. A corporate CEO

b. The Pope

c. The US President

d. A civil rights leader

The answer to this question is on:

page 135, second frame, right side.

GAME 46

1. Which disturbing film was adapted from a Chuck Palahniuk novel?

a. *Stigmata* (1999)

b. *Apt Pupil* (1998)

c. *Stir of Echoes* (1999)

d. *Fight Club* (1999)

The answer to this question is on:

page 135, third frame, right side.

GAME 66

1. What 1991 film was directed by eventual Oscar-winner Kathryn Bigelow?

a. *The Prince of Tides*

b. *Rambling Rose*

c. *Little Man Tate*

d. *Point Break*

The answer to this question is on:

page 135, bottom frame, right side.

GAME 15

12. Which film sees a small-town high school basketball coach lead his team to an unlikely championship?

a. *He Got Game* (1988)

b. *Hoosiers* (1986)

c. *Blue Chips* (1994)

d. *The Air Up There* (1994)

GAME 15 Q11 ANSWER c
Along with Stoltz and Cage, this 1982 film marked the early appearance of many future stars, including Sean Penn, Judge Reinhold, Phoebe Cates, and Forest Whitaker. Seasoned actor Ray Walston, who played uptight history teacher Mr. Hand, earned two Emmy Awards in the 1990s for his portrayal of Judge Henry Bone on the TV show *Picket Fences*.

GAME 35

12. Which actor has *not* portrayed Jesus Christ on film?

a. Victor Garber

b. Ted Neeley

c. José Ferrer

d. Robert Powell

GAME 35 Q11 ANSWER a
Before Bowie, Sting had been cast as Pilate in this 1988 Martin Scorsese film—one of the most controversial of all time. The film's realistic portrayal of the human side of Jesus struggling with life's temptations—including his decision to marry Mary Magdalene rather than die on the cross—invoked a huge uprising from multiple religious groups.

GAME 55

12. Which 2004 movie won the Oscar for Best Foreign Language Film?

a. *The Secret in Their Eyes*

b. *The Sea Inside*

c. *The Lives of Others*

d. *La Strada*

GAME 55 Q11 ANSWER a
Born in Spain in 1900, Buñuel directed (and co-wrote) his first film *Un Chien Andalou* (1929) with surrealist artist Salvador Dalí. After working in black and white for more than twenty years, he switched to color for *Robinson Crusoe*. Dan O'Herlihy received a Best Actor Oscar nomination for his work as the film's title character.

GAME 75

12. Which real-life ice skating star has a cameo appearance in *Ice Princess*?

a. Michelle Kwan

b. Nancy Kerrigan

c. Sarah Hughes

d. Kristi Yamaguchi

GAME 75 Q11 ANSWER c
Belushi's performance as Captain Wild Bill Kelso is one of the most memorable parts of this film about American paranoia during World War II. While his only listed role in the film is that of Kelso, Belushi also appears in a cameo—he is seated in an Italian restaurant and done up as Marlon Brando's "Vito Corleone."

GAME 6

2. What causes George Bailey's suicidal depression in the Christmas classic *It's a Wonderful Life* (1946)?

a. Job transfer

b. Marital strife

c. Mother's death

d. Financial crisis

GAME 6 Q1 ANSWER b

In this classic film starring Humphrey Bogart as detective Sam Spade, the role of Kasper Gutman was played by Sydney Greenstreet, who weighed over 350 pounds at the time. It was Greenstreet's first movie as well as John Huston's directorial debut. The film earned an Oscar nod for Best Picture and Greenstreet received one for Best Supporting Actor.

GAME 26

2. Which actor played Agent 007 in the most consecutive James Bond films?

a. Timothy Dalton

b. Roger Moore

c. Sean Connery

d. Pierce Brosnan

GAME 26 Q1 ANSWER c

Clint Eastwood is a secret service agent in search of an ex-government agent who is trying to kill the President. For his role as the psychopathic would-be assassin, John Malkovich earned an Oscar nomination for Best Supporting Actor (lost to Tommy Lee Jones for *The Fugitive*). This is the last film that Eastwood starred in but did not also direct.

GAME 46

2. Who plays a bitter handyman in the film *Giant* (1956)?

a. Nick Adams

b. James Dean

c. Marlon Brando

d. Montgomery Clift

GAME 46 Q1 ANSWER d

When Laura Ziskin of 20th Century Fox purchased the rights to Palahniuk's *Fight Club,* she wanted Buck Henry to write the screenplay because she considered *Fight Club* similar to *The Graduate,* one of Henry's many successes. But when newcomer Jim Uhls expressed his interest in the project, he got the job—and, as a result, made a name for himself.

GAME 66

2. Which director recreated Las Vegas for *One from the Heart* (1982)?

a. Francis Ford Coppola

b. Robert Zemeckis

c. Oliver Stone

d. Tim Burton

GAME 66 Q1 ANSWER d

Bigelow's 1991 film was *Point Break* starring Keanu Reeves and Patrick Swayze. In 2010, she became the first female American filmmaker to win a Best Director Oscar for *The Hurt Locker.* In 1991, Barbra Streisand directed *The Prince of Tides;* Martha Coolidge directed *Rambling Rose;* and Jodie Foster directed her first feature film *Little Man Tate.*

GAME 15

11. Which of the following actors did *not* appear in *Fast Times at Ridgemont High*?

a. Eric Stoltz

b. Nicolas Cage

c. Judd Nelson

d. Ray Walston

GAME 15 Q10 ANSWER c
This 1998 movie, which was actually filmed in Florida, did incredibly well at the box office. This success, however, must be footnoted. When the film was released, it was preceded by the preview for the upcoming *Phantom Menace* (1999). Many *Star Wars* fans bought tickets just to watch the preview, and then left the theater.

GAME 35

11. Which rock star is Pontius Pilate in *The Last Temptation of Christ*?

a. David Bowie

b. Sting

c. Neil Young

d. Pete Townshend

GAME 35 Q10 ANSWER a
Along with directing the film, Huston played Noah—a role he offered to Charlie Chaplin. Chaplin turned down the role, claiming that he didn't want to be in any film that he didn't direct himself. *The Bible*, which recounted stories from the Book of Genesis, was to be the first of a series to cover the entire Old Testament. The "series" ended here.

GAME 55

11. What is the first film that Spanish director Luis Buñuel shot in color?

a. *The Adventures of Robinson Crusoe* (1954)

b. *Simon of the Desert* (1965)

c. *Belle de Jour* (1967)

d. *Tristana* (1970)

GAME 55 Q10 ANSWER c
Herzog's tumultuous work with the actor began with *Aguirre, the Wrath of God* (1972), and continued with two 1979 films: *Nosferatu the Vampyre* (a remake of the 1922 German silent-film classic *Nosferatu*) and *Woyzeck*. The last two films they did together before Kinski's death in 1991 were *Fitzcarraldo* (1982) and *Cobra Verde* (1987).

GAME 75

11. Which actor has a cameo *and* a starring role in Steven Spielberg's *1941*?

a. Tim Matheson

b. Dan Aykroyd

c. John Belushi

d. John Candy

GAME 75 Q10 ANSWER a
Abdul-Jabbar appears as himself midway through the film in a dream that Chase's character Irwin "Fletch" Fletcher has about playing for the Los Angeles Lakers. He also appears in the zany 1980 disaster-movie spoof *Airplane!* as flight pilot Roger Murdock—who has to keep telling a kid on the plane that he's *not* Kareem Abdul-Jabbar!

GAME 6

3. Which actor played pool shark Minnesota Fats in *The Hustler* (1961)?

a. Rod Steiger

b. Jackie Gleason

c. Anthony Quinn

d. Marlon Brando

GAME 6 Q2 ANSWER d

When a large deposit from his loan company is misplaced, allowing an evil millionaire to take over the town, George Bailey (James Stewart) becomes a broken man. He decides to "end it all" until an angel shows him the many lives he has touched. The film was up for five Oscars including Best Picture, Best Actor (Stewart), and Best Director (Frank Capra).

GAME 26

3. Which actress plays a government assassin in *Point of No Return* (1993)?

a. Linda Hamilton

b. Sharon Stone

c. Bridget Fonda

d. Jennifer Jason Leigh

GAME 26 Q2 ANSWER b

Connery and Moore both played Bond seven times. Connery's consecutive streak of four films ended in 1969 when George Lazenby played Bond in *On Her Majesty's Secret Service*. Moore's streak of six ended in 1983 with *Octopussy*—the same year that Connery returned in *Never Say Never Again*. Moore's last Bond film was *A View to a Kill* (1985).

GAME 46

3. Which Shakespearean play received a contemporary big-screen twist in 1996?

a. *Hamlet*

b. *Julius Caesar*

c. *Romeo and Juliet*

d. *Twelfth Night*

GAME 46 Q2 ANSWER b

Based on the Edna Ferber novel, this film starring Elizabeth Taylor and Rock Hudson, provided Dean with his second Oscar nomination and his very last role —he died before all his work on the film had been completed. Director George Stevens had to hire Dean's friend and fellow *Rebel Without a Cause* actor Nick Adams to overdub some of Dean's lines.

GAME 66

3. Which of these Marlon Brando films was *not* directed by Elia Kazan?

a. *Viva Zapata!* (1952)

b. *On the Waterfront* (1954)

c. *A Streetcar Named Desire* (1951)

d. *Julius Caesar* (1953)

GAME 66 Q2 ANSWER a

In 1976, two years after winning Oscars both as director and producer of *The Godfather, Part II* and winning the Palme d'Or award at the Cannes Film Festival for *The Conversation*, Coppola went to the Philippines to shoot his Vietnam war epic *Apocalypse Now* (1979). After that film's turmoil, Coppola wanted *One from the Heart* to be a happier project.

GAME 15

10. In *The Waterboy*, Adam Sandler plays for a lousy college football team from:

a. Quebec

b. Florida

c. Louisiana

d. Indiana

GAME 15 Q9 ANSWER c
This classic campus comedy, which highlights the improvisational brilliance of comic actor John Belushi, focuses on the antics of a group of college frat boys. Considered the movie that launched the gross-out genre, *Animal House* was to be filmed at the U of Missouri until the school president read the script. It was filmed at the U of Oregon instead.

GAME 35

10. What role did John Huston play in *The Bible* (1966)?

a. Noah

b. Adam

c. Jesus

d. Methuselah

GAME 35 Q9 ANSWER c
The movie, which was the first English-language film for the Swedish actor, experienced many production setbacks. Joanna Dunham (Mary) became pregnant, necessitating costume redesigns and creative camera shots to hide her condition. Joseph Schildkraut (Nicodemus) died before the film was completed, so his parts had to be rewritten.

GAME 55

10. Which actor made five films with German director Werner Herzog?

a. Paul Henreid

b. Groucho Marx

c. Klaus Kinski

d. Max Schreck

GAME 55 Q9 ANSWER a
All four of these movies were directed by Japanese animation filmmaker Hayao Miyasaki. In 1997, his *Princess Mononoke* was the biggest-grossing film in Japan—only to be defeated by director James Cameron's *Titanic* that same year. By 2002, however, *Spirited Away* surpassed *Titanic* as the top-selling movie in Japan to date.

GAME 75

10. In which Chevy Chase film does Kareem Abdul-Jabbar have a cameo?

a. *Fletch* (1985)

b. *Foul Play* (1978)

c. *The Three Amigos* (1986)

d. *Spies Like Us* (1985)

GAME 75 Q9 ANSWER b
In the film, Reed can be seen chatting briefly with Lois Lane (Margot Kidder). Rex Reed also plays a character who undergoes a sex change in *Myra Breckenridge* (1970), and has a voice cameo as a guest on Larry King's radio show during the opening credits of Albert Brooks' *Lost in America* (1985).

GAME 6

4. Which sentimental classic about a beloved teacher starred Robert Donat and Greer Garson?

a. *Goodbye, Mr. Chips* (1939)

b. *Ninotchka* (1939)

c. *Dark Victory* (1939)

d. *Stagecoach* (1939)

GAME 6 Q3 ANSWER b
Gleason earned a Best Supporting Actor Oscar nomination for his role as the legendary pool master, while Paul Newman received a Best Actor nomination for his portrayal of the arrogant up-and-coming pool shark Fast Eddie Felsen. Both Gleason and Newman (who had never even held a pool cue before landing the role) did most of their own pool shots.

GAME 26

4. Who played an IRA gunman in the 1997 film *The Jackal*?

a. Richard Gere

b. Kevin Kline

c. Bruce Willis

d. Sylvester Stallone

GAME 26 Q3 ANSWER c
In this 1993 film, also known as *The Assassin*, Fonda plays a junkie who kills a cop, but is spared the death sentence in return for becoming a government assassin. She is the daughter of actor Peter Fonda, granddaughter of Henry, and niece of Jane. She has starred in a number of films, including *Singles* (1992) and *Single White Female* (1992).

GAME 46

4. Which box office hit was based on a 1992 novel by Michael Ondaatje?

a. *American Psycho* (2000)

b. *The Reader* (2008)

c. *The Green Mile* (1999)

d. *The English Patient* (1996)

GAME 46 Q3 ANSWER c
Set in fictional Verona Beach, *Romeo + Juliet* stars Leonardo DiCaprio and Claire Danes as modern star-crossed lovers. While the 1996 film retains Shakespeare's dialogue, swords are replaced with guns; horses, by cars; and an old-fashioned family feud, with warring industrialists. Not surprisingly, critical reaction to the film varied greatly.

GAME 66

4. Which director made *Metropolis*, *M*, and *You Never Live Once*?

a. Fritz Lang

b. Jean Renoir

c. Alfred Hitchcock

d. Luis Buñuel

GAME 66 Q3 ANSWER d
Brando's portrayal of Mark Anthony in director Joseph L. Manciewicz's film adaptation of Shakespeare's play led to a third consecutive Best Actor Oscar nomination for the star. Kazan first directed Brando in 1947 on Broadway in *A Streetcar Named Desire*, and it was Kazan's direction that led to Brando's first Oscar win for *On the Waterfront*.

GAME 15

9. Which film started the "Toga Party" craze on college campuses across America?

a. *Back to School* (1986)

b. *American Pie 2* (2001)

c. *Animal House* (1978)

d. *Porky's* (1982)

GAME 15 Q8 ANSWER c
When Williams took the role in this 1989 film, he said he wished he had had a teacher like John Keating. In *The Emperor's Club* (2002), Kevin Kline played the beloved Professor Hundert; while Richard Harris took on the role of Professor Dumbledore in the Harry Potter movies. Brian Cox played Dr. Guggenheim in the 1998 comedy-drama *Rushmore*.

GAME 35

9. Max von Sydow portrays Jesus in which George Stevens epic?

a. *King of Kings* (1961)

b. *Jesus of Nazareth* (1977)

c. *The Greatest Story Ever Told* (1965)

d. *Jesus Christ Superstar* (1973)

GAME 35 Q8 ANSWER b
In this movie starring Demi Moore, the seven signs of the Apocalypse from the biblical Book of Revelations begin to occur, signifying the end of the world. Ellen DeGeneres had a small role in the film, but her scene was cut. Had it been left in, it would have been her first film role. The clip was aired on *The Ellen DeGeneres Show* in May of 2007.

GAME 55

9. What was the first Japanese anime feature film to win an Oscar?

a. *Spirited Away* (2001)

b. *Princess Mononoke* (1997)

c. *Howl's Moving Castle* (2004)

d. *Castle in the Sky* (1986)

GAME 55 Q8 ANSWER d
After hiring Brigitte Bardot to be in this 1963 film, Godard cast Jack Palance as an American film producer who hires director Fritz Lang (appearing as himself) to make a movie of Homer's *Odyssey*. Godard made *Contempt* with the Italian producer Carlo Ponti, who insisted on having Brigitte Bardot—a well-known sex symbol—appear nude in the film.

GAME 75

9. Which film critic has a cameo in *Superman: The Movie* (1978)?

a. Roger Ebert

b. Rex Reed

c. Leonard Maltin

d. Gene Shalit

GAME 75 Q8 ANSWER d
This hilarious film features Brooks as a director named Mel Funn who hopes to recruit big-name stars for his very own modern-day "silent movie." In addition to Newman and Caan, there are delightful cameos by Burt Reynolds, Liza Minnelli, and Brooks' real-life wife Anne Bancroft—as well as a classic cameo by famous mime Marcel Marceau.

GAME 6

5. Who played the little girl in the 1947 Christmas classic *Miracle on 34th Street*?

a. Natalie Wood
b. Shirley Temple
c. Faye Dunaway
d. Raquel Welch

GAME 6 Q4 ANSWER a
Based on the novel by James Hilton, *Goodbye, Mr. Chips* tells the story of Charles Chipping, an aging classics teacher and school headmaster, as he looks back at the people and events of his decades-long career. Donat took home the Best Actor Oscar for his role as the beloved teacher, who was modeled after one of Hilton's former teachers.

GAME 26

5. Which star plays a spy in *Confessions of a Dangerous Mind* (2002)?

a. Al Pacino
b. Meryl Streep
c. Julia Roberts
d. Drew Barrymore

GAME 26 Q4 ANSWER a
Richard Gere plays Mulqueen, who works with the FBI to stop an anonymous assassin known only as "The Jackal." Initially, Gere was offered the role of the assassin, but turned it down and requested to play the hero. Liam Neeson, Matthew McConaughey, and Sean Connery also rejected the role of the Jackal, which was given to Bruce Willis.

GAME 46

5. Who directed the 1992 film adaptation of Bram Stoker's *Dracula*?

a. Francis Ford Coppola
b. Tim Burton
c. Kenneth Branagh
d. Steven Spielberg

GAME 46 Q4 ANSWER d
The *English Patient* was a winner both at the box office, and also at the awards ceremonies. It captured Academy Awards for Best Picture, Best Art Direction, Best Cinematography, Best Costume Design, Best Director, Best Film Editing, Best Original Score, and Best Sound, and Juliette Binoche took home an Oscar for Best Supporting Actress.

GAME 66

5. Which movie director made the 1964 nuclear war drama *Fail Safe*?

a. John Frankenheimer
b. Sidney Lumet
c. William Friedkin
d. Franklin J. Schaffner

GAME 66 Q4 ANSWER a
Before he and his family fled Germany in 1934, Lang was known best for directing legendary actor Peter Lorre in the 1931 thriller *M*. His 1927 science-fiction classic *Metropolis* was a favorite film of Adolf Hitler, though Lang himself was Jewish. Lang's 1937 American film *You Never Live Once* stars Henry Fonda and is considered a film-noir classic.

GAME 15

8. In *Dead Poet's Society*, who played the inspirational English teacher John Keating?

a. Richard Harris
b. Kevin Kline
c. Robin Williams
d. Brian Cox

GAME 15 Q7 ANSWER a
When Finn (played by Jack Black) loses his spot in the band, he becomes a substitute teacher at a prep school and forms another band with his students. In the film, the kids really play their instruments and the backup singers are real. Black plays some of his guitar parts in the movie, but doesn't actually perform the "self-indulgent" solos.

GAME 35

8. In which film does Jesus return to earth as the world is about to end?

a. *Dogma* (1999)
b. *The Seventh Sign* (1988)
c. *The Prophecy* (1995)
d. *Constantine* (2005)

GAME 35 Q7 ANSWER c
Peck was chosen for the role in this film because producer Darryl Zanuck thought he had a "biblical face." During his illustrious career, Peck starred in a number of legendary films, and garnered many Oscar nominations. His only win, however, was for his superlative role as the lawyer Atticus Finch in *To Kill a Mockingbird* (1962).

GAME 55

8. Which American actor appears in Jean-Luc Godard's film *Contempt* ?

a. Jack Nicholson
b. Warren Beatty
c. Marlon Brando
d. Jack Palance

GAME 55 Q7 ANSWER b
Co-written by Federico Fellini, this movie about the life and works of St. Francis of Assisi and the Franciscans has real-life monks in the leading roles. In 1995, it was named by the Vatican as one of the best films ever made. Rossellini was married to actress Ingrid Bergman, with whom he had three children, including actress Isabella Rossellini.

GAME 75

8. James Caan and Paul Newman have cameos in which Mel Brooks' film?

a. *High Anxiety* (1977)
b. *Young Frankenstein* (1974)
c. *The Producers* (1968)
d. *Silent Movie* (1976)

GAME 75 Q7 ANSWER a
Lovett met actress Julia Roberts (who also has a cameo in the film) when he portrayed an odd policeman in this Robert Altman classic. The two were married in 1993, the same year that Lovett played a vengeful baker in Altman's film *Short Cuts*. Lovett also appeared in Altman's *Prêt-à-Porter* (1994) and *Cookie's Fortune* (1999).

GAME 6

6. Who starred with Mickey Rooney in the 1938 classic film *Boys Town* ?

a. Deanna Durbin
b. Judy Garland
c. Spencer Tracy
d. Clark Gable

GAME 6 Q5 ANSWER a
Natalie Wood was just nine years old when this movie was released, but it wasn't her first film. At age four, she had an uncredited role in *Happy Land* (1943) as a crying little girl who had just dropped her ice cream cone. As an adult, Wood's film career ran hot and cold. A drowning accident brought her life to a tragic end at age forty-three.

GAME 26

6. Which baseball player was the hypnotized assassin in *The Naked Gun*?

a. Reggie Jackson
b. Johnny Bench
c. Ozzie Smith
d. Jose Canseco

GAME 26 Q5 ANSWER c
She played the seductive spy in this George Clooney-directed biopic. The movie is based on a book by TV game show host Chuck Barris, who claimed he was a CIA assassin. As a favor to Clooney, Roberts and Drew Barrymore worked for scale. Brad Pitt and Matt Damon, who cameoed as bachelors on *The Dating Game*, worked for free.

GAME 46

6. Which baseball movie is based on the novel *Shoeless Joe* ?

a. *Field of Dreams* (1989)
b. *The Natural* (1984)
c. *Bull Durham* (1988)
d. *Eight Men Out* (1988)

GAME 46 Q5 ANSWER a
Although Coppola called his film *Bram Stoker's Dracula*, there are major differences between the book and this adaptation. Perhaps most jarring to lovers of the novel is that the film provides overtly sexual scenes, while the novel only mildly hints at sexual situations. The movie also includes plot twists that are not true to Stoker's work.

GAME 66

6. Which of director Ang Lee's films features a blond male transvestite?

a. *Hulk* (2003)
b. *Brokeback Mountain* (2005)
c. *Taking Woodstock* (2009)
d. *Lust, Caution* (2007)

GAME 66 Q5 ANSWER b
Sidney Lumet was one of the most prolific directors of early TV productions in the 1950s. His first feature film, *12 Angry Men* (1957), earned three Oscar nominations (including one for Lumet's direction). *Fail Safe* showed Lumet's skill at getting solid performances from actors like Henry Fonda, Walter Matthau, and even the comic actor Dom DeLuise.

GAME 15

7. In *School of Rock* (2003), why does Dewey Finn get kicked out of his band?

a. Self-indulgent solos
b. Excessive salary demands
c. Obnoxious girlfriend
d. Love of disco

GAME 15 Q6 ANSWER d
Based on the Steven King novel, *Carrie* (1976) starred Sissy Spacek as the girl with telekinetic powers. The high school name is a reference to Norman Bates, the creepy motel owner in the1960 horror classic *Psycho*. King based Carrie's character on two girls he knew from school. Both were social outcasts and had strong religious upbringings.

GAME 35

7. Who starred as King David in *David and Bathsheba* (1951)?

a. Paul Newman
b. Robert Taylor
c. Gregory Peck
d. William Holden

GAME 35 Q6 ANSWER c
Cecil B. De Mille directed them in the 1949 epic film *Samson and Delilah*. De Mille had wanted Steve Reeves to play Samson, and was disappointed when Mature was cast as the biblical strongman. Ironically, Mature refused to wrestle the lion in the movie's classic scene. It was tame and had no teeth, but Mature said he feared being gummed to death.

GAME 55

7. Which Roberto Rossellini film features real monks?

a. *Rome, Open City* (1945)
b. *The Flowers of St. Francis* (1950)
c. *Paisà* (1946)
d. *Germany Year Zero* (1948)

GAME 55 Q6 ANSWER c
Though it looks like actors Anita Ekberg and Marcello Mastroianni are splashing about in Rome's actual Trevi Fountain, director Federico Fellini shot this iconic scene on a studio soundstage. In addition to Anouk Aimée, Yvonne Furneaux, and Magali Noël, *La Dolce Vita* features a small role by Velvet Underground singer Nico.

GAME 75

7. In which movie does singer Lyle Lovett make a cameo appearance?

a. *The Player* (1992)
b. *Reality Bites* (1994)
c. *French Kiss* (1995)
d. *Get Shorty* (1995)

GAME 75 Q6 ANSWER c
Having previously acted as Mr. Pink in Quentin Tarantino's breakthrough film *Reservoir Dogs* (1992), Buscemi appears in 1994's *Pulp Fiction* as the waiter who serves Uma Thurman and John Travolta at the retro diner Jack Rabbit Slim's. Meanwhile, Gary Busey gave an Oscar-nominated performance as Buddy Holly in 1978's *The Buddy Holly Story*.

GAME 6

7. Which classic film of the 1930s ends with the line, "Is this the end of Rico?"

a. *Little Caesar* (1931)

b. *Trader Horn* (1931)

c. *A Farewell to Arms* (1932)

d. *It Happened One Night* (1934)

GAME 6 Q6 ANSWER c
The day after Tracy won the Best Actor Oscar for his role as Father Flanagan in this film, MGM released a statement (without consulting Tracy) that the actor would donate his Oscar statuette to the real Boys Town in Nebraska. Tracy agreed, but only if the Academy sent him a replacement. When it arrived, the award read, "Best Actor — Dick Tracy."

GAME 26

7. What is the real name of CIA operative Jason Bourne?

a. John Smith

b. Felix Leiter

c. David Webb

d. Matt Helm

GAME 26 Q6 ANSWER a
Jackson played the Angels' right fielder in this 1988 comedy. The movie is the first of a series that centered on the adventures of incompetent police Lieutenant Frank Drebin, played by Leslie Nielsen. The film series is based on the 1982 TV series *Police Squad!*, which spoofed police dramas, and also starred Neilsen as the bumbling detective.

GAME 46

7. Which movie shares its title with both a novel and a famous painting?

a. *Girl with a Pearl Earring* (2003)

b. *Felicia's Journey* (1999)

c. *Flowers in the Attic* (1987)

d. *The Tailor of Panama* (2001)

GAME 46 Q6 ANSWER a
The working title of the movie was the same as the name of the book—*Shoeless Joe*—but when test audiences expressed their dislike of the "hobo" connotation, Universal Studios chose *Field of Dreams* instead. This was fine with novelist W.P. Kinsella because the title of his book had been *Dream Fields* until his publisher renamed it *Shoeless Joe*.

GAME 66

7. Which Martin Scorsese movie was the first to star Leonardo DiCaprio?

a. *The Aviator*

b. *Gangs of New York*

c. *Shutter Island*

d. *The Departed*

GAME 66 Q6 ANSWER c
Based on the memoir of Elliot Tiber, this film gave Ang Lee a chance to make his first comedy since 1993's *The Wedding Banquet*. Although Lee is perhaps best known for his work on 2005's gay cowboy film *Brokeback Mountain*, he has directed a wide range of movies, from 1995's costume drama *Sense and Sensibility* to 2003's superhero movie *Hulk*.

GAME 15

6. Which character attends Bates High School?

a. Regan
b. Damien
c. Norman
d. Carrie

GAME 15 Q5 ANSWER c
When Lohan auditioned for this 2004 film, she wanted the role of Regina— queen bee of the Plastics. Then she decided against it, fearing the public would perceive her as that character. Ironically, Rachel McAdams tried out for Cady, the "good girl," but got Regina instead. Obviously, she wasn't typecast, as her next role was Allie in the *The Notebook*.

GAME 35

6. Which biblical pair was portrayed by Victor Mature and Hedy Lamarr?

a. Adam/Eve
b. Abraham/Sarah
c. Samson/Delilah
d. Jesus/Mary Magdalene

GAME 35 Q5 ANSWER a
In this film, Gibson—a traditional Roman Catholic—presents a brutally violent portrayal of Christ's final hours. He wanted to shock viewers into realizing the enormity of Christ's sacrifice. In a personal effort to show that Christ died for his sins (the sins of man), Gibson filmed his own hands nailing Jesus to the cross during the crucifixion.

GAME 55

6. Who dances in the Trevi Fountain in *La Dolce Vita* (1963)?

a. Anouk Aimée
b. Yvonne Furneaux
c. Anita Ekberg
d. Magali Noël

GAME 55 Q5 ANSWER b
Director Lasse Hallström's work on this film earned him Oscar nominations for Best Director and Best Adapted Screenplay. His first notable American success was for the 1993 film *What's Eating Gilbert Grape*, followed by 1999's *The Cider House Rules* (for which he received another Oscar nod for Best Director) and 2000's *Chocolat*.

GAME 75

6. Who has a cameo as a waiter dressed as Buddy Holly in *Pulp Fiction*?

a. Quentin Tarantino
b. Gary Busey
c. Steve Buscemi
d. Christopher Walken

GAME 75 Q5 ANSWER a
In *Dead Again*—directed by British actor/ filmmaker Kenneth Branagh—Williams plays the eccentric Dr. Cozy Carlisle. He also plays Dr. Malcolm Sayer in Penny Marshall's 1990 film *Awakenings;* the befuddled Dr. Kosevich in *Nine Months* (1995); and the voice of computerized character Dr. Know in Steven Spielberg's *AI: Artificial Intelligence* (2001).

GAME 6

8. Which male star wears a woman's negligee in the classic comedy *Bringing Up Baby* (1938)?

a. Cary Grant
b. Henry Fonda
c. W.C. Fields
d. Jack Benny

GAME 6 Q7 ANSWER a
There were two versions of this line said by the gangster Rico (played by James Cagney): "Mother of God, is this the end of Rico?" and "Mother of mercy, is this the end of Rico?" After much consideration, it was determined that the words "Mother of God" coming from a murderous gangster were potentially blasphemous, so "Mother of mercy" was used.

GAME 26

8. Who played secret agent Harry Palmer in *The Ipcress File* (1965)?

a. Lee Marvin
b. Rod Steiger
c. Steve McQueen
d. Michael Caine

GAME 26 Q7 ANSWER c
Matt Damon has played the agent in the *Bourne* movies, which are based on Robert Ludlam novels. In *Mr. & Mr. Smith* (2005), Brad Pitt played assassin John Smith. Felix Leiter's character appeared in several James Bond films as 007's liason. And in a series of 1960's films that parodied James Bond-style movies, Dean Martin played Matt Helm.

GAME 46

8. Which Joe Wright film is based on a novel by Ian McEwan?

a. *The Soloist* (2009)
b. *Atonement* (2007)
c. *The End* (1998)
d. *Crocodile Snap* (1997)

GAME 46 Q7 ANSWER a
Based on the 1999 novel by Tracy Chevalier, *Girl with a Pearl Earring* gives a fictionalized account of the events that may have inspired one of Johannes Vermeer's most enduring works. The film's visual beauty—so much like the Dutch master's paintings—led to Oscar nominations for Best Art Direction, Best Cinematography, and Best Costume Design.

GAME 66

8. Who was the first Hollywood director to use a megaphone on a movie set?

a. Alfred Hitchcock
b. D.W. Griffith
c. Charlie Chaplin
d. Cecil B. De Mille

GAME 66 Q7 ANSWER b
Filmed at the famous Cinecittá Studios in Rome, *Gangs of New York* (2002) marked the first time that Scorsese worked with actor Leonardo DiCaprio. Just as he has worked repeatedly on movies with actor Robert De Niro, Scorsese continued to direct DiCaprio in his next three films: *The Aviator* (2004), *The Departed* (2006), and *Shutter Island* (2010).

GAME 15

5. In *Mean Girls,* Lindsay Lohan's character joins a high school clique dubbed the:

a. Wicked Stepdaughters

b. Debs

c. Plastics

d. Viragos

GAME 15 Q4 ANSWER a
Swanson plays the high school cheerleader who is guided by fate to battle vampires and other forces of nature. The more famous Buffy is Sarah Michelle Gellar, who starred in the TV series that began its seven-season run in 1997. Alyssa Milano was originally set for the role in the movie, which was also the first film for actress Hilary Swank.

GAME 35

5. Which biblical movie was directed by Mel Gibson?

a. *The Passion of the Christ* (2004)

b. *The Nativity Story* (2006)

c. *The Last Temptation of Christ* (1988)

d. *Godspell* (1973)

GAME 35 Q4 ANSWER b
Along with the story of Abraham, this film recounts a number of stories from the Book of Genesis. It was one of the first American films to feature male-female nudity with Michael Parks and Ulla Bergry as Adam and Eve. Richard Harris and Franco Nero play the enemy brothers Cain and Abel; they are rivals again as Arthur and Lancelot in *Camelot* (1967).

GAME 55

5. Which Swedish film tells the tale of a twelve-year-old living in the 1950s?

a. *Wild Strawberries* (1957)

b. *My Life as a Dog* (1985)

c. *Fannie and Alexander* (1982)

d. *Persona* (1966)

GAME 55 Q4 ANSWER d
The autobiographical character of Antoine Doinel first appeared in Truffaut's directorial debut *The 400 Blows* (1959). Truffaut revisited Doinel again in *Antoine and Colette* (one of five short films in the 1962 feature *Love at Twenty*), and three more times with *Stolen Kisses* in 1968, *Bed and Board* in 1970, and *Love on the Run* in 1979.

GAME 75

5. Which film features a cameo by Robin Williams as a psychologist?

a. *Dead Again* (1991)

b. *Awakenings* (1990)

c. *Insomnia* (2002)

d. *Nine Months* (1995)

GAME 75 Q4 ANSWER a
Brett Favre plays ex-boyfriend to Mary (Cameron Diaz) in this 1998 comedy from Bobby and Peter Farrelly (aka The Farrelly Brothers). Another legendary quarterback, Dan Marino, plays himself in a few films, including 1994's *Ace Ventura: Pet Detective.* Meanwhile, NFL coach Mike Ditka appears in the Will Ferrell comedy *Kicking & Screaming* (2005).

GAME 6

9. In the MGM 1939 classic *The Wizard of Oz*, what does Dorothy carry with her in Oz?

a. Purse

b. Rabbit's foot

c. Umbrella

d. Picnic basket

GAME 6 Q8 ANSWER a

In this film costarring Katharine Hepburn, when Grant's character is asked why he is wearing a woman's dressing gown, he responds, "Because I went gay all of a sudden!" The line is considered one of the first uses of the word "gay" (in the modern sense) in an American studio film. Interestingly, the line was an ad lib from Grant himself.

GAME 26

9. In which film does Chevy Chase try to foil a plot to assassinate the Pope?

a. *Spies Like Us* (1985)

b. *Foul Play* (1978)

c. *Fletch* (1985)

d. *Modern Problems* (1983)

GAME 26 Q8 ANSWER d

Based on the 1962 Len Deighton novel, this film was the first of the "Harry Palmer" series to launch Michael Caine's career. Because the book's character is nameless, Caine and producer Harry Saltzman came up with Harry Palmer (inspired by a boring classmate of Caine's). The movie was a major influence on the *Mission Impossible* TV series (1966).

GAME 46

9. From which Jane Austen novel does 1995's *Clueless* borrow its plot?

a. *Sense and Sensibility*

b. *Persuasion*

c. *Mansfield Park*

d. *Emma*

GAME 46 Q8 ANSWER b

McEwan named his book *Atonement* because it tells the story of a successful writer who spends her life trying to make amends for the error she committed as a young girl. In the film, the remorseful Briony Tallis is played at age thirteen by Saoirse Ronan, at age eighteen by Ramola Garai, and as a mature woman by veteran actress Vanessa Redgrave.

GAME 66

9. Mel Brooks' *High Anxiety* (1977) parodies the films of which director?

a. John Huston

b. David Lean

c. Orson Welles

d. Alfred Hitchcock

GAME 66 Q8 ANSWER d

De Mille's first silent film, *The Squaw Man* (1914), was a Western. When he first made *The Ten Commandments* as a silent black-and-white feature in 1923, De Mille required larger movie sets and had to use a megaphone to be heard by all the technicians and movie extras. De Mille's last film was the 1956 color remake of *The Ten Commandments*.

GAME 15

4. In *Buffy the Vampire Slayer* (1992), who stars as the title character?

a. Kristy Swanson

b. Sara Michelle Gellar

c. Alyssa Milano

d. Hilary Swank

GAME 15 Q3 ANSWER d

To increase the animosity between the two campus groups, Lee had the actors stay in different hotels during filming— and he gave the "Wannabees" noticeably better accommodations. This added to the tension on the set and made the hostility between the groups appear more realistic in this 1988 film that stars Laurence Fishburne.

GAME 35

4. In which biblical epic does George C. Scott portray Abraham?

a. *Ben-Hur* (1959)

b. *The Bible* (1966)

c. *King of Kings* (1961)

d. *The Story of Ruth* (1960)

GAME 35 Q3 ANSWER b

Heston won an Academy Award for his role as Judah Ben-Hur in this epic film, which received a record total of eleven Oscars. *Titanic* (1997) and *The Lord of the Rings: The Return of the King* (2003) are the only other films to win the same number of Oscars. Of the three films, however, only *Ben-Hur* won for acting performances.

GAME 55

4. What was director Francois Truffaut's first "Antoine Doinel" film?

a. *Bed and Board*

b. *Stolen Kisses*

c. *Love on the Run*

d. *The 400 Blows*

GAME 55 Q3 ANSWER c

Directed by Japanese filmmaker Ishiro Honda, *Gojira* was released in the US in 1956 (with several edits) under the title *Godzilla, King of the Monsters!* This version of the film featured *Perry Mason* TV star Raymond Burr as an American reporter named Steve Martin. Ishiro Honda also directed movies with the Japanese monsters Rodan and Mothra.

GAME 75

4. Which NFL great appears as himself in *There's Something About Mary*?

a. Brett Favre

b. Mike Ditka

c. Dan Marino

d. Steve Young

GAME 75 Q3 ANSWER b

This 1964 film about the Cheyenne's 1878 migration was the last Western made by legendary director John Ford, who remains best-known for classic Westerns like *Stagecoach* (1939) and *The Searchers* (1956). Before Jimmy Stewart's portrayal of Wyatt Earp, Ford directed Henry Fonda in that same role in *My Darling Clementine* (1946).

GAME 6

10. What helps sets the mood for the climactic airport scene in *Casablanca* (1942)?

a. Gusty wind

b. Heavy fog

c. Gentle snowfall

d. Torrential rain

GAME 6 Q9 ANSWER d
The picnic basket serves as a refuge for Dorothy's dog, Toto, played by a Cairn terrier named Terry. She was paid $125 a week, more than some of the other characters, including the Munchkins, who received $50 a week. By the end of the movie, after spending so much time with Terry, Garland wanted to adopt her, but the dog's owner wouldn't give her up.

GAME 26

10. Which film legend played a spy who applies lipstick before facing a firing squad?

a. Greta Garbo

b. Lana Turner

c. Marlene Dietrich

d. Rita Hayworth

GAME 26 Q9 ANSWER b
Chase stars with Goldie Hawn in this comedy that pays homage to director Alfred Hitchcock—several of his films are referenced throughout. The movie's theme song, "Ready to Take a Chance Again," written by Charles Fox and Norman Gimbel and performed by Barry Manilow, lost the Best Song Oscar to "Last Dance" from *Thank God It's Friday*.

GAME 46

10. Which Audrey Hepburn film is based on a play about a chauffeur's daughter?

a. *Funny Face* (1957)

b. *Charade* (1963)

c. *Roman Holiday* (1953)

d. *Sabrina* (1954)

GAME 46 Q9 ANSWER d
Starring Alicia Silverstone as a modern-day Emma, the teen flick *Clueless* surprised the industry by grossing over $11 million on its first weekend and over $60 million during its theatrical run. *Entertainment Weekly* called the film a "New Classic," and Alicia Silverstone's performance won her a multimillion-dollar deal with Columbia Pictures.

GAME 66

10. Who directed such films as *The French Connection* (1971) and *Bug* (2006)?

a. William Friedkin

b. Peter Bogdanovich

c. Michael Winner

d. John Frankenheimer

GAME 66 Q9 ANSWER d
There are references to more than a dozen Alfred Hitchcock movies in this Mel Brooks comedy, including *Vertigo* (1958) and a reenactment of the famous "shower scene" from *Psycho* (1960) that features writer/director Barry Levinson as a crazed bellhop. Hitchcock's matte artist Albert Whitlock even appears in the film as the character Arthur Brisbane.

GAME 15

3. In Spike Lee's *School Daze*, the two opposing groups are the "Jigaboos" and the:

a. "Gottabees"

b. "Gimmes"

c. "Upper-tunities"

d. "Wannabees"

GAME 15 Q2 ANSWER a
A reference to teen idol Bobby Rydell, the school in the film was shot at three different California high schools. The interior shots were filmed at Huntington Park HS; exteriors were shot at Venice HS (where *American History X* was filmed); and the carnival finale was shot at John Marshall HS (also the school filmed in *Buffy the Vampire Slayer*).

GAME 35

3. Which film starring Charlton Heston won the Best Picture Oscar?

a. *Quo Vadis* (1951)

b. *Ben-Hur* (1959)

c. *The Ten Commandments* (1956)

d. *El Cid* (1961)

GAME 35 Q2 ANSWER a
Hayworth has claimed that the erotic "Dance of the Seven Veils" she performed in this film was the most demanding of her career. The movie itself faced much criticism for its altering of the story as told in Scriptures. In the Bible, Salome dances for Herod in exchange for the head of John the Baptist. In the movie, she dances to *save* him.

GAME 55

3. The 1954 Japanese picture *Gojira* belongs to which film genre?

a. War

b. Western

c. Science fiction

d. Historical drama

GAME 55 Q2 ANSWER b
Though he directed the great silent film *Greed* (1924), von Stroheim is best known for acting in films like *La Grande Illusion* and American filmmaker Billy Wilder's 1950 film *Sunset Boulevard* (for which he received a Best Supporting Actor Oscar nomination). *La Grande Illusion* was the first foreign film to be nominated for a Best Picture Oscar.

GAME 75

3. Jimmy Stewart makes a cameo as which character in *Cheyenne Autumn*?

a. Jesse James

b. Wyatt Earp

c. George Custer

d. Wild Bill Hickok

GAME 75 Q2 ANSWER d
Fellow British pop stars Elton John and Bob Geldof also appeared in this feature film about The Spice Girls. Elton John also appeared along with Eric Clapton in Ken Russell's 1975 film adaptation of The Who's rock opera *Tommy*. Boomtown Rats singer Bob Geldof also starred in Alan Parker's film of *Pink Floyd The Wall* (1981).

GAME 6

11. In which movie classic did James Cagney smash a grapefruit into his leading lady's face?

a. *Little Caesar* (1931)
b. *The Public Enemy* (1931)
c. *The Roaring Twenties* (1939)
d. *Scarface* (1932)

GAME 6 Q10 ANSWER b
Although this romantic drama's final scene between Humphry Bogart and Ingrid Bergman takes place at an airport in Morocco, it was actually filmed at the Van Nuys Airport in California. (Built in 1928, the "Casablanca Hangar" was torn down in 2007.) In 2007, the American Film Institute ranked *Casablanca* # 3 as the Greatest Movie of All Time.

GAME 26

11. What is the name of the secret society of assassins in the movie *Wanted* (2008)?

a. League of Shadows
b. Brethren Court
c. The Fraternity
d. The Sith

GAME 26 Q10 ANSWER c
In the 1931 romantic spy film *Dishonored*, Dietrich's plays Marie Kolverer/Agent X-27—an Austrian prostitute who offers her services to spy on the Russians during World War I. The sultry German actress was discovered in Berlin by director Josef van Sternberg, who took her to Hollywood. She became the highest paid actress of her time.

GAME 46

11. The 2005 film *Sahara* is very loosely based on whose novel?

a. Stephen King
b. John Grisham
c. Clive Cussler
d. James Patterson

GAME 46 Q10 ANSWER d
Samuel A. Taylor's romantic comedy *Sabrina Fair* premiered on Broadway in 1953 and was praised for its clever dialogue. Since Taylor collaborated on the screen adaptation, it's not surprising that the same wit is evident in 1954's film *Sabrina*—along with critically acclaimed performances by Humphrey Bogart, Audrey Hepburn, and William Holden.

GAME 66

11. Which 1939 film did Orson Welles watch to study filmmaking techniques?

a. *Gone With the Wind*
b. *Stagecoach*
c. *The Wizard of Oz*
d. *Only Angels Have Wings*

GAME 66 Q10 ANSWER a
Though he won the Best Director Oscar for *The French Connection*, Friedkin is best known as the director of the 1973 movie version of William Peter Blatty's terrifying novel *The Exorcist*. During *The Exorcist* filming, Friedkin was said to fire a handgun on the movie set to get frightened reactions on film from some of the actors.

GAME 15

2. What is the name of the high school in 1978's *Grease*?

a. Rydell
b. Ridgemont
c. Rogers
d. Riverside

GAME 15 Q1 ANSWER d
In this popular film, Emilio Estevez, Anthony Michael Hall, Molly Ringwald, Ally Sheedy, and Judd Nelson star as five stereotypical teens (an athlete, a brain, a princess, a basket case, and a criminal), who find they have much in common. Unfortunately, Judd Nelson didn't get along with Ringwald or director John Hughes, so there was no hope for a sequel.

GAME 35

2. Who played the title role in the 1953 biblical epic *Salome*?

a. Rita Hayworth
b. Marilyn Monroe
c. Lana Turner
d. Ava Gardner

GAME 35 Q1 ANSWER c
After his 1923 silent version of this film, the Oscar-winning director decided to part the Red Sea once more in 1956. For his updated version, De Mille chose Charlton Heston to play Moses because he felt Heston resembled Michelangelo's statue of Moses. The American Film Institute has ranked the movie (De Mille's last) at #10 in the epic genre.

GAME 55

2. Which director stars in Jean Renoir's 1937 war film *La Grande Illusion*?

a. Charlie Chaplin
b. Erich von Stroheim
c. Jean Renoir
d. Buster Keaton

GAME 55 Q1 ANSWER b
This film earned Fellini the first of two Best Foreign Director Oscar nominations (the other was for the 1974 film *Amarcord*). He was given a Lifetime Achievement Oscar a few months before he died in October 1993. His Oscar-winning film *8 1/2* (1963) inspired the 1982 Broadway musical *Nine*, which was later released as a 2009 movie musical.

GAME 75

2. Which singer makes a cameo appearance in *Spice World* (1997)?

a. Sting
b. Eric Clapton
c. Bob Dylan
d. Elvis Costello

GAME 75 Q1 ANSWER d
After directing John Belushi and Dan Aykroyd in his World War II comedy *1941* (1979), Spielberg played a small part at the end of their *Blues Brothers* movie directed by John Landis. In 2001, he appeared briefly with Tom Cruise in Cameron Crowe's *Vanilla Sky*, and again with Cruise in 2002's *Austin Powers in Goldmember*.

GAME 6

12. "Where's the rest of me?" is a line from which film?

a. *Kings Row* (1942)
b. *Gone With the Wind* (1939)
c. *Meet John Doe* (1941)
d. *The Wizard of Oz* (1939)

GAME 6 Q11 ANSWER b
This infamous scene, which was done only as a practical joke for the reaction of the film crew, was left in by director William A. Wellman. It caused an uproar among women's groups who protested the on-screen abuse of Mae Clarke. For years, when dining out, Cagney would receive grapefruit from fellow patrons. He would customarily eat them.

GAME 26

12. Who costarred with Robert Redford in the 2001 movie *Spy Game*?

a. Ben Affleck
b. Matt Damon
c. Kevin Costner
d. Brad Pitt

GAME 26 Q11 ANSWER c
This film, which is loosely based on the comic book series, stars James McAvoy as a young office worker who discovers that his father belonged to The Fraternity. The League of Shadows was the secret society in *Batman Begins* (2005); the Brethren Court was in *Pirates of the Caribbean: At World's End* (2007); and The Sith was from the *Star Wars* series.

GAME 46

12. Which Robert Nathan work was turned into a David O. Selznick film?

a. *The Bishop's Wife*
b. *Portrait of Jenny*
c. *The River Journey*
d. *A Star in the Wind*

GAME 46 Q11 ANSWER c
The screenplay of *Sahara* took such liberties with the book's storyline that best-selling novelist Clive Cussler sued Philip Anschutz, the film's producer. Anchutz won the lawsuit and was awarded millions of dollars to cover legal fees. He was not as lucky at the box office, where *Sahara's* revenues fell short of its astronomical production costs.

GAME 66

12. Who directed the 1987 thriller *Fatal Attraction*?

a. John Carpenter
b. Brian De Palma
c. Adrian Lyne
d. Tobe Hooper

GAME 66 Q11 ANSWER b
Though his claim that he had watched *Stagecoach* forty times may have been an embellishment, Orson Welles' respect for the work of John Ford was not. John Ford remains one of America's best-celebrated film directors. He has even influenced foreign directors such as Ingmar Bergman, Akira Kurosawa, Satyajit Ray, and Jean-Luc Godard.

GAME 15	**1. Which movie takes place during a Saturday detention?** **a.** *Lucas* (1986) **b.** *Heathers* (1989) **c.** *Dazed and Confused* (1993) **d.** *The Breakfast Club* (1985)	The answer to this question is on: **page 154,** **top frame,** **right side.**
GAME 35	**1. Which movie did Cecil B. De Mille direct twice?** **a.** *The Greatest Show on Earth* **b.** *The King of Kings* **c.** *The Ten Commandments* **d.** *Samson and Delilah*	The answer to this question is on: **page 154,** **second frame,** **right side.**
GAME 55	**1. Which Federico Fellini film is set in ancient Rome?** **a.** *Fellini's Roma* (1972) **b.** *Fellini's Satyricon* (1969) **c.** *Ginger and Fred* (1985) **d.** *La Strada* (1954)	The answer to this question is on: **page 154,** **third frame,** **right side.**
GAME 75	**1. Which film does *not* feature a cameo by director Steven Spielberg?** **a.** *Vanilla Sky* (2001) **b.** *The Blues Brothers* (1980) **c.** *Austin Powers in Goldmember* (2002) **d.** *The Muse* (1999)	The answer to this question is on: **page 154,** **bottom frame,** **right side.**

GAME 7
Musicals

Turn to page 159 for the first question.

GAME 6 Q12 ANSWER a
Ronald Reagan played Drake McHugh in this film. He uttered these words (the most memorable of his career) upon discovering that his legs had been amputated by a sadistic doctor. *King's Row*, which has been described as grim and tragic, was also considered Reagan's best work. He even used this famous quote for the title of his 1965 biography.

GAME 27
Mr. President

Turn to page 159 for the first question.

GAME 26 Q12 ANSWER d
Redford plays Nathan Muir, a veteran CIA agent on the verge of retirement, who tries to rescue a rogue operative (played by Pitt) who has been captured in China. The film was directed by Tony Scott, who also directed such films as *Top Gun* (1986), *True Romance* (1993), and *Enemy of the State* (1998). His brother is film director Ridley Scott.

GAME 47
Breakout Roles

Turn to page 159 for the first question.

GAME 46 Q12 ANSWER b
Robert Nathan's novella about a struggling artist and a lovely girl slipping through time became a 1948 film starring Joseph Cotten and rising star Jennifer Jones. The haunting quality of Nathan's romantic fantasy was enhanced by cinematographer Joseph H. August, who shot certain scenes through canvas to make them look like paintings.

GAME 67
Historical Epics

Turn to page 159 for the first question.

GAME 66 Q12 ANSWER c
As a top movie director, Adrian Lyne is known for stylish and erotic films such as *Flashdance* (1983), *9 1/2 Weeks* (1986), and *Indecent Proposal* (1993). His 2002 film, *Unfaithful*, featuring Richard Gere and Diane Lane, was a remake of a similar 1968 French film by director Claude Chabrol. Lane earned an Oscar nod for her performance in this film.

GAME 15

School Days

*Turn to page 156
for the first question.*

Turn to page 156
for the first question.

GAME 14 Q12 ANSWER c
Featuring Marion Cotillard in an Oscar-winning role, this 2007 biopic about French singing sensation Edith Piaf was directed by Olivier Dahan and costarred the popular French actor Gérard Depardieu. When she won the Oscar for this role, Cotillard became the first actor to win an Oscar for a role performed in the French language only.

GAME 35

The Bible

*Turn to page 156
for the first question.*

Turn to page 156
for the first question.

GAME 34 Q12 ANSWER d
The Wrong Man was based on the true story of bass player "Manny" Balestrero (played by Henry Fonda in the film). Shot in New York City, this crime drama was a major influence on Martin Scorsese's film *Taxi Driver* (1976). *The Wrong Man* and *Taxi Driver* both featured musical scores by composer Bernard Herrmann.

GAME 55

More Foreign Films

*Turn to page 156
for the first question.*

Turn to page 156
for the first question.

GAME 54 Q12 ANSWER c
Released a year after Neil Simon's 1986 semi-autobiographical film *Brighton Beach Memoirs*, Woody Allen's *Radio Days* is a warm and nostalgic look at a time in America when radio was king. Although Allen narrates the movie, he is never seen on screen. The young Allen, called "Joe" in the film, is portrayed by actor Seth Green.

GAME 75

Cameo Corner

*Turn to page 156
for the first question.*

Turn to page 156
for the first question.

GAME 74 Q12 ANSWER a
Kevin Spacey plays the methodical murderer in this disturbing crime thriller. When the actor shaved his head for the role, director David Fincher shaved his own in support. Spacey also requested that his name be removed from the film's opening credits and advertising, so that his surprise entrance as the killer would not be spoiled for audiences.

GAME 7

1. Who directed and starred in the 1949 musical *On the Town*?

a. Bing Crosby
b. Fred Astaire
c. Donald O'Connor
d. Gene Kelly

The answer to this question is on:

**page 161,
top frame,
right side.**

GAME 27

1. In *Independence Day* (1996), who plays the President?

a. Michael Douglas
b. Jeff Bridges
c. Glenn Close
d. Bill Pullman

The answer to this question is on:

**page 161,
second frame,
right side.**

GAME 47

1. In which film did Ashley Judd make her big-screen debut?

a. *Heat*
b. *A Time to Kill*
c. *Kiss the Girls*
d. *Ruby in Paradise*

The answer to this question is on:

**page 161,
third frame,
right side.**

GAME 67

1. What was the first feature film released in CinemaScope?

a. *Spartacus* (1960)
b. *The Robe* (1953)
c. *Cleopatra* (1963)
d. *Exodus* (1960)

The answer to this question is on:

**page 161,
bottom frame,
right side.**

GAME 14

12. Which French singer's life is depicted in the 2007 film *La Vie en Rose*?

a. Nana Mouskouri
b. Regine
c. Edith Piaf
d. Josephine Baker

GAME 14 Q11 ANSWER b
Richard Gere starred opposite Diane Lane in *Unfaithful* (2002), a remake of *The Unfaithful Wife* (1968). He also appeared in a 1983 remake of Jean Luc-Godard's 1960 film *Breathless*, and in 1993's *Sommersby*, a remake of *The Return of Martin Guerre* (1982). *The Wages of Fear* won the Palme D'Or award at the 1953 Cannes Film Festival.

GAME 34

12. Which Alfred Hitchcock film tells the story of a nightclub musician accused of a robbery?

a. *North by Northwest* (1959)
b. *Strangers on a Train* (1951)
c. *Suspicion* (1941)
d. *The Wrong Man* (1956)

GAME 34 Q11 ANSWER a
In *Psycho*, Marion Crane (Janet Leigh) leaves her lonely life in Phoenix, Arizona, after stealing $40,000 from her employer. She ends up, however, losing her life at the hands of Norman Bates's "mother" while staying in Cabin 1 at the Bates Motel—only fifteen miles away from her boyfriend Sam's house in Fairvale, California.

GAME 54

12. Which Woody Allen film ends on a rooftop on New Year's Eve?

a. *Stardust Memories* (1980)
b. *Purple Rose of Cairo* (1985)
c. *Radio Days* (1987)
d. *Interiors* (1978)

GAME 54 Q11 ANSWER b
Although best known as the director of such films as *The Way We Were* (1973) and *Out of Africa* (1985), Sydney Pollack actually began his show business career as an actor. In addition to working with Woody Allen, he appeared in Robert Altman's 1992 Hollywood satire *The Player* and in Stanley Kubrick's final film, *Eyes Wide Shut* (1999).

GAME 74

12. What is the serial killer's name in the 1995 movie *Seven*?

a. John Doe
b. Jack Sprat
c. Hannibal
d. Socrates

GAME 74 Q11 ANSWER d
Though she had been acting since childhood, Heigl achieved recognition in 2005, after being cast as Dr. Isobel "Izzie" Stevens on the hit show *Grey's Anatomy*. She followed that success by playing the female lead in director Judd Apatow's 2006 comedy *Knocked Up*. In her personal life, the dog-lover involves herself in many animal rescue projects.

GAME 7

2. "I'm Gonna Wash That Man Right Outta My Hair" is in which film's musical score?

a. *South Pacific* (1958)
b. *Annie Get Your Gun* (1950)
c. *Gigi* (1958)
d. *Show Boat* (1951)

GAME 7 Q1 ANSWER d
Kelly, Frank Sinatra, and Jules Munshin play sailors on a one-day leave in this movie, which was filmed on location in New York City. To keep the filming low-key, many of the scenes were shot from cameras hidden in the back of a station wagon. Regardless, during the final scene, hundreds of fans can be seen in the background watching the actors.

GAME 27

2. In 1993's *Dave*, who plays both the President and his stand-in?

a. Kevin Kline
b. Tim Hutton
c. Woody Harrelson
d. Robert De Niro

GAME 27 Q1 ANSWER d
Bill Pullman plays fictional US President Thomas J. Whitmore in this big-budget disaster movie. Sets of the White House interior seen in the film were originally built for *The American President* (1995), and had just been used for *Nixon* (1995). They would soon double for the famous building in another alien invasion picture, *Mars Attacks!* (1996).

GAME 47

2. Whose breakout role came as a single mom in *Jerry Maguire* (1996)?

a. Renée Zellweger
b. Kirsten Dunst
c. Debra Messing
d. Melissa Gilbert

GAME 47 Q1 ANSWER d
Director Victor Nunez wrote this 1993 film as a tribute to Jane Austen's classic 1817 novel *Northanger Abbey*. Like Catherine Morland of the novel, Ruby (Judd's character) leaves home and relocates to a summer resort town for a new start. Judd has since played many strong women in such films as *Double Jeopardy* (1999) and *Simon Birch* (1998).

GAME 67

2. Whom does Brad Pitt play in the 2004 movie *Troy*?

a. Achilles
b. Hercules
c. Odysseus
d. Hector

GAME 67 Q1 ANSWER b
When 20th Century Fox decided to shoot *The Robe* using CinemaScope, a wide-screen process, it enabled the director, Henry Koster, to more lavishly display the film's actors and their surroundings. A special Academy Award was given to 20th Century for its "imagination, showmanship, and foresight" in introducing this new technology to the public.

GAME 14

11. Richard Gere starred in American remakes of each of these French films except:

a. *The Unfaithful Wife*

b. *The Wages of Fear*

c. *Breathless*

d. *The Return of Martin Guerre*

GAME 14 Q10 ANSWER c
The White Balloon is a gentle, fanciful film that centers around a child's misadventures during the Iranian New Year holiday of Nowruz. It received critical acclaim and earned numerous awards, including the Golden Camera Award (Prix de la Camera d'Or) at the Cannes Film Festival in 1995.

GAME 34

11. *Psycho* begins in which US city?

a. Phoenix

b. Washington, DC

c. New York

d. San Francisco

GAME 34 Q10 ANSWER b
Alfred Hitchcock's Sealyham terrier was named Johnnie, which was also the name of Cary Grant's character in *Suspicion*. More than twenty years later in his film *The Birds,* the obligatory Hitchcock cameo called for the director to walk past lead actress Tippi Hedren while leaving a pet shop with two Sealyham terriers on leashes.

GAME 54

11. Who plays Judy Davis's husband in 1992's *Husbands and Wives*?

a. Liam Neeson

b. Sydney Pollack

c. Woody Allen

d. Joe Mantegna

GAME 54 Q10 ANSWER a
Featuring the black-and-white cinematography of Gordon Willis—who worked with Allen in 1979 on another black-and-white film, *Manhattan*—1984's *Broadway Danny Rose* was Allen's ode to his own early days in New York show business. The Oscar-nominated movie includes cameos by talk-show legend Joe Franklin and early TV star Milton Berle.

GAME 74

11. Who plays the perpetual bridesmaid in the 2008 comedy *27 Dresses*?

a. Katie Holmes

b. Ashley Judd

c. Drew Barrymore

d. Katherine Heigl

GAME 74 Q10 ANSWER c
After scoring a few bit parts in daytime soap operas, Perry gained wider popularity in the early '90s playing Dylan McKay on television's *Beverly Hills 90210*. Hoping to branch out, he took the part of bull rider Lane Frost in this biopic. In order to perform some of his own stunt work, the actor actually learned how to ride a bull.

GAME 7

3. "Tradition" is one of the classic songs in which hit musical?

a. *Man of La Mancha* (1972)
b. *Mame* (1974)
c. *Fiddler on the Roof* (1971)
d. *Funny Girl* (1968)

GAME 7 Q2 ANSWER a
Mitzi Gaynor, who plays Ensign Nellie Forbush in the movie, washes her hair while singing the popular song. During the scene, the soap on her shoulders disappears and then reappears, creating a continuity problem. Gaynor was considered for the role along with such iconic actresses as Judy Garland, Elizabeth Taylor, Doris Day, and Audrey Hepburn.

GAME 27

3. 1976's *All the President's Men* refers to which US President?

a. Gerald Ford
b. John F. Kennedy
c. Richard Nixon
d. Lyndon Johnson

GAME 27 Q2 ANSWER a
Kline has become a pro at handling dual roles on film. A few years after filming this Ivan Reitman comedy, he played corporate CEO Rod McCain and son Vince McCain in 1997's *Fierce Creatures*. He then went on to portray US Marshal Artemus Gordon and US President Ulysses Grant in the Will Smith action-adventure movie *Wild Wild West* in 1999.

GAME 47

3. After his breakout role in *The Graduate*, what was Dustin Hoffman's next film?

a. *Kramer vs. Kramer*
b. *Madigan's Millions*
c. *The Producers*
d. *Midnight Cowboy*

GAME 47 Q2 ANSWER a
Her character, Dorothy Boyd, delivered one of the film's memorable lines, "You had me at hello," to Jerry Maguire (Tom Cruise). The line served as the inspiration for country singer Kenny Chesney's 1999 song "You Had Me From Hello." Eventually, the two met at a tsunami relief concert and were married in May 2005 (the marriage lasted four months).

GAME 67

3. Which event is the climax of the 1959 movie epic *Ben-Hur*?

a. Gladiator fight
b. Battle at sea
c. Birth of Christ
d. Chariot race

GAME 67 Q2 ANSWER a
Brad Pitt spent more than six months getting in shape for the role of Achilles, and even quit smoking. Little wonder when you consider that the mythological hero whom Pitt portrays was the fiercest of warriors, was very nearly immortal (only one heel was vulnerable to attack), and was regarded as the most handsome of all of Troy's foes.

GAME 14

10. Which "balloon" movie was the debut feature film of Iranian director Jafar Panahi?

a. Flight of the Red Balloon (2008)

b. The Red Balloon (1956)

c. The White Balloon (1995)

d. The Black Balloon (2008)

GAME 14 Q9 ANSWER d
Though her close affiliation with Hitler's Third Reich has forever tainted her legacy, Riefenstahl's *Triumph of the Will* is still regarded as a masterpiece of documentary filmmaking. Riefenstahl's fellow German director Fritz Lang made the classic science-fiction film *Metropolis* in 1927—a silent movie that was reputed to be one of Hitler's favorite films.

GAME 34

10. Alfred Hitchcock's dog appeared in which of his following films?

a. *Young and Innocent* (1937)

b. *Suspicion* (1941)

c. *The Birds* (1963)

d. *Rear Window* (1954)

GAME 34 Q9 ANSWER c
Carroll appeared in a total of five Alfred Hitchcock films—*Rebecca, Spellbound, Suspicion, Strangers on a Train,* and *North by Northwest.* James Stewart is in second place with starring roles in four Hitchcock films, while Cary Grant and Grace Kelly were each in two separately and in one—*To Catch a Thief*—together.

GAME 54

10. Which Woody Allen character is a talent agent who runs afoul of mobsters?

a. Danny Rose

b. Alvy Singer

c. Leonard Zelig

d. Sid Waterman

GAME 54 Q9 ANSWER a
Dianne Wiest's first role in a Woody Allen movie was in the 1985 comedy-fantasy *The Purple Rose of Cairo.* She went on to win a Best Supporting Actress Oscar for 1986's *Hannah and Her Sisters.* After appearing in Allen's *September* and *Radio Days* in 1987, Wiest won another Oscar for her work in Allen's 1994 film *Bullets Over Broadway.*

GAME 74

10. What does Luke Perry portray in the 1994 movie *8 Seconds*?

a. High school teacher

b. Undercover cop

c. Rodeo rider

d. Baseball player

GAME 74 Q9 ANSWER c
Though De Mille's name is generally synonymous with such massive productions, it was actually Todd who brought this sweeping tale to the big screen. Still regarded as one of the biggest undertakings in Hollywood history, it was the former Broadway producer's first film. The movie required 74,685 costumes and employed a staggering 68,894 extras.

GAME 7

4. Who costarred with Steve Martin in the musical *Pennies from Heaven*?

a. Linda Ronstadt

b. Sheryl Lee Ralph

c. Julie Andrews

d. Bernadette Peters

GAME 7 Q3 ANSWER c
Great care was given to accurately portray Orthodox traditions in this movie about a poor Jewish family in pre-revolutionary Russia; but some minor mistakes were made. In the wedding scene, for instance, the bride and groom dancing together was depicted as scandalous. Actually, it is standard for the newlyweds to share a wedding dance.

GAME 27

4. Who plays a presidential candidate in the 2003 movie *Head of State*?

a. Chris Rock

b. Charlie Sheen

c. Jerry Seinfeld

d. Ray Romano

GAME 27 Q3 ANSWER c
Robert Redford and Dustin Hoffman play journalists Bob Woodward and Carl Bernstein respectively, in this Oscar-nominated film based on their investigative reporting of the 1972 Watergate Scandal for *The Washington Post*. The two actors spent months in the *Post's* offices in preparation for their roles as the future Pulitzer Prize winners.

GAME 47

4. Which blockbuster was Aussie Hugh Jackman's first American film?

a. *Someone Like You*

b. *Van Helsing*

c. *Kate & Leopold*

d. *X-Men*

GAME 47 Q3 ANSWER b
Shot before *The Graduate* (1967), this box office flop was released shortly after in 1968. Interestingly, Hoffman had also been cast in Mel Brooks 1968 hit *The Producers* as Nazi playwright Franz Liebkind, but dropped out to play what became his Oscar-nominated role in *The Graduate*. Ironically, he starred in it with Mel Brooks' wife, Anne Bancroft.

GAME 67

4. Which epic film begins with an idyllic scene in a wheat field?

a. *Dr. Zhivago* (1965)

b. *Gladiator* (2000)

c. *Quo Vadis* (1951)

d. *Braveheart* (1995)

GAME 67 Q3 ANSWER d
Even by today's standards, *Ben-Hur's* chariot race is a spectacular action sequence. Over 15,000 extras were employed on the largest movie set ever built (eighteen acres) for a scene that took over five weeks to film. Stars Charlton Heston (in the title role) and Stephen Boyd (playing Messala) even drove their own chariots instead of using stuntmen.

GAME 14

9. What was female director Leni Riefenstahl's 1935 Nazi propaganda film?

a. *The Sorrow and the Pity*

b. *Metropolis*

c. *The Tin Drum*

d. *Triumph of the Will*

GAME 14 Q8 ANSWER c
The Seventh Seal is Ingmar Bergman's allegory of a medieval knight on a quest for truth in the face of Death (played, literally, by Swedish actor Bengt Ekerot). The knight is played by actor Max von Sydow, who may be known best as Father Merrin from 1973's *The Exorcist*.

GAME 34

9. Which actor appeared in more Hitchcock films than any other?

a. Cary Grant

b. James Stewart

c. Leo G. Carroll

d. Grace Kelly

GAME 34 Q8 ANSWER d
In *Marnie*, the magazine is being read by Sean Connery's character Mark Rutland, who owns a printing company. This was not the only film in which Hitchcock used print media as a prop—in *Lifeboat*, he achieved his customary cameo by showing up in a newspaper's weight-loss ad.

GAME 54

9. For which Woody Allen movie did Dianne Wiest win a Supporting Actress Oscar?

a. *Hannah and Her Sisters*

b. *September*

c. *The Purple Rose of Cairo*

d. *Radio Days*

GAME 54 Q8 ANSWER d
Filmed on location in the Hamptons of Long Island, New York, *Interiors* is often remembered as being a black-and-white film if only because it remains one of Allen's bleakest works to date. The film earned five Oscar nominations, including Best Actress for Geraldine Page and Best Supporting Actress for Maureen Stapleton.

GAME 74

9. Who produced the epic *Around the World in Eighty Days* (1956)?

a. Darryl Zanuck

b. Cecil B. De Mille

c. Michael Todd

d. Billy Wilder

GAME 74 Q8 ANSWER a
In addition to being one of the world's most famous leading men, Ford is also a licensed airplane and helicopter pilot. His character flies a DeHaviland Beaver aircraft in the film, which the actor actually owns in real life. Proving himself a true hero, Ford has been known to provide helicopter rescue to stranded hikers near his ranch in Wyoming.

GAME 7

5. Which post-impressionist artist was a character in the movie musical *Moulin Rouge*?

a. Edouard Vuillard

b. Henri de Toulouse-Lautrec

c. Paul Cezanne

d. Vincent van Gogh

GAME 7 Q4 ANSWER d
Although Martin was offered the role of Indiana Jones in *Raiders of the Lost Ark*, he chose to do this film instead. In one scene, "pennies," which were actually penny-sized sequins, rained from the sky. After filming was over, the sequins blew out the stage door. A year later, they were still found sparkling on the street corners of the MGM studios.

GAME 27

5. Fictional US President Merkin Muffley appears in which '60s movie?

a. *Fail-Safe* (1964)

b. *Lawrence of Arabia* (1962)

c. *The Graduate* (1967)

d. *Dr. Strangelove* (1964)

GAME 27 Q4 ANSWER a
Rock's first film role came along thanks to fellow comedian Eddie Murphy, who had seen his stand-up act and decided to give him a small part in *Beverly Hills Cop II* (1987). He went on to play bigger roles in such films as *Dogma* (1999), and created the television show *Everybody Hates Chris* in 2005. *Head of State* was his directorial debut.

GAME 47

5. Whose big film break came for playing a teenage murderess?

a. Joan Cusack

b. Emily Watson

c. Kate Winslet

d. Heather Graham

GAME 47 Q4 ANSWER d
His role as Wolverine in this 2000 film, based on a Marvel Comics series, made him an instant star. Because Jackman is over six feet tall—more than a foot taller than the comic book character he portrays—he was often shot from the waist up to appear shorter than he actually is. To further help the illusion, his costars wore platform shoes.

GAME 67

5. In which historical film is William Wallace the central character?

a. *The Name of the Rose* (1986)

b. *A Man for All Seasons* (1966)

c. *Braveheart* (1995)

d. *The Lion in Winter* (1968)

GAME 67 Q4 ANSWER b
Gladiator's opening shot helps establish the fact that main character Maximus Decimus Meridius (Russell Crowe) began life as a peaceable farmer—a creator of life, not a warrior. But in the film, circumstances turn Maximus into a general in the Roman Army, a slave, and finally a gladiator, who uses his skills to deadly effect in Rome's Colosseum.

8. Which "seven" film brought acclaim to Swedish director Ingmar Bergman?

a. *The Seventh Sign* (1988)

b. *Seven Brides for Seven Brothers* (1954)

c. *The Seventh Seal* (1957)

d. *The Seventh Sin* (1957)

GAME 14 Q7 ANSWER b
Though he made several short films in Poland after graduating from film school, *Knife in the Water* earned Polanski his first Oscar nomination in 1963 for Best Foreign Language Film. In 1965, he made *Repulsion*—the first of his "apartment paranoia" movies—which was later followed by *Rosemary's Baby* (1968) and *The Tenant* (1976).

---

8. Which Alfred Hitchcock film features a copy of the book publishing magazine *Publishers Weekly*?

a. *Lifeboat* (1944)

b. *Psycho* (1960)

c. *North by Northwest* (1959)

d. *Marnie* (1964)

GAME 34 Q7 ANSWER b
Ted Knight played the *uncredited* part of a policeman who stands watch over Norman Bates. Meanwhile, *Dallas* star Barbara Bel Geddes was featured in Hitchcock's *Vertigo*, and *Dynasty* star John Forsythe was cast in *The Trouble With Harry*. Suzanne Pleshette from *The Bob Newhart Show* appeared in Hitchcock's 1963 classic *The Birds*.

---

8. Which Woody Allen movie was *not* shot in black and white?

a. *Stardust Memories* (1980)

b. *Manhattan* (1979)

c. *Broadway Danny Rose* (1984)

d. *Interiors* (1978)

GAME 54 Q7 ANSWER b
In this existential black-and-white comedy, Woody Allen portrays the neurotic protagonist Kleinman, while Madonna plays the sword-swallowing wife of a strong man in a traveling circus. The cast also includes other big-name actors such as John Malkovich, John Cusack, Donald Pleasence, Mia Farrow, Lily Tomlin, Jodie Foster, and Kathy Bates.

---

8. Who stars with Anne Heche in *Six Days, Seven Nights* (1998)?

a. Harrison Ford

b. Sean Connery

c. Michael Douglas

d. Sylvester Stallone

GAME 74 Q7 ANSWER d
The movie features Laurence Olivier as Professor Moriarty, and Robert Duvall as Dr. Watson. The "seven" in the film's title refers to the percentage of cocaine in the famous detective's own concoction, with which he habitually injects himself. Although the film uses Arthur Conan Doyle's literary characters, it is not based on one of his stories.

GAME 7

6. Who does Diana Ross portray in the 1972 movie *Lady Sings the Blues*?

a. Bessie Smith
b. Josephine Baker
c. Billie Holiday
d. Ella Fitzgerald

GAME 7 Q5 ANSWER b
Due to a genetic disorder, Toulouse-Lautrec was only five feet tall. John Leguizamo, who played the artist in this 2001 movie, stood on his knees during most scenes. In the final musical number, however, he squatted the entire time in order to have greater mobility. This necessitated several weeks of physical therapy after the filming ended.

GAME 27

6. Who plays US President Staton in the 2006 film *American Dreamz*?

a. Hugh Grant
b. Dennis Quaid
c. Mark Wahlberg
d. Richard Dreyfuss

GAME 27 Q5 ANSWER d
Peter Sellers plays three roles in Stanley Kubrick's political satire. Financing of the film was contingent on Sellers playing four different parts, but a sprained ankle prevented him from portraying Air Force Major TJ "King" Kong. The actor does, however, play Group Captain Lionel Mandrake, President Merkin Muffley, and Dr. Strangelove himself.

GAME 47

6. Whose movie break came for playing Sodapop Curtis in *The Outsiders*?

a. Ben Affleck
b. Rob Lowe
c. Charlie Sheen
d. Sean Astin

GAME 47 Q5 ANSWER c
In 1994's *Heavenly Creatures*—the true story of teenagers Pauline Parker and Juliet Hulme who murdered Parker's mother—Winslet plays the assertive Juliet. The film was also the debut for Melanie Lynskey, who plays the shy Pauline. Directed and co-written by Peter Jackson, the movie was shot at most of the places where the actual events occurred.

GAME 67

6. Of which war is *Last Samurai* character Nathan Algren a veteran?

a. American Civil War
b. World War I
c. War of 1812
d. Revolutionary War

GAME 67 Q5 ANSWER c
In *Braveheart*, thirteenth-century Scottish warrior William Wallace is played by Mel Gibson, who was also the film's director and producer. Initially, Gibson felt that he was too old for the lead, and wanted to cast Jason Patric instead. But Gibson's company, Icon Productions, could get financial backing only if the older actor took the starring role.

GAME 14

7. What was the first feature film that Roman Polanski made in Poland?

a. *Repulsion*

b. *Knife in the Water*

c. *Cul-de-Sac*

d. *The Tenant*

GAME 14 Q6 ANSWER c
One of Japan's greatest film directors, Akira Kurosawa evoked medieval 16th-century Japan in both *Seven Samurai* and *Throne of Blood* (an adaptation of Shakespeare's *Macbeth*). In 1985, Kurosawa revisited Shakespeare with his ambitious take on the play *King Lear* in the film *Ran*.

GAME 34

7. Which *Mary Tyler Moore Show* regular appeared briefly at the end of *Psycho*?

a. Barbara Bel Geddes

b. Ted Knight

c. Suzanne Pleshette

d. John Forsythe

GAME 34 Q6 ANSWER d
In one of the most alluring entrances in American movies, Grace Kelly playfully reveals her name to be Lisa Carol Fremont while turning on three different lights in the living room of her boyfriend, L.B. "Jeff" Jeffries (played by James Stewart). At film's end, a love song called "Lisa" is heard playing in a nearby apartment.

GAME 54

7. Which of these Woody Allen comedies features Madonna?

a. *Sweet and Lowdown* (1999)

b. *Shadows and Fog* (1992)

c. *Crimes and Misdemeanors* (1989)

d. *Scoop* (2006)

GAME 54 Q6 ANSWER c
In 1989's *Crimes and Misdemeanors*, Allen features film clips of screen legends like Betty Hutton singing "Murder He Says" from *Happy Go Lucky* and Edward G. Robinson in *The Last Gangster*. A clip from *Duck Soup* appears in another Allen film, *Hannah and Her Sisters* (1986), where it persuades Allen's character to abandon thoughts of suicide.

GAME 74

7. Which of these "seven" films features Sherlock Holmes?

a. *Seven Pounds* (2008)

b. *Seven Sweethearts* (1942)

c. *Seven* (1995)

d. *The Seven-Per-Cent Solution* (1976)

GAME 74 Q6 ANSWER b
Jeff Daniels plays Roger, owner of Pongo the Dalmation, in this live-action version of the 1961 Disney animated film *One Hundred and One Dalmatians*. To entice the loveable puppies into licking him, Daniels rubbed his face with raw hot dogs. Filmmakers also used steak juice on the human actors to encourage their canine costars to act accordingly.

GAME 7

7. Which actor starred in the 1983 version of the musical *The Pirates of Penzance*?

a. William Hurt
b. Tom Berenger
c. Kevin Kline
d. Mel Gibson

GAME 7 Q6 ANSWER c
Ross's performance of the rise and fall of legendary blues singer Billie Holiday earned her an Oscar nomination. Actually, this was the first movie about an African-American to receive *any* Academy Award nomination (it garnered five!). A number of other actresses were considered for the title role, including Diahann Carroll and Cicely Tyson.

GAME 27

7. Which former US President boasts a 1944 Oscar-winning biopic?

a. Lincoln
b. Jefferson
c. Wilson
d. Hoover

GAME 27 Q6 ANSWER b
Quaid is known is for his work in such films as *Great Balls of Fire!* (1989), *Wyatt Earp* (1994), and *Far From Heaven* (2002). A real jack-of-all-trades, the actor also plays in a band called the Sharks, has his pilot's license, and is a highly regarded amateur golfer. He even hosts an annual celebrity golf tournament for charity in Austin, Texas.

GAME 47

7. Which film gave Anne Hathaway her big break?

a. *The Princess Diaries*
b. *Ella Enchanted*
c. *Becoming Jane*
d. *The Devil Wears Prada*

GAME 47 Q6 ANSWER b
In addition to Lowe, this 1983 movie, based on the S.E. Hinton novel of the same name and directed by Francis Ford Coppola, is noted for being the breakout film of many future stars. Other cast members—most of whom were in their teens during filming—include Matt Dillon, Tom Cruise, Emilio Estevez, Diane Lane, Ralph Macchio, and Patrick Swayze.

GAME 67

7. Which film's funeral scene features 300,000 performers onscreen?

a. *The Fall of the Roman Empire* (1964)
b. *Schindler's List* (1993)
c. *War and Peace* (1939)
d. *Gandhi* (1982)

GAME 67 Q6 ANSWER a
The creators of *The Last Samurai* (2003) did not seek strict historical accuracy. Although the title role of Nathan Algren (portrayed by Tom Cruise) is an American Civil War veteran, the film was actually inspired by a French artillery officer named Jules Brunet, who—like the fictitious Algren—fought alongside the samurai in nineteenth-century Japan.

GAME 14

6. Which Akira Kurosawa film has a contemporary setting?

a. *Throne of Blood* (1957)

b. *Seven Samurai* (1954)

c. *High and Low* (1963)

d. *Ran* (1985)

GAME 14 Q5 ANSWER d
Translated from the French as *Les Invasions Barbares*, this film is the sequel to director Denys Arcand's 1986 film *The Decline of the American Empire*. It stands as the first Canadian movie to win the Best Foreign Language Film Oscar; it also won a Best Screenplay award at the Cannes Film Festival in 2003.

GAME 34

6. What is Grace Kelly's character in Alfred Hitchcock's 1954 thriller *Rear Window*?

a. Judy

b. Madeleine

c. Marion

d. Lisa

GAME 34 Q5 ANSWER c
Gaslight was directed by George Cukor and starred Ingrid Bergman and Charles Boyer, with Joseph Cotten and Angela Lansbury in her debut film role (for which she received her first Oscar nomination). Hitchcock directed Cotten in *Shadow of a Doubt* (1943), Bergman in *Spellbound* (1945) and *Notorious* (1946), and both actors in *Under Capricorn* (1949).

GAME 54

6. Which movie is *not* shown in *Crimes and Misdemeanors*?

a. *Happy Go Lucky* (1942)

b. *Mr. & Mrs. Smith* (1941)

c. *Duck Soup* (1933)

d. *The Last Gangster* (1937)

GAME 54 Q5 ANSWER b
Shadows and Fog (1992) was based on Allen's one-act play *Death*. *Shadow Play* is a 1996 French film starring Helena Bonham Carter, who appeared in Woody Allen's 1995 film *Mighty Aphrodite*. *Shadow of Evil* is a 1995 TV movie starring Oscar-winner Cliff Robertson, while *Shadow of the Hawk* is a 1976 movie starring Jan-Michael Vincent.

GAME 74

6. What are Roger and Anita's dalmatians named in *101 Dalmatians* (1996)?

a. Charlie and Chloe

b. Perdita and Pongo

c. Milo and Otis

d. Max and Terry

GAME 74 Q5 ANSWER c
In the film, Bullock's character chooses 28 days in rehab over jail time. The actress spent time in an actual rehabilitation clinic in preparation for her role as an alcoholic undergoing treatment. To add to the realism of her portrayal, she downed three shots of espresso whenever a scene called for her to shake uncontrollably from withdrawal.

8. What is the occupation of Sweeney Todd in the musical of the same name?

a. Dentist
b. Photographer
c. Barber
d. Minister

GAME 7 Q7 ANSWER c
This Gilbert and Sullivan operetta also featured Linda Ronstadt and Rex Smith. As an experiment, when the movie was released in theaters, it was simultaneously broadcast on an LA television channel. This infuriated most theater owners, who boycotted the movie in protest. Abysmal box office sales resulted, even though the reviews were positive.

8. Who becomes the US President in 2006's *Man of the Year*?

a. A defense lawyer
b. A TV chef
c. A baseball coach
d. A talk show host

GAME 27 Q7 ANSWER c
Alexander Knox earned a Best Actor nomination at the Oscars for his performance as Woodrow Wilson in the critically acclaimed *Wilson*. Originally from Canada, he had been acting in England before he was cast to play the former Democratic leader. He returned to England after being blacklisted in Hollywood during the McCarthy Era.

8. Whose performance in 1954's *Magnificent Obsession* shot him to stardom?

a. Jack Lemmon
b. Paul Newman
c. Richard Burton
d. Rock Hudson

GAME 47 Q7 ANSWER a
When auditioning for the role of the klutzy princess Mia Thermopolis in this 2001 Disney family comedy, Hathaway accidentally fell off a chair, which apparently helped her get the part. Her role in *The Princess Diaries,* as well as its 2004 sequel, kicked off what has become a stellar acting career for Hathaway.

8. Whom does Angelina Jolie play in the 2004 film *Alexander*?

a. Alexander's daughter
b. Alexander's sister
c. Alexander's mother
d. Alexander's lover

GAME 67 Q7 ANSWER d
Before computer imaging, filmmakers had to use real people to depict teeming throngs, so in the 1982 epic *Gandhi,* director Richard Attenborough employed about 200,000 volunteers and nearly 100,000 paid extras to stage the funeral of India's civil rights leader. The sequence was filmed on the thirty-third anniversary of the actual event, January 31, 1982.

GAME 14

5. The 2003 Oscar for Best Foreign Language Film went to *The ____ Invasions.*

a. Mongol

b. Roman

c. Viking

d. Barbarian

GAME 14 Q4 ANSWER b

Bicycle Thieves is a classic example of Italian *neo-realism* cinema (films that achieve realism by casting non-professionals rather than trained actors). Directed by Vittorio De Sica, this movie won an Honorary Oscar as Most Outstanding Foreign Film in 1950. It was also featured in Robert Altman's Hollywood satire *The Player* (1992).

GAME 34

5. Which of these classic 1940s thrillers was *not* directed by Alfred Hitchcock?

a. *Foreign Correspondent* (1940)

b. *Notorious* (1946)

c. *Gaslight* (1944)

d. *Suspicion* (1941)

GAME 34 Q4 ANSWER c

Rebecca was the first film that Alfred Hitchcock made in America under contract to famed Hollywood producer David O. Selznick. When the film won Best Picture, Selznick made history by winning the award two years in a row (he first won in 1939 for *Gone with the Wind*). Hitchcock never received an Oscar for Best Director.

GAME 54

5. Which "shadow" film was directed by Woody Allen?

a. *Shadow of the Hawk*

b. *Shadows and Fog*

c. *Shadow of Evil*

d. *Shadow Play*

GAME 54 Q4 ANSWER d

Having become a teen idol after starring in James Cameron's Oscar-winning *Titanic* (1997), DiCaprio was quick to change his screen image. In *Celebrity*, he plays the obnoxious *l'enfant terrible* actor Brandon Darrow, who deludes Kenneth Branagh's character, Lee Simon, into thinking that he is actually interested in Lee's movie script.

GAME 74

5. What must Sandra Bullock do in *28 Days* (2000)?

a. Graduate college

b. Join the army

c. Spend time in rehab

d. Get married

GAME 74 Q4 ANSWER a

Garner first achieved fame on television, playing CIA agent Sydney Bristow in the spy drama *Alias*. She has since embarked on a promising film career, with roles in 2002's *Catch Me if You Can*, 2007's *Juno*, and 2009's *Ghosts of Girlfriends Past*. The actress married her *Daredevil* (2003) costar Ben Affleck in 2005.

GAME 7

9. Which movie musical is based on the life of comedienne Fanny Brice?

a. *Star 80* (1983)

b. *Cabaret* (1972)

c. *New York, New York* (1977)

d. *Funny Girl* (1968)

GAME 7 Q8 ANSWER c
This film, starring Johnny Depp as the murderous barber of Fleet Street, was in production for nearly twenty-five years. During that time, purportedly hundreds of actors had been attached to the role of Sweeney Todd, including Al Pacino, Robert Redford, Warren Beatty, Harrison Ford, Tim Curry, Jack Nicholson, Kevin Kline, and Steve Martin.

GAME 27

9. Who has been portrayed by Walter Huston, Henry Fonda, and Raymond Massey?

a. Franklin D. Roosevelt

b. Abraham Lincoln

c. Harry S. Truman

d. Dwight Eisenhower

GAME 27 Q8 ANSWER d
In the movie, Robin Williams plays Tom Dobbs, a TV personality who decides to run for President and wins. The character is loosely based on political comedians such as Jon Stewart, Bill Maher, and Stephen Colbert. Originally, the part was offered to radio shock jock Howard Stern, whose commitments to his day job prevented him from taking the role.

GAME 47

9. For which film did Emma Thompson win her first Oscar?

a. *Sense and Sensibility* (1995)

b. *Howard's End* (1992)

c. *Dead Again* (1991)

d. *The Remains of the Day* (1993)

GAME 47 Q8 ANSWER d
In this film, Hudson's starring role as a handsome playboy helped shape his image as a romantic lead, which is how he was often cast during the '50s and '60s. His romantic comedies with costar Doris Day were arguably the most notable. During his fruitful career of over forty years, Hudson earned one Oscar nod for his role in *Giant* (1956).

GAME 67

9. Who received screen credit for directing *Gone With the Wind* (1939)?

a. Victor Fleming

b. George Cukor

c. David O. Selznick

d. Sam Wood

GAME 67 Q8 ANSWER c
Director Oliver Stone wanted a strong, passionate woman to play Olympias, the mother of Alexander the Great, King of Macedonia. Stone chose Angelina Jolie despite the fact that she was only a year older than "son" Colin Farrell, who had the title role. Unfortunately for both the director and the actors, the film was considered a box office failure.

GAME 14

4. The 1948 film *Bicycle Thieves* is from which country?

a. Germany
b. Italy
c. France
d. Japan

GAME 14 Q3 ANSWER c
As cabaret singer Lola-Lola, Dietrich captured the imagination of Sternberg and moviegoers everywhere in this film. They made six movies together, including the classics *Shanghai Express* and *Blonde Venus*. Dietrich's Lola-Lola character was spoofed in Mel Brooks' *Blazing Saddles* (1974) by Madeline Kahn's character Lili Von Shtüpp.

GAME 34

4. What is the only Alfred Hitchcock film to win a Best Picture Oscar?

a. *Psycho* (1960)
b. *Spellbound* (1945)
c. *Rebecca* (1940)
d. *Rear Window* (1954)

GAME 34 Q3 ANSWER c
The first Hitchcock cameo dates back to his 1927 British film *The Lodger*. Hitchcock made more movie cameos as he grew more famous. His last cameo in his final film *Family Plot* (1976) showed him only in silhouette. The only time he ever looked directly at the camera was during his cameo in the 1964 thriller *Marnie*.

GAME 54

4. Which actor trashes a hotel room in Woody Allen's 1998 comedy *Celebrity* ?

a. Johnny Depp
b. Nicolas Cage
c. Jim Carrey
d. Leonardo DiCaprio

GAME 54 Q3 ANSWER a
This Japanese spy film—on which Woody Allen and co-writer Mickey Rose constructed an absurd plot centered on egg salad—was first released in 1965 as *Key of Keys*. After production, much to Allen's displeasure, several incongruent musical sequences featuring '60s band The Lovin' Spoonful were spliced into the film to beef up the running time.

GAME 74

4. Who plays the older Jenna in the 2004 movie *13 Going on 30*?

a. Jennifer Garner
b. Jennifer Aniston
c. Reese Witherspoon
d. Jenna Elfman

GAME 74 Q3 ANSWER a
Despite its explosive subject matter, director Kathryn Bigelow's fact-based 2002 film was itself a bomb. Only a few years later, her next movie, *The Hurt Locker* (2009), not only went on to win the Academy Award for Best Picture, but also helped Bigelow make Oscar history. She became the first woman ever to win Best Director for her work on that film.

GAME 7

10. "Thank Heaven" is the last line from which movie musical?

a. *Gigi* (1958)
b. *South Pacific* (1958)
c. *The Wizard of Oz* (1939)
d. *The Sound of Music* (1965)

GAME 7 Q9 ANSWER d
In her film debut, Barbra Streisand reprised her Broadway role of the comedienne and former Ziegfeld Girl—and earned a Best Actress Oscar for her portrayal. Frank Sinatra had been in serious contention for the role of Nicky Arnstein (Brice's husband), but was passed over because Streisand refused to work with him. The part went to Omar Sharif.

GAME 27

10. Who plays a former US President in *Welcome to Mooseport* (2004)?

a. Kevin Kline
b. Gene Hackman
c. Dustin Hoffman
d. Burt Reynolds

GAME 27 Q9 ANSWER b
Walter Huston plays Lincoln in 1930's *Abraham Lincoln;* Henry Fonda plays the former leader in his early years in *Young Mr. Lincoln* (1939); and Raymond Massey plays the Great Emancipator in both *Abe Lincoln in Illinois* (1940) and *How the West Was Won* (1962). Other actors to wear the President's top hat include F. Murray Abraham and Hal Holbrook.

GAME 47

10. In which film did Al Pacino land his first starring role?

a. *Serpico*
b. *The Godfather*
c. *The Panic in Needle Park*
d. *Dog Day Afternoon*

GAME 47 Q9 ANSWER b
Although she had been in previous films, Thompson's critically acclaimed performance in *Howard's End* marked her as a serious actress. She also received Oscar nods for the 1993 films *The Remains of the Day* and *In the Name of the Father,* as well as 1995's *Sense and Sensibility,* for which she won a writing Oscar for Best Adapted Screenplay.

GAME 67

10. Which film follows four generations of an American family?

a. *Giant* (1956)
b. *Birth of a Nation* (1915)
c. *Last of the Mohicans* (1992)
d. *How the West Was Won* (1962)

GAME 67 Q9 ANSWER a
Producer David O. Selznick ran through several directors when creating this Academy Award-winning epic. George Cukor, the first director, was fired and replaced with Victor Fleming after less than three weeks of shooting. Although Fleming completed most of the project, Sam Wood and William Cameron Menzies directed certain scenes, as well.

GAME 14

3. Which screen beauty starred in Josef von Sternberg's German film classic *The Blue Angel* (1930)?

a. Greta Garbo

b. Hedy Lamarr

c. Marlene Dietrich

d. Louise Brooks

GAME 14 Q2 ANSWER d
Roberto Benigni won the Best Actor Oscar along with the Best Foreign Language Film Oscar in 1998 for his popular Italian film *Life Is Beautiful*. In addition to the Italian films *La Strada* (1954), *Nights of Cabiria* (1957), and *Amarcord* (1973), Federico Fellini's *8 1/2* (1963) also won an Oscar for Best Foreign Language Film.

GAME 34

3. Alfred Hitchcock was famous for which gimmick?

a. Subliminal advertising

b. 3-D

c. Cameo appearances

d. Threatening journalists

GAME 34 Q2 ANSWER d
James Stewart made his first of four Hitchcock appearances in this 1948 thriller—he later starred in *Rear Window* (1954), *The Man Who Knew Too Much* (1956), and *Vertigo* (1958). As a technical experiment, Hitchcock filmed *Rope* in a series of ten-minute takes that were constructed to avoid visible edits.

GAME 54

3. Which Woody Allen film is a Japanese movie dubbed over with comic dialogue?

a. *What's Up, Tiger Lily?* (1966)

b. *Radio Days* (1987)

c. *Love and Death* (1974)

d. *Vicki Cristina Barcelona* (2008)

GAME 54 Q2 ANSWER c
Play It Again, Sam was Woody Allen's second play. It opened on Broadway in 1969—two years after his first play, *Don't Drink the Water*—and featured Allen along with his actor friends Diane Keaton and Tony Roberts, and Jerry Lacy as Bogart. The 1972 film adaptation of *Play It Again, Sam* also starred Allen, Keaton, Roberts, and Lacy.

GAME 74

3. In the movie *K-19: The Widowmaker*, what exactly is K-19?

a. Nuclear submarine

b. Locomotive

c. Space satellite

d. Radio tower

GAME 74 Q2 ANSWER d
After serving a one-year stint in the US Army, Duvall—a native Californian—relocated to New York to pursue an acting career. In order to make ends meet, he worked as a post office clerk and even shared an apartment with fellow struggling actor Dustin Hoffman. Coincidentally, both men would go on to win Academy Awards for their film work.

GAME 7

11. In the 1978 musical *Grease,* what is Rizzo's first name?

a. Betty
b. Sue
c. Carol
d. Wendy

GAME 7 Q10 ANSWER a
Generally regarded as MGM's last traditional musical, *Gigi* was nominated for and won nine Academy Awards—a record number at that time. The day after the awards ceremony, MGM employees answered the phone with, "Hello, M-Gigi-M." With its four letter name, *Gigi* is the movie with the shortest title to win an Oscar for Best Picture.

GAME 27

11. In which film are Henry Fonda and Cliff Robertson presidential rivals?

a. *The Best Man* (1964)
b. *Winter Kills* (1979)
c. *State of the Union* (1948)
d. *Fail-Safe* (1964)

GAME 27 Q10 ANSWER b
Hackman and fellow actor Dustin Hoffman were voted "Least Likely to Succeed" by their classmates at the Pasadena Playhouse in California. Hackman moved to New York to prove them wrong, and Hoffman soon followed. Coincidentally, Hoffman was the original choice to play President Monroe Cole in this comedy directed by Donald Petrie.

GAME 47

11. Which ex-Mouseketeer's film debut was in *Honey I Blew Up the Kid*?

a. Britney Spears
b. Ryan Gosling
c. Keri Russell
d. Justin Timberlake

GAME 47 Q10 ANSWER c
His role as a heroin addict in this 1971 film caught the eye of director Francis Ford Coppola, who then cast him as Michael Corleone in the 1972 hit *The Godfather.* The studio had wanted a better-known actor for the role—Robert Redford and Warren Beatty were considered—but Coppola chose Pacino, who received an Oscar nomination.

GAME 67

11. Which "spectacular" ran at a loss, yet was the year's highest grossing film?

a. *Cleopatra* (1963)
b. *Dr. Zhivago* (1965)
c. *Quo Vadis* (1951)
d. *Ben-Hur* (1959)

GAME 67 Q10 ANSWER d
How the West Was Won follows four generations of the Prescotts as they move westward from New York State to California over a fifty-year span of time. The sweeping epic was nominated for eight Academy Awards; won three; and, due to its historical significance, was selected for preservation by the National Film Registry.

GAME 14

2. Which Oscar-winning Best Foreign Language Film was *not* directed by Federico Fellini?

a. *Amarcord*

b. *Nights of Cabiria*

c. *La Strada*

d. *Life Is Beautiful*

GAME 14 Q1 ANSWER b

In 1959, a new kind of French film movement called "The French New Wave" emerged with films like Francois Truffaut's *The 400 Blows* and Alain Resnais' *Hiroshima Mon Amour.* A year later in *Breathless,* Godard—previously a film critic along with Truffaut—introduced the use of hand-held cameras and jump-cut editing to mainstream moviemaking.

GAME 34

2. *Rope* was the first Alfred Hitchcock film:

a. Located in the US

b. Without a murder

c. Considered a comedy

d. Shot in color

GAME 34 Q1 ANSWER b

While still making films in his native Great Britain, Alfred Hitchcock's first version of *The Man Who Knew Too Much* (1934) featured legendary screen villain Peter Lorre. The 1956 American remake was shot in color and starred James Stewart and Doris Day, who sang the famous song "Que Sera, Sera" at two points in the film.

GAME 54

2. Which Woody Allen character interacts with an imaginary Humphrey Bogart?

a. Harry Block

b. Isaac Davis

c. Allan Felix

d. Fielding Mellish

GAME 54 Q1 ANSWER d

The comedy *Take the Money and Run* was the first movie that Woody Allen actually directed. The film features a playful musical score by Marvin Hamlisch, who later composed the score for Allen's second film, *Bananas* (1971). Watch for Allen's second wife—*Mary Hartman, Mary Hartman* star Louise Lasser—in a small but humorous role.

GAME 74

2. Who plays the title role in 1971's *THX 1138*?

a. John Hurt

b. Kurt Russell

c. Tom Skerritt

d. Robert Duvall

GAME 74 Q1 ANSWER a

Carrey plays Walter Sparrow, a man who begins to believe that every event in life can somehow be connected to the number 23, in the aptly titled *The Number 23.* He was the perfect choice for the role, having already been fascinated by the theory—dubbed the "23 Enigma"—for years. Carrey even named his production company JC 23 Entertainment.

GAME 7

12. Which film adaptation of a Broadway musical stars Catherine Zeta-Jones and Renée Zellweger?

a. *A Chorus Line* (1985)

b. *Evita* (1997)

c. *Chicago* (2002)

d. *My Fair Lady* (1964)

GAME 7 Q11 ANSWER a
In this fun-loving musical, Stockard Channing plays Betty Rizzo—the leader of a female "gang" from Rydell High called the Pink Ladies. Although most of the cast included teenagers, many of the actors who played them were older. Channing, for example, was 33; Olivia Newton-John was 🎀; John Travolta was 23; and Jeff Conaway was 26.

GAME 27

12. Who plays US President Mackenzie in *First Daughter* (2004)?

a. Warren Beatty

b. Harrison Ford

c. Michael Keaton

d. Bruce Greenwood

GAME 27 Q11 ANSWER a
The film was written by Gore Vidal, who based it on his 1960 Tony Award-winning stage play of the same name. Lee Tracy puts in an Oscar-nominated performance as fictional former US President Art Hockstader, a role he originated on Broadway. Actor Ronald Reagan was actually rejected for a part in the movie for not looking presidential enough.

GAME 47

12. Which Oscar winner's first starring role was in *The Next Karate Kid*?

a. Hilary Swank

b. Halle Berry

c. Angelina Jolie

d. Gwyneth Paltrow

GAME 47 Q11 ANSWER c
After leaving *The New Mickey Mouse Club*, Russell was cast in this 1992 Disney family flick as Mandy the babysitter, but her breakout role was as the title character in the TV series *Felicity*. She has appeared in movies such as *The Upside of Anger* (2005), *Waitress* (2007), *August Rush* (2007), and *Extraordinary Measures* (2010).

GAME 67

12. Who plays Moses' wife in the 1956 version of *The Ten Commandments*?

a. Anne Baxter

b. Yvonne De Carlo

c. Nina Foch

d. Debra Paget

GAME 67 Q11 ANSWER a
Starring Elizabeth Taylor in the title role, *Cleopatra* started with a budget of $2 million, but eventually cost a record-breaking $44 million to produce due to elaborate sets and costumes, extensive filming delays, casting issues, and a host of other problems. When the film earned only $26 million, 20th Century Fox very nearly went bankrupt.

GAME 14

1. Which of these films was directed by French filmmaker Jean-Luc Godard?

a. *Hiroshima Mon Amour* (1959)

b. *Breathless* (1960)

c. *The 400 Blows* (1959)

d. *Les Diaboliques* (1954)

The answer to this question is on:

page 180, top frame, right side.

GAME 34

1. Which of his own films did director Alfred Hitchcock remake in the '50s?

a. *Rope*

b. *The Man Who Knew Too Much*

c. *Strangers on a Train*

d. *Spellbound*

The answer to this question is on:

page 180, second frame, right side.

GAME 54

1. In which film does Woody Allen play inept thief Virgil Starkwell?

a. *Small Time Crooks* (2000)

b. *Bananas* (1971)

c. *Sleeper* (1973)

d. *Take the Money and Run* (1969)

The answer to this question is on:

page 180, third frame, right side.

GAME 74

1. Which number was significant in a 2007 film starring Jim Carrey?

a. 23

b. 13

c. 18

d. 21

The answer to this question is on:

page 180, bottom frame, right side.

GAME 8

GRAB BAG

*Turn to page 185
for the first question.*

GAME 28

GRAB BAG

*Turn to page 185
for the first question.*

GAME 48

GRAB BAG

*Turn to page 185
for the first question.*

GAME 68

GRAB BAG

*Turn to page 185
for the first question.*

GAME 7 Q12 ANSWER c
While attending a Christmas party, producer Marty Richards heard Catherine Zeta-Jones singing carols. Wowed by her voice, he offered her the role of Roxie Hart in the film version of *Chicago*. Zeta-Jones, who was unfamiliar with the play, said she'd consider the role of Velma Kelly, who sang the only song she knew from the show, "All That Jazz."

GAME 27 Q12 ANSWER c
Only one of these actors has not appeared as a US President on film. Ford plays fictional President James Marshall in 1997's *Air Force One;* Greenwood portrays Commander in Chief John F. Kennedy in 2000's *Thirteen Days;* but Beatty's character, Senator Bulworth, is assassinated as a mere presidential candidate in 1998's *Bulworth.*

GAME 47 Q12 ANSWER a
Five years before her Oscar-winning breakout performance in *Boys Don't Cry* (1999), Hillary Swank first hit the big screen as Mr. Miyagi's troubled teenage student in this fourth movie of the *The Karate Kid* series. Swank received a second Oscar for her role as amateur boxer Maggie Fitzgerald in Clint Eastwood's *Million Dollar Baby* (2004).

GAME 67 Q12 ANSWER b
Despite her exotic image, Yvonne De Carlo was born Peggy Middleton in Vancouver, Canada. For several years after moving to Hollywood, De Carlo won only uncredited roles in very minor films. When she starred opposite Charlton Heston in *The Ten Commandments,* the actress became part of one of the most financially successful movies ever produced.

GAME 14

Foreign Films

*Turn to page 182
for the first question.*

Turn to page 182
for the first question.

GAME 13 Q12 ANSWER a

The film stars Nick Nolte as a San Quentin inmate who captures media attention by writing and staging a play in prison. *Weed's* director and cowriter, John D. Hancock, was once the director of the San Francisco Actors Workshop. There, he met a convict who had organized a San Quentin theater group—and who served as the film's inspiration.

GAME 34

Alfred Hitchcock

*Turn to page 182
for the first question.*

Turn to page 182
for the first question.

GAME 33 Q12 ANSWER b

In this film about a comet colliding with the Earth, Freeman joins the ranks of esteemed actors who have portrayed fictional United States Presidents. They include John Travolta in *Primary Colors* (1998), Billy Bob Thornton in *Love Actually* (2003), Jack Nicholson in *Mars Attacks!* (1996), and Michael Douglas in *The American President* (1995).

GAME 54

Woody Allen

*Turn to page 182
for the first question.*

Turn to page 182
for the first question.

GAME 53 Q12 ANSWER c

Fresh from the success of *American Graffiti* (1973), George Lucas wrote an ambitious space-age saga (called "The Star Wars" in an early draft). Realizing the scope of his vision, Lucas placed the first film near the midway point in the larger tale. *Star Wars* became a huge hit, which enabled Lucas to make the remaining five movies in the series.

GAME 74

**Movies
By the Numbers**

*Turn to page 182
for the first question.*

Turn to page 182
for the first question.

GAME 73 Q12 ANSWER d

Sheedy, who had struggled with her own addiction to sleeping pills, was so eager to play character Lucy Berliner that she flew to the film's auditions at her own expense. The actress's outstanding performance was met with a flurry of honors, including the Independent Spirit Award and the Los Angeles Film Critics Association Award for Best Actress.

GAME 8

1. Who appeared as a singing waitress in *The Blues Brothers*?

a. Koko Taylor

b. Etta James

c. Aretha Franklin

d. Gladys Knight

The answer to this question is on:

page 187, top frame, right side.

GAME 28

1. Which disco artist stars in *Thank God It's Friday* (1978)?

a. Freda Payne

b. Gloria Gaynor

c. Donna Summer

d. Evelyn "Champagne" King

The answer to this question is on:

page 187, second frame, right side.

GAME 48

1. Which Jim Carrey character loves a socialite named Mary Swanson?

a. Ace Ventura

b. Bruce Nolan

c. Lloyd Christmas

d. Stanley Ipkiss

The answer to this question is on:

page 187, third frame, right side.

GAME 68

1. Which actor portrays a photographer in *Apocalypse Now* (1979)?

a. Tommy Lee Jones

b. John Malkovich

c. Dennis Hopper

d. Harry Dean Stanton

The answer to this question is on:

page 187, bottom frame, right side.

GAME 13

12. Which prison film centers on a convict who founds a theater group?

a. *Weeds* (1987)

b. *The Shawshank Redemption* (1995)

c. *The Longest Yard* (1974)

d. *Brubaker* (1980)

GAME 13 Q11 ANSWER c
Robert Strauss received a Best Supporting Actor Oscar nomination for his performance as Stanislas "Animal" Kasava in this Billy Wilder film. Wilder was himself nominated for Best Director, as well as star William Holden, who got the nod for Best Actor. Only Holden won, accepting the award with two words ("Thank you") due to the show's cut-off time.

GAME 33

12. What role does Morgan Freeman play in the 1998 disaster movie *Deep Impact*?

a. An astronaut

b. A US President

c. An astronomer

d. A reporter

GAME 33 Q11 ANSWER d
In this British film adaptation of a science fiction novel by John Wyndham, salt water is used to dissolve the plant-like beings that threaten human life after arriving in a meteor shower. In 2002, moviegoers saw a similar substance used to defeat the aliens in M. Night Shyamalan's *Signs*. This time, though, the water was fresh, not salted.

GAME 53

12. Which episode began the six-film *Star Wars* saga?

a. Episode I

b. Episode VI

c. Episode IV

d. Episode II

GAME 53 Q11 ANSWER d
In an ironic twist, Anakin Skywalker actually builds C-3PO while he is a young slave on Tatooine. By the time Anakin has turned into Darth Vader, C-3PO has joined with R2D2 and the Rebel Alliance. In *The Empire Strikes Back*, Darth Vader's bounty hunter Boba Fett smashes C-3PO into pieces with a laser gun.

GAME 73

12. In which indie film does Ally Sheedy play a drug addict?

a. *Claire Dolan* (1998)

b. *Sugar Town* (1999)

c. *The Addiction* (1995)

d. *High Art* (1998)

GAME 73 Q11 ANSWER a
Sammy Cahn and Jimmy Van Heusen wrote the score for this updated version of the Robin Hood legend. Although more of the film's songs are sung by cast member Bing Crosby than by any of the Rat Packers, "My Kind of Town" is performed by Frank Sinatra, and is also heard playing during the opening and closing credits.

GAME 8

2. In which film does the villain strike the San Andreas Fault with a nuclear missile?

a. *Batman Returns* (1992)

b. *Superman* (1978)

c. *Die Hard* (1988)

d. *Total Recall* (1990)

GAME 8 Q1 ANSWER c
The legendary "Queen of Soul" plays Mrs. Murphy, the singing waitress at the Soul Food Café. Franklin isn't the only musical talent to appear in this 1980 movie starring John Belushi and Dan Ackroyd as Jake and Elwood Blues. Others include James Brown, Cab Calloway, Ray Charles, John Lee Hooker, Joe Walsh, and Steve Lawrence.

GAME 28

2. In *The Godfather* (1972), where do hit men turn Sonny into Swiss cheese?

a. Church

b. Restaurant

c. Barber's chair

d. Tollbooth

GAME 28 Q1 ANSWER c
Dubbed "The Queen of Disco," Donna Summer stars in this film that takes place in a Hollywod disco. Although panned by critics, the film did win a Best Original Song Oscar for "Last Dance" (it also earned Summer her first Grammy). The soundtrack, which includes songs from artists like Diana Ross and Thelma Houston, was also a commercial success.

GAME 48

2. What's the name of the fictional drug company in *Mission Impossible II* ?

a. Biocyte

b. Cyberdyne Systems

c. Multi-National United

d. Buy and Large

GAME 48 Q1 ANSWER c
Carrey was initially offered $700,000 to play the role in 1994's *Dumb & Dumber,* but his salary increased to $7 million after *Ace Ventura: Pet Detective* opened earlier that year at #1. His film *The Mask* also opened in the #1 spot that year, as did *Dumb & Dumber.* This made Carrey the first actor to have three films open at #1 in the same year.

GAME 68

2. In which film does Tom Hanks play the character Jimmy Dugan?

a. *Philadelphia* (1993)

b. *Dragnet* (1987)

c. *Punchline* (1988)

d. *A League of Their Own* (1992)

GAME 68 Q1 ANSWER c
Hopper's role in director Francis Ford Coppola's war epic was a return to mainstream success for the actor, who had garnered much acclaim ten years earlier for his 1969 road movie *Easy Rider.* He would gain further recognition for his performance in *Blue Velvet* (1986), as well as a Best Supporting Oscar nomination for his role in *Hoosiers* (1986).

GAME 13

11. Who is worshipped by a POW named "Animal" in *Stalag 17* (1953)?

a. Roseanne Barr

b. Vivien Leigh

c. Betty Grable

d. Judy Garland

GAME 13 Q10 ANSWER d
Stephen King sold the rights to adapt his novella *Rita Hayworth and Shawshank Redemption* to director Frank Darabont for one dollar. Calling the deals his "Dollar Babies," the author has made a habit of granting budding filmmakers permission to film his short stories for the paltry sum. As a movie lover, it is his way of giving back to the art form.

GAME 33

11. What is used to destroy the aliens in the 1962 classic *Day of the Triffids*?

a. Bacteria

b. An atom bomb

c. Sulfuric acid

d. Water

GAME 33 Q10 ANSWER b
Throughout this film, which was edited to look like it was shot with a handheld camera, famous New York landmarks such as the Statue of Liberty, the Brooklyn Bridge, and Coney Island are destroyed by a monster. However, part of the movie was filmed in Los Angeles, and the title, *Cloverfield*, is actually the name of a boulevard in Santa Monica.

GAME 53

11. Which *Star Wars* character created C-3PO?

a. Boba Fett

b. Chewbacca

c. Luke Skywalker

d. Anakin Skywalker

GAME 53 Q10 ANSWER d
All of these women are connected to Anakin Skywalker's life. Shmi is Anakin's mother, who is freed from slavery on Tatooine only to be captured and killed by Tuskan Raiders (aka Sand People). Beru is the wife of Anakin's stepbrother, Owen Lars, while Padme is Anakin's doomed wife. Leia is Anakin and Padme's daughter.

GAME 73

11. Which Rat Pack film features the song "My Kind of Town"?

a. *Robin and the 7 Hoods* (1964)

b. *Ocean's 11* (1960)

c. *4 for Texas* (1963)

d. *Sergeants 3* (1962)

GAME 73 Q10 ANSWER b
Zoolander had the ill fortune to open only two weeks after the terrorist attacks of September 11, 2001. While this initially resulted in a disappointing box office performance, the offbeat film—which also features Ben Stiller's father, Jerry Stiller—eventually developed a solid cult following and generated significant DVD sales.

GAME 8

3. Who paints Danielle's portrait in the romantic fantasy *Ever After* (1998)?

a. Vincent Van Gogh
b. Pierre Renoir
c. Michelangelo
d. Leonardo da Vinci

GAME 8 Q2 ANSWER b
Through this act, Lex Luthor attempts to create his own coastline by separating the Golden State from the mainland. Jack Nicholson and Gene Wilder were both considered for the role of Luthor, which was ultimately played by Gene Hackman. Initially, Hackman was reluctant to take the role, fearing it might damage his reputation as a serious actor.

GAME 28

3. Which character says, "As God is my witness, I'll never be hungry again"?

a. Norma Desmond
b. Scarlett O'Hara
c. Jane Eyre
d. Mildred Pierce

GAME 28 Q2 ANSWER d
Sonny Corleone, played by James Caan, is machine-gunned to death in this shockingly brutal scene (he's shot nearly 1,000 times). During the filming of the scene, which was done in one take, over 100 squibs (tiny firecrackers) were attached to Caan's clothes and set to go off so that it looked as if his body was being hit by rapid machine-gun fire.

GAME 48

3. "We'll go on forever, Pa. We're the people," is spoken in which film?

a. *The Pearl* (1947)
b. *The Red Pony* (1949)
c. *Of Mice and Men* (1939)
d. *The Grapes of Wrath* (1940)

GAME 48 Q2 ANSWER a
Biocyte Pharmaceuticals creates a genetically modified virus called Chimera in this 2000 sequel to *Mission: Impossible*. Cyberdyne Systems, which is responsible for the eventual creation of the evil SkyNet, is in *Terminator 2* (1991); Multi-National United is in *District 9* (2009); and Buy and Large Corporation is in the Pixar-animated *WALL-E* (2008).

GAME 68

3. Who plays the title character in *What's Eating Gilbert Grape* (1993)?

a. Johnny Depp
b. Kiefer Sutherland
c. Brad Pitt
d. Keanu Reeves

GAME 68 Q2 ANSWER d
After a few box-office bombs—including *The 'Burbs* (1989), *Joe Versus the Volcano* (1990), and *Bonfire of the Vanities* (1990)—Hanks began his evolution into an acclaimed dramatic actor by playing a reluctant baseball manager in this hit film. He continued his success with Oscar-winning performances in *Philadelphia* (1993) and *Forrest Gump* (1994).

GAME 13

10. Which prison drama features inmates drinking beer on a rooftop?

a. *Dead Man Walking* (1995)

b. *Midnight Express* (1978)

c. *The Longest Yard* (1974)

d. *The Shawshank Redemption* (1994)

GAME 13 Q9 ANSWER d

Lancaster and Savalas received Academy Award nominations for their performances in this fictionalized account of the life of prison inmate Robert Stroud. Despite its title, the film is set primarily in Leavenworth prison, where Stroud adopted and studied hundreds of birds over the course of his stay. He eventually published two books on the subject.

GAME 33

10. What city gets destroyed in the 2008 sci-fi film *Cloverfield*?

a. Sydney

b. New York

c. London

d. Los Angeles

GAME 33 Q9 ANSWER c

As the result of a massive marketing campaign that began with a Super Bowl commercial, this film about an alien invasion of Earth was eagerly awaited by moviegoers. Although it was scheduled for release on July 3, 1996, many theaters, responding to the public, started showing *Independence Day* on July 2— the day on which the film's action begins.

GAME 53

10. In the *Star Wars* movies, who is Anakin Skywalker's mother?

a. Padme

b. Leia

c. Beru

d. Shmi

GAME 53 Q9 ANSWER b

After delivering Princess Leia and the stolen plans to the Death Star back to the rebels, Luke joins the Red Squadron as an X-Wing fighter in this 1977 film. He is reunited with his friend Biggs from Tatooine, who states his battle number as "Red Three." During this fight with the Galactic Empire, Biggs is killed by Darth Vader.

GAME 73

10. In which film do Frat Packers Ben Stiller and Owen Wilson play models?

a. *The Independent* (2000)

b. *Zoolander* (2001)

c. *Duplex* (2003)

d. *Envy* (2004)

GAME 73 Q9 ANSWER c

California-born Molly Ringwald began her acting career by appearing in stage plays and local TV commercials in the Sacramento area. She then was cast in various television series before moving to the big screen. *Spacehunter: Adventures in the Forbidden Zone* was Ringwald's second film, produced two years before the formation of the Brat Pack.

GAME 8

4. Who played the ape Cornelius in the film *Planet of the Apes*?

a. Charlton Heston
b. Roddy McDowall
c. James Whitmore
d. Gene Wilder

GAME 8 Q3 ANSWER d
Drew Barrymore plays Danielle in this "historical" version of Cinderella. Complete with horrid stepmother (Anjelica Huston) and life as a servant, Danielle also befriends Leonardo da Vinci, who helps her find her happily-ever-after ending. The portrait he paints of her in the film is based on a real da Vinci work called *La Scapigliata* (Female Head).

GAME 28

4. What's the rank of Richard Crenna's character in the *Rambo* series?

a. Colonel
b. General
c. Major
d. Lieutenant

GAME 28 Q3 ANSWER b
The famous line is spoken by actress Vivien Leigh in *Gone With the Wind*—the 1939 film adaptation of the Margaret Mitchell novel. The epic film contains another line that was ranked at #1 by the American Film Institute in 2005: "Frankly, my dear, I don't give a damn," were the departing words of Rhett Butler (Clark Gable) to Scarlett O'Hara.

GAME 48

4. In which film does Marlon Brando square off against Jack Nicholson?

a. *The Last Detail* (1973)
b. *The Freshman* (1990)
c. *The Score* (2001)
d. *The Missouri Breaks* (1976)

GAME 48 Q3 ANSWER d
Based on John Steinbeck's Pulitzer Prize-winning 1939 novel of the same name, *The Grapes of Wrath* tells the story of the Joads, a family that loses its farm during the Great Depression and migrates to California. This film was one of the first twenty-five chosen by the Library of Congress to be preserved in the National Film Registry in 1989.

GAME 68

4. In which movie does Bridget Fonda play paleontologist Kelly Scott?

a. *Mr. Jealousy* (1997)
b. *The Lost World* (1997)
c. *A Simple Plan* (1998)
d. *Lake Placid* (1999)

GAME 68 Q3 ANSWER a
Known for his quirky and peculiar characters, Depp first gained recognition on the television series *21 Jump Street* and soon became a teen idol. Not one to rest on that status, the actor has played such memorable roles as Edward Scissorhands, Ichabod Crane, and Sweeney Todd—not to mention his Oscar-nominated turn as pirate Jack Sparrow.

GAME 13

9. Who plays Burt Lancaster's jailhouse pal in 1962's *Birdman of Alcatraz*?

a. Ed Begley
b. Peter Falk
c. Spencer Tracy
d. Telly Savalas

GAME 13 Q8 ANSWER a
Three days after the movie wrapped, actress Judy Tyler—who plays Elvis' love interest Peggy Van Alden in the film—died tragically in a car accident while driving from Los Angeles to New York. She had starred in her first film—*Bop Girl Goes Calypso* (1957)—earlier that year. Sadly, Tyler would never see either performance on the big screen.

GAME 33

9. Which movie opens with R.E.M.'s "It's the End of the World As We Know It"?

a. *Armageddon* (1998)
b. *The Day After Tomorrow* (2004)
c. *Independence Day* (1996)
d. *Mars Attacks!* (1996)

GAME 33 Q8 ANSWER d
When plants begin releasing a neurotoxin that causes humans to kill themselves, scientists realize that the Earth is rejecting humans as pests. Some critics of M. Night Shyamalan's film called this plot "too thoughtful" for a summer flick, while others praised Shyamalan's efforts to make the public take notice of Earth's environmental problems.

GAME 53

9. In *A New Hope,* what is Luke Skywalker's Red Squadron battle number?

a. Red Three
b. Red Five
c. Red Eleven
d. Red Twelve

GAME 53 Q8 ANSWER b
Calrissian (Billy Dee Williams) loses his ship to fellow gambler Han Solo (Harrison Ford)—an offscreen event that is referred to by Lando in *The Empire Strikes Back* (1980). When asked to fight on the Endor moon, Han gives the *Millennium Falcon* back to Lando, who leads an attack on the new Death Star in 1983's *Return of the Jedi.*

GAME 73

9. Which campy sci-fi movie stars Brat Pack actress Molly Ringwald?

a. *Weird Science* (1985)
b. *Explorers* (1985)
c. *Spacehunter* (1983)
d. *Space Camp* (1986)

GAME 73 Q8 ANSWER c
Based on a series of books created by espionage writer Donald Hamilton, four movies—produced between 1966 and 1969—starred Dean Martin as US secret agent Matt Helm. Although the films used some of the books' titles and very general plot elements, they did not remain true to the books' atmosphere and themes, nor to the Matt Helm character.

GAME 8

5. Which rock icon appeared in *Pat Garrett and Billy the Kid* (1973)?

a. Bob Dylan
b. John Lennon
c. Elvis Presley
d. Mick Jagger

GAME 8 Q4 ANSWER b
McDowall played Cornelius in this first of five "Planet of the Apes" movies. A makeup team of over eighty members painstakingly transformed the actors into realistic-looking apes. The mask-like makeup took hours to apply, and had to be left on during breaks and meals, which, by the way, had to be liquified for the actors to drink through straws.

GAME 28

5. Which American film was the first to show a toilet flushing?

a. *Great Expectations* (1946)
b. *Modern Times* (1936)
c. *The Blob* (1958)
d. *Psycho* (1960)

GAME 28 Q4 ANSWER a
Crenna is perhaps best known for the role of Colonel Samuel Trautman—the former commanding officer of John Rambo's Special Forces unit. Initially, Kirk Douglas had the part, but quit after only one day of filming *First Blood* (1982)—the first movie of the series. Crenna spoofed his famous character in the 1993 comedy *Hot Shots! Part Deux.*

GAME 48

5. In *Big*, what's the name of the toy company where Tom Hanks works?

a. Wonder World
b. Zoltar's
c. MacMillan
d. Thompson

GAME 48 Q4 ANSWER d
In this Western, Nicholson plays a horse thief who is sought after by a bounty hunter (Brando). Unfortunately, the filming of the movie was not monitored by the American Humane Society (AHA), and several horses were injured during production—one actually drowned. As a result, the AHA placed this film on its list of unacceptable titles.

GAME 68

5. For which genre is Keystone Studios known?

a. Musical
b. Comedy
c. Western
d. Sci-fi

GAME 68 Q4 ANSWER d
At the time of its release, this goofy horror film was one of a number of animal-inspired monster movies to find its way to theaters. Prior to this tale of a monstrous alligator, moviegoers were treated to the story of a giant (and hungry) snake in 1997's *Anaconda.* Not to be outdone, 2000's *Crocodile* brought viewers (surprise!) a giant crocodile.

GAME 13

8. On what charge is Elvis Presley convicted in *Jailhouse Rock* (1957)?

a. Manslaughter

b. Armed robbery

c. Hit and run

d. Assault and battery

GAME 13 Q7 ANSWER c
The film was based on a true story and was the last collaboration between director Don Siegel and actor Clint Eastwood. The two had previously worked together on four movies—*Coogan's Bluff* (1968), *Two Mules for Sister Sara* (1970), *Dirty Harry* (1971), and *The Beguiled* (1971). As a director, Eastwood dedicated *Unforgiven* (1992) to Siegel.

GAME 33

8. Which disaster movie implies that we need to take better care of our planet?

a. *The Mist* (2007)

b. *Sunshine* (2007)

c. *Without Warning* (1994)

d. *The Happening* (2008)

GAME 33 Q7 ANSWER d
Director James Cameron originally considered several established actors to take the role of the penniless Jack Dawson, and ultimately chose DiCaprio in part because he wanted a youthful performer. Although DiCaprio initially did not care for the role, he finally accepted, and critics described the twenty-two-year-old's performance as "captivating."

GAME 53

8. Which *Star Wars* character loses the *Millennium Falcon* in a card game?

a. Chewbacca

b. Lando Calrissian

c. Greedo

d. Jabba the Hutt

GAME 53 Q7 ANSWER b
Count Dooku (aka Darth Tyranus) is portrayed by British actor Christopher Lee, who played Dracula to Peter Cushing's Van Helsing in the Hammer Films' horror movies of the 1960s. Cushing actually appeared in a *Star Wars* movie before Lee, when he was hired to play Grand Moff Tarkin in 1977's *A New Hope*.

GAME 73

8. Which fictitious private eye was portrayed on film by Dean Martin?

a. Sam Spade

b. Ellery Queen

c. Matt Helm

d. Mike Hammer

GAME 73 Q7 ANSWER b
Most of Mare Winningham's early work was in television, but in 1985, the young actress appeared in *St. Elmo's Fire*, making her a true Brat Packer. Although the popular film earned Winningham greater fame, it did not win her a slew of big-screen offers. Instead, she returned to TV in a Hallmark Hall of Fame production entitled *Love Is Never Silent*.

GAME 8

6. Which actor played the title role in *The Omega Man* (1971)?

a. Kirk Douglas

b. Charlton Heston

c. Donald Pleasence

d. George Kennedy

GAME 8 Q5 ANSWER a
For the film's soundtrack, Dylan recorded "Knockin' on Heaven's Door," an instant hit that reached #12 on the Billboard Top 100. Born Robert Allen Zimmerman, Dylan is considered one of the greatest rock musicians of all time. That's why it is so ironic that in his Music Appreciation class at the University of Minnesota, he received a grade of D+.

GAME 28

6. Which movie first paired Charlie Chaplin and Buster Keaton?

a. *Modern Times* (1936)

b. *The General* (1926)

c. *The Gold Rush* (1925)

d. *Limelight* (1952)

GAME 28 Q5 ANSWER d
Legendary director Alfred Hitchcock knew that filmmakers—to appease censors—had never filmed a toilet in a scene, let alone one that was being flushed. In *Psycho*, he had Marion Crane (played by Janet Leigh) rip a piece of paper—an incriminating bit of evidence—and flush it down the toilet. Although the censors complained, it was left in.

GAME 48

6. "If you build it, he will come" is a line from which movie?

a. *Field of Dreams* (1989)

b. *Evan Almighty* (2007)

c. *Moonstruck* (1987)

d. *Out of Africa* (1985)

GAME 48 Q5 ANSWER c
When thirteen-year-old Josh Baskin (David Moscow) is granted his wish "to be big," he is transformed into an adult (Tom Hanks) and gets a job at MacMillan Toys. To help Hanks play the part of a young teen, all his scenes were first shot with Moscow. This allowed Hanks to watch and then mimic Moscow's mannerisms. Hanks got an Oscar nod for the role.

GAME 68

6. Which film's leading man won an Oscar posthumously?

a. *Network* (1976)

b. *Broadcast News* (1987)

c. *Dr. Strangelove* (1964)

d. *On Golden Pond* (1981)

GAME 68 Q5 ANSWER b
Keystone Studios was founded by Mack Sennett in 1912 and quickly become a leading innovator in the world of comedic movies. After its successful Keystone Kops series popularized the art of slapstick, the studio began to foster the early careers of many silent film legends, including Charlie Chaplin, Harold Lloyd, Gloria Swanson, and Fatty Arbuckle.

GAME 13

7. In which film do three prisoners disappear without a trace?

a. *Papillon* (1973)

b. *Con Air* (1997)

c. *Escape from Alcatraz* (1979)

d. *The Shawshank Redemption* (1994)

GAME 13 Q6 ANSWER c

Kennedy spent sixteen years in the US Army before a back injury caused him to retire from military service. Born into a show-biz family, he soon made his name in the movie industry with performances in such films as *Charade* (1963), *The Flight of the Phoenix* (1965), and 1967's *Cool Hand Luke*—a role that won him the Best Supporting Actor Oscar.

GAME 33

7. Which actor was originally slated for the role of Jack in *Titanic* (1997)?

a. Brad Pitt

b. Matt Damon

c. Leonardo DiCaprio

d. Matthew McConaughey

GAME 33 Q6 ANSWER b

According to a book on the making of the movie, the computer-generated imagery (CGI) cow picked up by the tornado in this film was originally a CGI zebra from the 1995 movie *Jumanji*. Viewers must have appreciated the final effect, because *Twister* was the second-highest grossing film of 1996 and also received two Oscar nominations.

GAME 53

7. What is Count Dooku also known as in the *Star Wars* films?

a. Darth Maul

b. Darth Tyranus

c. Darth Sidious

d. Darth Plagueis

GAME 53 Q6 ANSWER d

In *The Empire Strikes Back* (1980), Luke Skywalker is told by Obi-Wan Kenobi to begin Jedi training with Yoda on Dagobah. Coruscant is home first to the evil Galactic Empire and then the good New Republic. Tatooine is home both to Anakin Skywalker and Luke Skywalker, while Alderaan is Princess Leia Organa's destroyed home planet.

GAME 73

7. Who portrays shy and innocent Wendy Beamish in *St. Elmo's Fire*?

a. Andie MacDowell

b. Mare Winningham

c. Demi Moore

d. Ally Sheedy

GAME 73 Q6 ANSWER a

Lead character Randy Dupree, portrayed by Frat Pack actor-comedian Owen Wilson, may be an insensitive housemate, but he has a soft spot in his heart for professional cyclist Lance Armstrong. That's why the film includes Armstrong in three cameos—first, in Dupree's biking video; then, in a dream sequence; and finally, in an after-the-credits scene.

GAME 8	**7.** Which movie has the image of a bicycle soaring across the background of the moon? **a.** *E.T.* (1982) **b.** *The Neverending Story* (1984) **c.** *Cocoon* (1985) **d.** *Pee-wee's Big Adventure* (1985)	**GAME 8 Q6 ANSWER b** In this movie, which is based on the novel *I Am Legend* by Richard Matheson, Heston plays the last survivor in the aftermath of a biological war. This story was first filmed in 1964 as *The Last Man on Earth*, starring Vincent Price. In 2007, a third adaptation was released using the actual title of the book—*I Am Legend*, starring Will Smith.
GAME 28	**7.** What reduces the kids to pea-sized beings in *Honey, I Shrunk the Kids*? **a.** Nuclear fallout **b.** Experimental ray gun **c.** Witch's spell **d.** Tainted candy	**GAME 28 Q6 ANSWER d** Written and directed by Chaplin, *Limelight* was the only feature film in which the rival comics appeared—they did the final musical number together. At first, Chaplin felt the part was too small for Keaton, but when he learned Keaton was going through hard times, he wanted him in the film. Chaplin also composed the movie's Oscar-winning score.
GAME 48	**7.** Which *Blazing Saddles* character falls for the exploding candygram? **a.** Captain Oveur **b.** Lili Von Shtupp **c.** Hedley Lamarr **d.** Mongo	**GAME 48 Q6 ANSWER a** This Oscar-nominated sports drama starring Kevin Costner is an adaptation of W.P. Kinsella's 1982 novel *Shoeless Joe*. "If you build it, he will come," was ranked #39 on the American Film Institute's list of best movie quotes. It is also one of the most misquoted lines, often cited as, "If you build it, *they* will come."
GAME 68	**7.** What is hijacked in *The Taking of Pelham One Two Three* (1974, 2009)? **a.** Subway train **b.** Battleship **c.** City bus **d.** Airplane	**GAME 68 Q6 ANSWER a** This movie was the first in Academy history to win three of the four acting awards. Faye Dunaway won the Oscar for Best Actress in a Leading Role; Beatrice Straight was honored as Best Supporting Actress; and though Peter Finch had died before the ceremony took place, he was still deemed the year's best actor, with his widow accepting the award.

GAME 13

6. Who won an Oscar in 1967 for playing a prisoner named Dragline?

a. John Wayne

b. Jim Brown

c. George Kennedy

d. Gene Hackman

GAME 13 Q5 ANSWER b
Sean Penn received his first Oscar nomination for his performance as death-row inmate Matthew Poncelet in this Tim Robbins film. He went on to be recognized by the Academy for his work in such movies as *Sweet and Lowdown* (1999) and *I Am Sam* (2001). Penn has won Best Actor Oscars for his roles in the 2003 drama *Mystic River* and 2008's *Milk*.

GAME 33

6. What animal is picked up by a tornado in the 1996 movie *Twister*?

a. A zebra

b. A cow

c. A goat

d. A dog

GAME 33 Q5 ANSWER a
Armageddon debuted less than three months after the similarly themed *Deep Impact*. Astronomers declared *Deep Impact* more accurate, but *Armageddon* beat it at the box office. It also received four Oscar nominations, including Best Sound Effects Editing, Best Visual Effects, Best Original Song ("I Don't Want to Miss a Thing"), and Best Sound.

GAME 53

6. What *Star Wars* planet is known for its swamps?

a. Coruscant

b. Tatooine

c. Alderaan

d. Dagobah

GAME 53 Q5 ANSWER b
Played by British actor Anthony Daniels, C-3PO is a protocol droid with a gold-colored body and a neurotic personality. Though he is seen only briefly in *Episode I: The Phantom Menace* (1999), C-3PO appears in every *Star Wars* movie with his eventual droid counterpart R2D2. The pair is often compared to the comedy duo Laurel and Hardy.

GAME 73

6. Which real-life athlete is featured in the 2006 film *You, Me and Dupree*?

a. Lance Armstrong

b. Wayne Gretzky

c. Tiger Woods

d. Michael Jordan

GAME 73 Q5 ANSWER c
The last film to feature five members of the Rat Pack, *Sergeants 3* cast Frank Sinatra in the role originally filled by Victor McLaglen, Peter Lawford in the Douglas Fairbanks, Jr. role, and Dean Martin in the Cary Grant part. Sammy Davis, Jr. plays Sam Jaffe's character, and Joey Bishop—portraying a fourth sergeant—completes the Pack.

GAME 8

8. Who played alcoholic Glen Whitehouse in the movie *Affliction* (1997)?

a. Jack Lemmon

b. Martin Sheen

c. James Coburn

d. Paul Newman

GAME 8 Q7 ANSWER a
That image became the emblem for Steven Spielberg's company Amblin Entertainment. When Reese's Pieces were used in the movie to lure the endearing little alien, sales of the candy skyrocketed, kicking off the craze of product placement in films. Originally, M&Ms were supposed to be used, but the Mars Company denied the request. Bet they're sorry.

GAME 28

8. Which film takes place in a Central American jungle?

a. *The Jungle Book* (1967)

b. *Cat People* (1982)

c. *Predator* (1987)

d. *Cat's Eye* (1985)

GAME 28 Q7 ANSWER b
Rick Moranis plays the science geek who invents the miniaturizer in this 1989 Disney film. Originally, the movie was called *Teenie Weenies,* but the producers felt it sounded too much like a kiddie film, so a line from the movie itself was used as the title. The film received positive reviews and spawned two movie sequels and a short TV series.

GAME 48

8. "I don't have to show you any stinking badges!" is spoken in which film?

a. *The Treasure of the Sierra Madre* (1948)

b. *Key Largo* (1948)

c. *First Blood* (1982)

d. *A Fistful of Dollars* (1964)

GAME 48 Q7 ANSWER d
Alex Karras plays the dimwitted Mongo in this 1974 Mel Brooks' comedy Western. The character was the idea of comedian Richard Pryor, who was slated for the lead role of Sheriff Bart. However, due to Pryor's controversial comedy routines, financers refused to back the movie if he had the role. So Brooks made Pryor one of the film's co-writers.

GAME 68

8. Which film tells the story of Marine officer Wilbur "Bull" Meechum?

a. *Drugstore Cowboy* (1989)

b. *The Mighty Quinn* (1989)

c. *The Great Santini* (1979)

d. *Stroker Ace* (1983)

GAME 68 Q7 ANSWER a
Hollywood has portrayed a number of illegally appropriated vehicles on the big screen over the years. In *Under Seige* (1992), Steven Seagal attempts to thwart a gang of mercenaries aboard a battleship; in *Speed* (1994), Dennis Hopper holds a city bus for ransom; and in *Air Force One* (1997), terrorists seize control of the US President's airplane.

GAME 13

5. What method of execution is used in 1995's *Dead Man Walking*?

a. Gas chamber

b. Lethal injection

c. Firing squad

d. Electric chair

GAME 13 Q4 ANSWER c
This Coen brothers movie spurred a resurgence of interest in folk music with its popular Depression-era soundtrack. Featuring such musical talents as Ralph Stanley, John Hartford, and Alison Krauss, the album spawned a concert tour and a documentary film (2000's *Down from the Mountain*), and won a Grammy for Album of the Year in 2002.

GAME 33

5. In which movie does NASA hire a drilling expert to destroy an asteroid?

a. *Armageddon* (1998)

b. *Space Cowboys* (2000)

c. *Deep Impact* (1998)

d. *The Rock* (1996)

GAME 33 Q4 ANSWER d
In this film about global warming and the coming of a new Ice Age, we also see giant hail pound Tokyo and tsunamis and blizzards whip New York. To ease the minds of terrified moviegoers, the Red Cross set up stands at theaters across the United States offering informative brochures about remaining safe during various natural disasters.

GAME 53

5. Which *Star Wars* character speaks over 6 million galactic languages?

a. Chewbacca

b. C-3PO

c. Princess Leia

d. Han Solo

GAME 53 Q4 ANSWER c
The Sleestak are humanoids from the classic TV show *Land of the Lost*. Meanwhile, the Jawas appear like the space-age equivalent to Walt Disney's Seven Dwarfs in the first *Star Wars* film from 1977. In 1983's *Return of the Jedi*, *Star Wars* fans meet both the terrible Rancor and the cuddly Ewoks.

GAME 73

5. Which Rat Pack film is a Western version of the 1939 classic *Gunga Din*?

a. *Some Came Running* (1958)

b. *4 for Texas* (1963)

c. *Sergeants 3* (1962)

d. *Texas Across the River* (1966)

GAME 73 Q4 ANSWER b
Considered one of the two "core" Brat Pack films—the other one is *St. Elmo's Fire* (1985)—*The Breakfast Club* also features Judd Nelson, Emilio Estevez, Molly Ringwald, and Anthony Michael Hall. A cult classic, this film has been referred to and imitated in countless coming-of-age movies, TV shows, commercials, and posters.

GAME 8

9. Which villain says, "I find your lack of faith disturbing."

a. Count Dracula
b. Goldfinger
c. The Joker
d. Darth Vader

GAME 8 Q8 ANSWER c
Coburn came out of retirement to appear in this film—and received a Best Supporting Actor Oscar for his riveting performance. The role was first offered to Paul Newman and James Garner, but both men turned it down because the character was so dark. During Coburn's forty-five-year career, he appeared in nearly seventy films.

GAME 28

9. Because of the movie, "lost weekend" has come to mean a weekend of:

a. Romance
b. Drunkenness
c. Housecleaning
d. Excessive spending

GAME 28 Q8 ANSWER c
Arnold Schwarzenegger leads a special task force that is targeted by an alien "predator" in this sci-fi thriller. Visual effects/makeup artist Stanley Winston (who worked on the *Terminator* and *Jurassic Park* films) designed the creature with a little help from well-known director James Cameron, who suggested that the creature have mandibles.

GAME 48

9. Which of the following characters is from the *Harry Potter* series?

a. Magneto
b. Count Dooku
c. Morpheus
d. Argus Filch

GAME 48 Q8 ANSWER a
Based on B. Traven's 1927 novel of the same name, this classic film won three Oscars, including Best Director for John Huston, and Best Supporting Actor for his father, Walter Huston. It was the first father/son Oscar win. John Huston has said that working with his father and his father winning the Oscar are among his fondest moments.

GAME 68

9. Which series features Ricardo Montalban and Robert Goulet as villains?

a. *The Naked Gun*
b. *Hot Shots*
c. *Beverly Hills Cop*
d. *Lethal Weapon*

GAME 68 Q8 ANSWER c
The role of flying ace Meechum resulted in Robert Duvall's first Academy Award nomination for Best Actor. He also received a Best Supporting Actor nomination that same year for his work in *Apocalypse Now* (1979). After four nominations, Duvall won an Oscar for his performance in 1983's *Tender Mercies*, which brought him the Best Actor honor.

GAME 13

4. What group makes a hit record in *O Brother, Where Art Thou* (2000)?

a. The Blue Mountain Men

b. The Fiddlers Three

c. The Soggy Bottom Boys

d. The Kingston Trio

GAME 13 Q3 ANSWER c
Redford first captured the public's attention by playing the Sundance Kid in 1969's *Butch Cassidy and the Sundance Kid*. Not long after, he ventured successfully into directing, winning a Best Director Oscar for his directorial debut, *Ordinary People* (1980). A longtime supporter of independent film, he is also chairman of the Sundance Film Festival.

GAME 33

4. What reduces Los Angeles to rubble in the 2004 film *The Day After Tomorrow*?

a. A blizzard

b. An earthquake

c. A tidal wave

d. Tornadoes

GAME 33 Q3 ANSWER a
This movie was based on the 1898 H.G. Wells novel of the same name, and was not the first dramatic presentation to draw its story from the book. The original *War of the Worlds* movie had appeared in 1953, and two decades earlier, a *War of the Worlds* radio adaptation had caused some listeners to believe that Martians had actually invaded the planet.

GAME 53

4. Which creature is *not* from the *Star Wars* universe?

a. Ewok

b. Jawa

c. Sleestak

d. Rancor

GAME 53 Q3 ANSWER a
While writing the first *Star Wars* film in 1977, George Lucas was paying homage both to Buck Rogers and mythologists like Joseph Campbell. Although he did earn a Best Original Screenplay Oscar nod for the film, he had screenwriters Leigh Brackett and Lawrence Kasdan write the script for the next film in the series, *The Empire Strikes Back* (1980).

GAME 73

4. Who plays "basket case" Allison Reynolds in 1985's *The Breakfast Club*?

a. Molly Ringwald

b. Ally Sheedy

c. Demi Moore

d. Mare Winningham

GAME 73 Q3 ANSWER d
Delivered by Vince Vaughn's character, Trent Walker, this line conveys the unappealing side of Walker's personality. Vaughn's performance not only won him the acclaim of moviegoers and film critics, but also attracted the attention of director Steven Spielberg, who soon cast the young Frat Packer in his 1997 sci-fi film *The Lost World: Jurassic Park*.

GAME 8

10. In which film does Barbara Hershey shoot Robert Redford?

a. *Sneakers* (1992)

b. *Havana* (1990)

c. *The Natural* (1984)

d. *Indecent Proposal* (1993)

GAME 8 Q9 ANSWER d

In *Star Wars* (1977) Darth Vader says this line while telekinetically choking a subordinate. James Earl Jones voiced the character, but asked not to be credited because he was an up-and-coming actor at the time and feared being typecast. David Prowse played Darth Vader onscreen and was unaware of the voice dubbing until the movie opened.

GAME 28

10. In which movie does a Model-T Ford drive airborne?

a. *The Absent-Minded Professor* (1961)

b. *Bedknobs and Broomsticks* (1971)

c. *The Love Bug* (1968)

d. *Phantom Tollbooth* (1969)

GAME 28 Q9 ANSWER b

Based on Charles R. Jackson's 1944 novel, *The Lost Weekend* (1945) stars Ray Milland as an alcoholic writer. Directed by Billy Wilder, the film was one of the first to focus on alcoholism. (The liquor industry tried to prevent its release by offering Paramount $5 million.) The film won Oscars for Best Picture, Director, Actor, and Writing.

GAME 48

10. Who plays Captain Ahab in *Moby Dick* (1956)?

a. Gary Cooper

b. Anthony Quinn

c. Gregory Peck

d. Raymond Massey

GAME 48 Q9 ANSWER d

David Bradley plays Filch—the Hogwarts caretaker in the films of the *Harry Potter* franchise. The sinister Magneto, played by Ian McKellen, is a recurring character in the *X-Men* series; Count Dooku is a *Star Wars* villain, portrayed by Christopher Lee; and Morpheus, played by Laurence Fishburne, is the protector of humans in *The Matrix* series.

GAME 68

10. Who plays a detective in the 2002 movie *Murder by Numbers*?

a. Kathleen Turner

b. Angelina Jolie

c. Sandra Bullock

d. Cameron Diaz

GAME 68 Q9 ANSWER a

After the swift cancellation of their 1982 television series *Police Squad!*, the filmmaking team of Zucker, Abrahams, and Zucker decided to bring the show's characters to the big screen in *The Naked Gun: From the Files of Police Squad!* (1988). Displaying the same slapstick humor found in their 1980 hit *Airplane!*, the film spawned two sequels.

GAME 13

3. Who plays an incarcerated General in *The Last Castle* (2001)?

a. Michael Douglas

b. Sean Connery

c. Robert Redford

d. Kevin Costner

GAME 13 Q2 ANSWER d
In this film, he plays a young American who is stuck in a foreign prison for drug possession. Phoenix's big-screen acting debut began at age twelve with the film *Space Camp* (1986). Since then, he has appeared in many films, and has received two Oscar nods to date—Best Supporting Actor for *Gladiator* (2000) and Best Actor for *Walk the Line* (2005).

GAME 33

3. What tagline was used for *War of the Worlds* (2005)?

a. "They're already here."

b. "They only want one thing—Destruction!"

c. "This time it's war."

d. "It's closer than you think."

GAME 33 Q2 ANSWER d
In *Volcano*, Jones plays the chief of Office of Emergency Management in Los Angeles, and Heche is a geologist who believes that a volcano is forming under Jones' city. The movie was released on the heels of *Dante's Peak*, which was also about a volcano. When *Eruption* appeared later that year, movie viewers got to choose from three lava-packed tales.

GAME 53

3. Who wrote the screenplay for 1977's *Star Wars: A New Hope*?

a. George Lucas

b. Leigh Brackett

c. Lawrence Kasdan

d. Gloria Katz

GAME 53 Q2 ANSWER a
Just like Yoda and Qui-Gon Jinn, Luke Skywalker wields a green lightsaber in *Return of the Jedi*. Anakin Skywalker and Obi-Wan Kenobi both had blue lightsabers before Anakin became Darth Vader and started using a red one. A purple lightsaber was used by Mace Windu, who was eventually killed by the Emperor in *Revenge of the Sith*.

GAME 73

3. Which Frat Pack film has the line, "She was smiling at how money I am"?

a. *Wedding Crashers* (2005)

b. *Meet the Parents* (2000)

c. *The Break-Up* (2006)

d. *Swingers* (1996)

GAME 73 Q2 ANSWER c
A popular stand-up comedian, late-night talk show host, and TV and movie actor, Joey Bishop was best known as a member of the famous Rat Pack. When he appeared in the 1990 comedy *Betsy's Wedding*, Bishop became the only Rat Pack performer to work with members of the Brat Pack—specifically, actresses Molly Ringwald and Ally Sheedy.

GAME 8

11. "I just felt like ___" is spoken by the title character in *Forrest Gump* (1994).

a. Shrimping
b. Mowing
c. Running
d. Helping

GAME 8 Q10 ANSWER c
Redford plays baseball player Roy Hobbs —a young prodigy whose career is put on hold when he is inexplicably shot by a mysterious woman he meets on a train. In a subsequent comeback years later, the middle-aged Hobbs magically takes a losing 1930s baseball team to the top of the league. *The Natural* earned four Academy Award nominations.

GAME 28

11. Which character wears a trademark white tuxedo jacket?

a. Addison DeWitt
b. Rick Blaine
c. Travis Bickle
d. Monty Berrigan

GAME 28 Q10 ANSWER a
In this popular Disney flick, Professor Ned Brainard (Fred MacMurray) invents a substance called Flubber ("flying rubber") that he uses to make his Model-T fly. The film was a big hit at the box office and was followed by the 1963 sequel *Son of Flubber*. The original movie was remade twice—as a 1988 TV movie, and as a 1997 theatrical film called *Flubber*.

GAME 48

11. Which child star got an Oscar nod at age fourteen for playing a hooker?

a. Jodie Foster
b. Helen Hunt
c. Drew Barrymore
d. Brooke Shields

GAME 48 Q10 ANSWER c
The villainous sea captain was different from the heroic characters that Peck usually played. After receiving poor reviews for his performance, he blamed the script, which was adapted from Herman Melville's 1851 novel. He later admitted that at thirty-eight, he had been too young to play Ahab, who, according to the novel, was an old man.

GAME 68

11. Who is Kevin Costner's character in *The Bodyguard* (1992)?

a. Peter Fallow
b. Steve Malone
c. Andrew Clark
d. Frank Farmer

GAME 68 Q10 ANSWER c
The film is loosely based on the criminal case of Leopold and Loeb, in which university students Nathan Leopold and Richard Loeb kidnapped and murdered a fourteen-year-old boy, believing they could commit the "perfect crime." A number of movies have been inspired by the true story, including *Rope* (1948), *Swoon* (1992), and *Funny Games* (1997).

GAME 13

2. In which country is Joaquin Phoenix imprisoned in *Return to Paradise* (1998)?

a. Iran

b. Canada

c. North Korea

d. Malaysia

GAME 13 Q1 ANSWER c
From Joseph Merrick in *The Elephant Man* (1980), to Winston Smith in *Nineteen Eighty-Four* (1984), to Kane in *Alien* (1979), this former Royal Academy of Dramatic Arts student has played countless memorable roles. The part of Turkish prison inmate Max in this critically acclaimed drama earned Hurt his first Oscar nod—for Best Supporting Actor.

GAME 33

2. What disaster movie stars Tommy Lee Jones and Ann Heche?

a. *Independence Day* (1996)

b. *Titanic* (1997)

c. *Dante's Peak* (1997)

d. *Volcano* (1997)

GAME 33 Q1 ANSWER b
Junger's *The Perfect Storm* recounts the story of the *Andrea Gail*, a fishing boat caught in the monster storm that hit the Eastern Seaboard in October 1991. Although both the book and the film were accused of factual errors, Junger's nonfiction work became a bestseller, and the movie, which starred George Clooney, grossed over $300 million worldwide.

GAME 53

2. What color is Master Yoda's lightsaber in the *Star Wars* movies?

a. Green

b. Purple

c. Blue

d. Red

GAME 53 Q1 ANSWER c
The first Death Star appears in *Revenge of the Sith* and *A New Hope*, while the second partially built Death Star is featured in *Return of the Jedi*. Luke Skywalker destroys the first one with two proton torpedoes in *A New Hope*, and Lando Calrissian and the Rebel Alliance destroy the second one in *Return of the Jedi*.

GAME 73

2. Which Rat Packer's films include *Betsy's Wedding*?

a. Peter Lawford

b. Frank Sinatra

c. Joey Bishop

d. Dean Martin

GAME 73 Q1 ANSWER d
This 1992 Disney film received mixed reviews from critics but ended up being a box office success. It inspired two sequels, released in 1994 and 1996, which were also quite popular. The movie even inspired a professional hockey team: In 1993, Disney founded the Mighty Ducks of Anaheim, currently known in the NHL as the Anaheim Ducks.

GAME 8

12. Harry Osborn is the best friend of which mysterious character?

a. Clark Kent

b. Lamont Cranston

c. Peter Parker

d. Bruce Wayne

GAME 8   Q11   ANSWER c
This is Forrest's simple reason for his epic cross-country run across America, which took "three years, two months, fourteen days and sixteen hours." Tom Hanks plays Forrest, but many of the running scenes were actually shot with Tom's brother, Jim Hanks. In 2007, the American Film Institute ranked this as the #76 Greatest Movie of All Time.

GAME 28

12. What type of film is 1931's *The Public Enemy*?

a. War drama

b. Mystery

c. Gangster flick

d. Detective story

GAME 28   Q11   ANSWER b
In 1942's *Casablanca*, Blaine, played by Humphrey Bogart, is always clad in the tuxedo jacket at his nightclub. Despite having an A-list cast and esteemed writers, no one involved in the film's production expected it to be anything special. But *Casablanca* was nominated for eight Oscars and won three—Best Picture, Director, and Screenplay.

GAME 48

12. Who is Jimmy Stewart's best friend in the 1950 film *Harvey*?

a. His mother

b. A fortune teller

c. An invisible rabbit

d. A talking horse

GAME 48   Q11   ANSWER a
The nomination was for her role as a pre-teen prostitute in *Taxi Driver* (1976). Foster began acting in commercials at age three, and debuted in her first film—Disney's *Napoleon and Samantha*—at age ten. She has earned Oscars for her roles as a rape victim in 1988's *The Accused* and as FBI agent Clarice Starling in 1991's *The Silence of the Lambs*.

GAME 68

12. "Gimme that baby, you warthog from hell!" is spoken in which comedy?

a. *Parenthood* (1989)

b. *Look Who's Talking* (1989)

c. *Raising Arizona* (1987)

d. *Ghostbusters* (1984)

GAME 68   Q11   ANSWER d
This romantic tale was originally intended to be made twenty years earlier with Steve McQueen and Diana Ross in the lead roles. Though that production fell through, the film was eventually shot in 1992 with Whitney Houston and Kevin Costner topping the bill. In honor of McQueen, Costner had his hair cut in the actor's trademark style for the part.

GAME 13

1. John Hurt plays an inmate in which prison drama?

a. *Escape from Alcatraz* (1979)
b. *The Longest Yard* (1974)
c. *Midnight Express* (1978)
d. *Brubaker* (1980)

The answer to this question is on:

page 206, top frame, right side.

GAME 33

1. What disaster film was based on a book by Sebastian Junger?

a. *Gray Lady Down* (1978)
b. *The Perfect Storm* (2000)
c. *The Poseidon Adventure* (1972)
d. *White Squall* (1996)

The answer to this question is on:

page 206, second frame, right side.

GAME 53

1. How many Death Stars are there in the *Star Wars* movies?

a. Four
b. Three
c. Two
d. One

The answer to this question is on:

page 206, third frame, right side.

GAME 73

1. What sport does Brat Packer Emilio Estevez coach in *The Mighty Ducks*?

a. Baseball
b. Football
c. Basketball
d. Hockey

The answer to this question is on:

page 206, bottom frame, right side.

GAME 9

The Directors

*Turn to page 211
for the first question.*

GAME 8 Q12 ANSWER c
Harry, played by James Franco, is the buddy of *Spider-Man* Peter Parker. For the part, Franco had his black hair dyed brown to look more like his onscreen father, played by Willem Dafoe. Speaking of hair, Kirsten Dunst, who played Mary Jane, wore a red wig over her blond tresses. She liked the color so much, she dyed her hair red for the sequels.

GAME 29

Film Firsts

*Turn to page 211
for the first question.*

GAME 28 Q12 ANSWER c
One of Hollywood's earliest gangster movies, *The Public Enemy* contains the famous "grapefruit scene" in which James Cagney smashes a grapefruit into the face of costar Mae Clark. Women's groups across the country rallied in protest of the abuse. In truth, the scene was staged as a practical joke, but the director decided to leave it in.

GAME 49

More Horror Movies

*Turn to page 211
for the first question.*

GAME 48 Q12 ANSWER c
This comedy-drama is based on Mary Chase's 1944 Pulitzer Prize-winning play of the same name. Stewart's portrayal of Elwood P. Dowd, a middle-aged man whose best friend is a mythological rabbit named Harvey, earned him a Best Actor nod. The film also stars Josephine Hull, who won the Best Supporting Actress Oscar for her role as Dowd's sister.

GAME 69

Movies about Writers

*Turn to page 211
for the first question.*

GAME 68 Q12 ANSWER c
Nicolas Cage and Holly Hunter play kidnapping newlyweds in this classic Coen Brothers comedy. In addition to casting the film's leads, the filmmakers also hired fifteen babies to play the Arizona quintuplets. Meant to portray the story's five crawling newborns, a few of the babies had to be let go during the shoot for taking their first steps.

GAME 13

Prison Films

*Turn to page 208
for the first question.*

Turn to page 208

GAME 12 Q12 ANSWER a

A former member of the Deadly Viper Assassination Squad, Thurman plays a woman out for revenge against her former partners in this Quentin Tarantino film. Tarantino offered her the leading role as a present on her thirtieth birthday. Due to the movie's nearly four-hour running time, it was released in two volumes (2003 and 2004).

GAME 33

Disaster Movies

*Turn to page 208
for the first question.*

GAME 32 Q12 ANSWER c

Although *Pete's Dragon* is set in Maine, it was filmed in California. The movie's lighthouse was constructed above Morro Bay and was built with such a large beacon that Disney had to get permission from the Coast Guard to operate it, so as to not confuse ships passing by. This was the first Disney film to be recorded using Dolby Stereo technology.

GAME 53

Star Wars

*Turn to page 208
for the first question.*

GAME 52 Q12 ANSWER b

The comedian actually got his start on television as a contestant on the popular 1980's talent competition *Star Search*. Though he did not win, he soon made his feature-film debut in Spike Lee's *Do the Right Thing* (1989). While starring in a number of comedic blockbusters, Lawrence also starred in his own TV show from 1992 to 1997 called *Martin*.

GAME 73

**Movie "Packs"
Rat, Brat & Frat**

*Turn to page 208
for the first question.*

GAME 72 Q12 ANSWER a

The film was co-written by Steve Martin and features his first starring role on the silver screen. The funny man had already become a stand-up comedy sensation, however, with sold-out arena shows throughout the US. In addition to being an actor and comedian, this Renaissance man is an accomplished writer, musician, and composer.

GAME 9

1. Who directed Denzel Washington in *He Got Game* (1998), *Malcolm X* (1992), and *Inside Man* (2006)?

a. John Singleton

b. Bill Duke

c. Spike Lee

d. Carl Franklin

The answer to this question is on:

page 213, top frame, right side.

GAME 29

1. What was the first movie released with digital sound?

a. *Fantasia*

b. *Jurassic Park*

c. *Return of the Jedi*

d. *The Last Starfighter*

The answer to this question is on:

page 213, second frame, right side.

GAME 49

1. Who is Katie's boyfriend in *Paranormal Activity* (2009)?

a. Micah

b. Kemper

c. Clay

d. Sam

The answer to this question is on:

page 213, third frame, right side.

GAME 69

1. Which writer does Sir Anthony Hopkins play in 1993's *Shadowlands*?

a. Mark Twain

b. C.S. Lewis

c. Balzac

d. T.S. Eliot

The answer to this question is on:

page 213, bottom frame, right side.

GAME 12

12. What is Uma Thurman's code name in the *Kill Bill* films?

a. Black Mamba
b. Cottonmouth
c. Copperhead
d. Sidewinder

GAME 12 Q11 ANSWER b
Tim Curry plays the transvestite doctor from Transsexual, Transylvania, in this British cult classic that has played to packed midnight movie crowds since 1976. Initially, the movie was negatively reviewed by critics due to its overt sexual nature; but its popularity grew with the midnight showings, which still take place in some US cities.

GAME 32

12. Which Disney film is set in the Maine village of Passamaquoddy?

a. *Candleshoe* (1977)
b. *Freaky Friday* (1976)
c. *Pete's Dragon* (1977)
d. *The Apple Dumpling Gang* (1975)

GAME 32 Q11 ANSWER a
George Clooney stars as Danny Ocean in 2001's *Ocean's Eleven*. A huge success in the box office, *Ocean's Eleven* boasts an all-star cast, including Matt Damon as Linus Caldwell, Brad Pitt as Rusty Ryan, Julia Roberts as Danny's ex-wife Tess Ocean, and Andy Garcia as casino owner Terry Benedict. Two successful sequels were subsequently released.

GAME 52

12. In which film does Martin Lawrence play a thief posing as a detective?

a. *National Security* (2003)
b. *Blue Streak* (1999)
c. *Boomerang* (1992)
d. *Bad Boys* (1995)

GAME 52 Q11 ANSWER a
Murray broke onto the scene as a member of the influential sketch-comedy show *Saturday Night Live* in 1976. He soon followed his television success with a string of hit movies, including 1979's *Meatballs*, 1980's *Caddyshack*, and 1981's *Stripes*. Outside of acting, Murray is an avid golfer and a vocal fan of his native Chicago's sports teams.

GAME 72

12. Which movie character states, "I was born a poor black child"?

a. *The Jerk* (1979)
b. *Loser* (2000)
c. *Slacker* (1991)
d. *Kingpin* (1996)

GAME 72 Q11 ANSWER a
When director Steven Spielberg expressed an interest in making a James Bond movie, fellow filmmaker George Lucas told him he had something even better in mind. That something was the archeologist-adventurer Indiana Jones. Though Tom Selleck was offered the part first, it was Harrison Ford who ended up wearing Jones' signature fedora.

GAME 9

2. Sydney Pollack won the Best Director Oscar for which film?

a. *Tootsie* (1982)

b. *Out of Africa* (1985)

c. *The Way We Were* (1973)

d. *Absence of Malice* (1981)

GAME 9 Q1 ANSWER c
Like Martin Scorsese and Oliver Stone before him, Spike Lee studied film at New York University. He first directed Denzel Washington in *Mo' Better Blues* (1990), appearing in the film himself as a supporting character. Lee also appeared as the comical sidekick "Shorty" in *Malcolm X*, for which Washington received a Best Actor Oscar nomination.

GAME 29

2. What was the first movie to win the Academy Award for Best Picture?

a. *Wings* (*1927*)

b. *Cimarron* (*1931*)

c. *Broadway Melody* (*1929*)

d. *The Jazz Singer* (*1927*)

GAME 29 Q1 ANSWER a
The animated film *Fantasia* was re-released several times after its 1940 debut. For the 1982 reissue, Disney completely re-recorded the film's soundtrack with a digital recording arranged by Irwin Kostal. This made it the first movie score to use entirely digital technology. A later reissue (1990) would restore the film's original soundtrack.

GAME 49

2. In the 2007 film *1408*, who is trapped in an evil hotel room?

a. Craig T. Nelson

b. Steven Weber

c. John Cusack

d. Timothy Hutton

GAME 49 Q1 ANSWER a
In this scary film, Micah and girlfriend Katie are played by actors Micah Sloat and Katie Featherston. As for the other answer choices, Kemper is the name of Jessica Biel's boyfriend in the 2003 remake of *The Texas Chainsaw Massacre*; Clay is Alison Lohman's boyfriend in *Drag Me to Hell* (2009), and Sam is Janet Leigh's boyfriend in *Psycho* (1960).

GAME 69

2. Which film features a college professor named Grady Tripp?

a. *Election* (1999)

b. *Finding Forrester* (2000)

c. *Wonder Boys* (2000)

d. *Iris* (2001)

GAME 69 Q1 ANSWER b
Hopkins has portrayed numerous prominent historical figures on screen, including Charles Dickens, Richard Nixon, and Pablo Picasso. The actor, however, is no stranger to fiction. His past roles also feature a number of literary characters, such as Quasimodo, Van Helsing, and Hannibal Lecter, the last of which won him the 1991 Best Actor Oscar.

GAME 12

11. Which film is set in the home of Dr. Frank N. Furter?

a. *Monsters Gone Wild* (2004)

b. *Rocky Horror Picture Show* (1975)

c. *Young Frankenstein* (1974)

d. *Jeepers Creepers* (2001)

GAME 12 Q10 ANSWER c
To date, Matlin, Wyman, and Hunter are the only actresses to receive Oscars for non-speaking roles. Wyman, for her portrayal of a deaf-mute in *Johnny Belinda* (1948); Maitlin (who is deaf in real life), for her American Sign Language performance in *Children of a Lesser God* (1986); and Hunter, for her British Sign Language role in *The Piano* (1993).

GAME 32

11. Which movie character is friends with Linus Caldwell and Rusty Ryan?

a. Danny Ocean

b. Travis Bickle

c. Clark Griswold

d. Jack Sparrow

GAME 32 Q10 ANSWER b
The Mask (1994) stars Jim Carrey as Stanley Ipkiss, who transforms into The Mask. The film also stars Cameron Diaz, who plays Tina Carlyle, in her first movie role. Anna Nicole Smith, Vanessa Williams, and Kristy Swanson were all considered for the part, but producers spotted Diaz as she was leaving a modeling agency and decided she was perfect.

GAME 52

11. Who plays Dustin Hoffman's roommate in *Tootsie* (1982)?

a. Bill Murray

b. Warren Beatty

c. John Candy

d. Tom Cruise

GAME 52 Q10 ANSWER c
This bumbling French detective was famously brought to life by the incomparable Peter Sellers. Also appearing in five sequels to the classic comedy, Sellers originated the character in Blake Edwards' 1963 film *The Pink Panther*. In 2006's *The Pink Panther*, comedian Steve Martin took on the role of Clouseau in a retelling of the series.

GAME 72

11. Of what is Indiana Jones intensely afraid?

a. Snakes

b. Germs

c. Heights

d. Spiders

GAME 72 Q10 ANSWER c
Known by Bond fans simply as "M," the character was first played by Bernard Lee in 1962's *Dr. No* through 1979's *Moonraker*. Robert Brown then took over the role in 1983's *Octopussy*. In 1995, Judi Dench became the first female to hold the title, playing a newly appointed "M" in *Goldeneye*.

GAME 9

3. Who directed The Beatles' first motion picture *A Hard Day's Night* (1964)?

a. Stanley Donen

b. Tony Scott

c. Richard Lester

d. Vincente Minnelli

GAME 9 Q2 ANSWER b
Sydney Pollack had his greatest success as a director with *Out of Africa,* which won a total of seven Oscars. Although he directed and/or produced more than forty films, Pollack also gave strong performances in films like Robert Altman's *The Player* (1992), Woody Allen's *Husbands and Wives* (1992), and Stanley Kubrick's *Eyes Wide Shut* (1999).

GAME 29

3. Which song was played in the first movie to feature rock music?

a. "Rock Around the Clock"

b. "Hard Day's Night"

c. "Love Me Tender"

d. "Where the Boys Are"

GAME 29 Q2 ANSWER a
Set in World War I, *Wings* stars Clara Bow, Charles "Buddy" Rogers, and Richard Arlen, and features Gary Cooper in a small role that was said to launch his career. *Wings* was not only the first movie to win the Best Picture Academy Award (then called Best Picture, Production), but also the only silent film to ever win that award.

GAME 49

3. Boris Karloff stars in which classic 1931 monster film?

a. *The Mummy's Curse*

b. *Nosferatu*

c. *Frankenstein*

d. *The Vampire Bat*

GAME 49 Q2 ANSWER c
Based on a short story by writer Stephen King, *1408* also stars Samuel L. Jackson as the hotel manager Gerald Olin. This is not the only time that Stephen King has written about a haunted hotel room. In his 1977 novel *The Shining,* young Danny Torrance is warned to avoid room 217 (changed to room 237 in Stanley Kubrick's 1980 film adaptation).

GAME 69

3. Which writer did Bill Murray portray in a major motion picture?

a. Jack Kerouac

b. Hunter S. Thompson

c. Ernest Hemingway

d. Norman Mailer

GAME 69 Q2 ANSWER c
Michael Douglas agreed to lower his usual salary in order to be given the role of the pot-smoking prof in this movie based on the Michael Chabon novel of the same name. Though he was known for playing slick executives, the part required Douglas to gain twenty-five pounds. He accomplished the feat by adopting a steady diet of junk food and beer.

GAME 12

10. Which actress did *not* win an Oscar for a non-speaking role?

a. Marlee Matlin
b. Jane Wyman
c. Katharine Hepburn
d. Holly Hunter

GAME 12 Q9 ANSWER b
The film won the Best Original Song Oscar for "Evergreen," which was written by Streisand and Paul Williams. The movie itself is a remake of two previous films—a 1937 drama starring Janet Gaynor and a 1954 musical with Judy Garland. The earlier films centered on the movie industry; the '76 film adapted the story to the music industry.

GAME 32

10. Which character says, "Hold on sugar, Daddy's got a sweet tooth tonight"?

a. Austin Powers
b. The Mask
c. Beetlejuice
d. James Bond

GAME 32 Q9 ANSWER d
Both Arsenio Hall and Eddie Murphy portrayed several characters in this film. It was the first time Murphy played multiple characters in a movie, and the practice soon became a trademark of his work. He portrayed several different people in 1996's *The Nutty Professor,* 2000's *The Nutty Professor II,* 1999's *Bowfinger,* and 2008's *Meet Dave.*

GAME 52

10. Which detective tracks down a jewel thief known as "the Phantom"?

a. Sam Spade
b. Frank Drebin
c. Inspector Clouseau
d. Philip Marlowe

GAME 52 Q9 ANSWER b
Although the action takes place in the fictional town of Woodsboro, this horror flick was shot in Santa Rosa, California. It reignited interest in the slasher movie genre during the '90s and spawned numerous imitators, including *I Know What You Did Last Summer* (1997) and *Urban Legend* (1998)—not to mention the *Scary Movie* series of parodies.

GAME 72

10. Which movie character's boss is Sir Miles Messervy?

a. Emma Peel
b. Charlie Chan
c. James Bond
d. The Saint

GAME 72 Q9 ANSWER b
Grant is remembered not only for his acting, but also for his business sense. By deciding not to renew his contract with Paramount, he became the first actor to break free from the established studio system. Allowing Grant the ability to work with any studio he chose, this action marked the beginning of the end of studio control over actors' careers.

GAME 9

4. George Stevens won an Oscar for directing which 1956 film?

a. *The Searchers*
b. *Giant*
c. *I Remember Mama*
d. *Shane*

GAME 9 Q3 ANSWER c
One of several brilliant British directors of the 1960s, Richard Lester's distinct style of filmmaking helped redefine British cinema. In 1965, he also directed the second Beatles movie, *Help!* His work on the Beatles films is often cited as the precursor to music videos. Lester also directed both *Superman II* (1980) and *Superman III* (1983).

GAME 29

4. What was the first film to win all five major Academy Awards?

a. *Gone With the Wind* (1939)
b. *The Last Emperor* (1987)
c. *Vertigo* (1958)
d. *It Happened One Night* (1934)

GAME 29 Q3 ANSWER a
Performed by Bill Haley & His Comets, "Rock Around the Clock" was run under the opening credits of the 1955 film *Blackboard Jungle* to represent the music that young people favored at the time. Although the song had been a commercial disappointment when released in 1954, it took off after the film's debut, eventually selling 25 million copies.

GAME 49

4. Who costars with Donald Pleasance in 1984's *Terror in the Aisles*?

a. Nancy Allen
b. Jamie Lee Curtis
c. Janet Leigh
d. Angie Dickinson

GAME 49 Q3 ANSWER c
Written by Mary Wollstonecraft Shelley and published in 1818 as *Frankenstein; or, The Modern Prometheus,* director Carl Laemmle Jr.'s 1931 film is just one of sixteen movies in which the legendary Karloff appeared. He went on to portray Frankenstein's monster again in *Bride of Frankenstein* (1935) and *Son of Frankenstein* (1939).

GAME 69

4. Who plays writer George Plimpton in the 1968 movie *Paper Lion*?

a. James Coburn
b. James Caan
c. Alan Alda
d. Tony Randall

GAME 69 Q3 ANSWER b
The "Gonzo journalist" has actually been portrayed on film twice. Murray plays Thompson in *Where the Buffalo Roam* (1980), while Johnny Depp plays Thompson's autobiographical character Raoul Duke in 1998's *Fear and Loathing in Las Vegas.* Depp is also scheduled to appear as another of Thompson's pseudonyms in the movie version of *The Rum Diary.*

GAME 12

9. Which Barbra Streisand movie features the song "Evergreen"?

a. *Funny Lady* (1975)
b. *A Star Is Born* (1976)
c. *The Way We Were* (1973)
d. *Yentl* (1983)

GAME 12 Q8 ANSWER c
After a group of street thugs break into his home, kill his wife, and rape his daughter, mild-mannered Paul Kersey (Bronson) becomes a man bent on revenge. Although the film was criticized for advocating vigilantism and for its graphic violence, it was a major commercial success, generating four sequels over the next twenty years.

GAME 32

9. Who plays Eddie Murphy's best friend in 1988's *Coming to America*?

a. Rick James
b. Richard Pryor
c. Wesley Snipes
d. Arsenio Hall

GAME 32 Q8 ANSWER b
This critically acclaimed film was inspired by a 1972 *Life* magazine article on bank robbers John Wojtowicz and Salvatore Naturile. The article described Wojtowicz as someone with the "good looks of an Al Pacino or Dustin Hoffman." Pacino was cast in the leading role, but at one point when he briefly quit the project, the part was offered to Hoffman.

GAME 52

9. Which film is set in the town of Woodsboro, California?

a. *Spider-Man* (2002)
b. *Scream* (1996)
c. *Buffy the Vampire Slayer* (1992)
d. *Scary Movie* (2000)

GAME 52 Q8 ANSWER b
Before becoming an actress and sex symbol, Welch modeled for department store Neiman Marcus and worked as a cocktail waitress. After a number of bit parts, she won a lead role in 1966's sci-fi smash *Fantastic Voyage*, which made her a star. She then landed other memorable parts in such films as *One Million Years B.C.* (1966) and *Bedazzled* (1967).

GAME 72

9. Which leading man retired after filming *Walk, Don't Run* (1966)?

a. Humphrey Bogart
b. Cary Grant
c. James Stewart
d. Burt Lancaster

GAME 72 Q8 ANSWER d
While fourteen hundred actresses were interviewed and four hundred were asked to read for the role, it was Vivien Leigh who got the part and went on to win the Best Actress Oscar for her performance. One Hollywood rumor suggests that the nationwide hunt for the film's lead was a publicity stunt and that Leigh had signed on before it even began.

GAME 9

5. How many major characters are there in Robert Altman's film *Nashville* (1975)?

a. 48
b. 36
c. 24
d. 1

GAME 9 Q4 ANSWER b
George Stevens was up for the Best Director Oscar that year along with John Ford, who had directed John Wayne in *The Searchers*. *Giant* featured the third and final screen performance by *Rebel Without a Cause* star James Dean, and also featured appearances by Dean's *Rebel Without a Cause* costars Dennis Hopper and Sal Mineo.

GAME 29

5. What was the first feature film shown in Technicolor?

a. *Becky Sharp* (1935)
b. *Jane Eyre* (1944)
c. *The Wizard of Oz* (1939)
d. *Gone With the Wind* (1939)

GAME 29 Q4 ANSWER d
Few people thought that *It Happened One Night* would garner five Oscars. Star Claudette Colbert didn't attend the awards ceremony because she felt she wouldn't win Best Actress, and was rushed to the Biltmore Hotel at the last moment to accept her statuette. The film also won awards for Best Actor, Best Director, Best Picture, and Best Screenplay.

GAME 49

5. Which "zombie" movie was *not* directed by George A. Romero?

a. *Land of the Dead* (2005)
b. *Dawn of the Dead* (1978)
c. *Day of the Dead* (1985)
d. *Zombieland* (2009)

GAME 49 Q4 ANSWER a
In addition to Pleasance (known best to horror fans as Dr. Loomis in John Carpenter's *Halloween* and *Halloween II*), *Terror in the Aisles* features Nancy Allen four years after appearing in husband Brian De Palma's 1980 masterpiece, *Dressed to Kill*. She also appeared in his films *Carrie* (1976) and *Blow Out* (1981) before they divorced in 1984.

GAME 69

5. Which movie chronicles the adventures of romance writer Joan Wilder?

a. *Nikita* (1990)
b. *The African Queen* (1951)
c. *Isn't She Great* (2000)
d. *Romancing the Stone* (1984)

GAME 69 Q4 ANSWER c
In an early film role, Alda plays the adventurous journalist who tried out for the 1963 Detroit Lions to discover how the average person might stack up against professionals. Having contracted polio as a child, the *M*A*S*H* star is fortunate to even walk properly. Thanks to early treatment of the disease, he was able to avoid its long-term effects.

GAME 12

8. In which film does Charles Bronson play a vigilante?

a. *Death Hunt* (1981)

b. *10 to Midnight* (1983)

c. *Death Wish* (1974)

d. *The Mechanic* (1972)

GAME 12 Q7 ANSWER a
Although 1973's *Enter the Dragon*, starring Bruce Lee, is still considered the most popular kung fu film, *Five Fingers of Death*—released earlier that same year—is credited with kicking off the craze. *Thunderfist*, also released in 1973, was a box office bomb, while 1983's *Revenge of the Ninja* is considered among the best of the genre.

GAME 32

8. In what motion picture are Sonny and Sal the criminal duo?

a. *The Usual Suspects* (1995)

b. *Dog Day Afternoon* (1975)

c. *Scarface* (1983)

d. *Mean Streets* (1973)

GAME 32 Q7 ANSWER a
Edward Scissorhands (1990) tells the story of Edward, an artificial man whose inventor dies before giving his creation real hands. This film was the first collaboration between Johnny Depp, who plays Edward, and director Tim Burton. To date, they have worked on six other films together, including *Sleepy Hollow* (1999) and *Alice in Wonderland* (2010).

GAME 52

8. What does Raquel Welch play in *Kansas City Bomber* (1972)?

a. A terrorist

b. A roller derby queen

c. A civil rights worker

d. A demolition expert

GAME 52 Q7 ANSWER a
Cary Grant plays advertising executive Roger Thornhill in this tale of mistaken identity. Having just starred in Hitchcock's 1958 movie *Vertigo*, actor Jimmy Stewart was keen on landing the role, but Hitchcock felt that he looked too old for the part, and gave it to Grant (who was actually four years older than Stewart).

GAME 72

8. Which film character is known for saying "Fiddledeedee"?

a. Nora Charles

b. Ma Kettle

c. Blondie

d. Scarlett O'Hara

GAME 72 Q7 ANSWER c
The Antarean life force rejuvenates a group of aging friends in this movie directed by Ron Howard. Wilford Brimley, Hume Cronyn, Jessica Tandy, and Don Ameche (who won an Oscar for the role) are among the film's stellar cast. During production, Brimley was only age fifty and had to dye his hair gray to appear much older.

GAME 9

6. Warren Beatty starred in and directed all of these films except:

a. *Love Affair* (1994)

b. *Bugsy* (1991)

c. *Reds* (1981)

d. *Heaven Can Wait* (1978)

GAME 9 Q5 ANSWER c
Robert Altman's *Nashville* is a complex tapestry of film narrative spun from the tangled lives of twenty-four separate characters. In 1978, he outdid himself with a cast of forty-eight characters in *A Wedding*. By 1984, Altman reversed course with *Secret Honor* (1984)—a film about President Nixon that starred only one actor (Philip Baker Hall).

GAME 29

6. What special-effects system was first used in the 1974 movie *Earthquake*?

a. Cinemascope

b. Sensurround

c. 3-D

d. Kaleidoscope

GAME 29 Q5 ANSWER a
Before *Becky Sharp's* 1935 release, three-strip Technicolor was used only for short movies, such as Disney's animated *The Three Little Pigs* (1933). Although *Becky* was not a great success, it made enough money to convince others that Technicolor was worth the added production costs, and the system dominated the industry until the 1950s.

GAME 49

6. Which actor appeared in the first of the *Saw* films in 2004?

a. Morgan Freeman

b. Danny Glover

c. Denzel Washington

d. Gregory Hines

GAME 49 Q5 ANSWER d
Directed by Ruben Fleischer and starring Woody Harrelson, *Zombieland* was one of 2009's top-grossing films. Ironically, the word "zombie" does not appear in the title of any of George A. Romero's famous zombie films. His first, *Night of the Living Dead* (1968), was shot in black and white on location in Pittsburgh, Pennsylvania.

GAME 69

6. Who plays suicidal writer Virginia Woolf in *The Hours* (2002)?

a. Elisabeth Shue

b. Nicole Kidman

c. Demi Moore

d. Cate Blanchett

GAME 69 Q5 ANSWER d
Feeling that the film's director, Robert Zemeckis, had done a poor job, 20th Century Fox studios removed him from his next film, *Cocoon* (1985). *Romancing's* unexpected success—and Zemeckis' suddenly free schedule—allowed the filmmaker to concentrate on his own project, *Back to the Future*, which went on to become the biggest hit of 1985.

GAME 12

7. Which martial arts film started the kung fu craze of the 1970s?

a. *Five Fingers of Death*
b. *Enter the Dragon*
c. *Thunderfist*
d. *Revenge of the Ninja*

GAME 12 Q6 ANSWER b

Hepburn won the award for her portrayal of Eleanor of Aquitaine in the historic 1968 film *The Lion in Winter*. Streisand earned hers for the role of Fanny Brice in *Funny Girl*. In 1931, there was also a tie for the Best Actor Oscar. Frederick March and Wallace Beery both won for their roles in *Dr. Jekyll and Mr. Hyde* and *The Champ* respectively.

GAME 32

7. Who replies "I can't" when his love asks to be held?

a. Edward Scissorhands
b. Forrest Gump
c. Chance the Gardener
d. Frankenstein's Monster

GAME 32 Q6 ANSWER d

Frank, who looks like a normal dog but is actually an alien, appears in both *Men in Black* (1997) and *Men in Black II* (2002). He is played by Mushu, a trained pug, and is voiced by puppeteer and voice actor Tim Blaney. Blaney has worked on many popular TV shows and movies, including *Short Circuit* (1986) and *How the Grinch Stole Christmas* (2000).

GAME 52

7. Which Hitchcock film's main character escapes an airplane attack?

a. *North by Northwest* (1959)
b. *Saboteur* (1942)
c. *The 39 Steps* (1935)
d. *Notorious* (1946)

GAME 52 Q6 ANSWER d

Born Winona Laura Horowitz, the Oscar-nominated actress changed her surname to Ryder for her movie debut in 1986's *Lucas*. She came to prominence, however, as teen goth Lydia Deetz in Tim Burton's 1988 ghost story *Beetlejuice*. She has since worked with other respected directors, including Francis Ford Coppola and Martin Scorsese.

GAME 72

7. From which planet do the peaceful aliens hail in 1985's *Cocoon*?

a. Etheria
b. Caladan
c. Antarea
d. Hyperion

GAME 72 Q6 ANSWER d

After working in a number of stage productions, Wilder was given a minor part in this true-crime story. He then won a leading role in 1968's *The Producers*, which marked the beginning of a fruitful filmmaking relationship with director Mel Brooks. Brooks would also direct him in the cult comedies *Blazing Saddles* (1974) and *Young Frankenstein* (1974).

GAME 9

7. Who directed the contemporary "film noir" classic *Chinatown* (1974)?

a. Jack Nicholson
b. Roman Polanski
c. John Huston
d. Robert Towne

GAME 9 Q6 ANSWER b
While he earned a Best Actor Oscar nomination for his work in *Bugsy*, the film was actually directed by Oscar-winner Barry Levinson. *Heaven Can Wait* (1978) was a remake of the 1941 film *Here Comes Mr. Jordan*, and it was Beatty's directorial debut. In 1982, Beatty won the Best Director Oscar for his film *Reds*.

GAME 29

7. Who starred in the first feature-length talking picture?

a. Pee-wee Herman
b. Charlie Chaplin
c. Al Jolson
d. Fatty Arbuckle

GAME 29 Q6 ANSWER b
Sensurround was developed in the 1970s to create realistic vibrations and tremors during the showing of *Earthquake* (1974). The process was controversial, as it caused damage to theaters and nearby buildings, and made some moviegoers sick. Nevertheless, Sensurround was also used in *Midway* (1976), *Rollercoaster* (1977), and *Saga of a Star World* (1978).

GAME 49

7. Which film does *not* involve a terrorized couple?

a. *The Vanishing* (1993)
b. *The Strangers* (2008)
c. *The Others* (2001)
d. *Dead Calm* (1989)

GAME 49 Q6 ANSWER b
Upon its release, *Saw* was seen as one of the first in a new wave of ultra-gory and brutally sadistic horror films that many critics derided as "torture porn." Nevertheless, *Saw* was a box-office smash and has led to a number of sequels. Glover appears in the film as detective David Tapp, and made a cameo as that character in 2008's *Saw V*.

GAME 69

7. Which film stars Nicolas Cage as a screenwriter and his twin brother?

a. *City of Angels* (1998)
b. *Leaving Las Vegas* (1995)
c. *Adaptation* (2002)
d. *Windtalkers* (2002)

GAME 69 Q6 ANSWER b
Kidman was director Stephen Daldry's first choice to portray the famous English novelist. Not only did the actress wear a prosthetic nose and learn to write with her right hand, she also read all of the late Woolf's personal letters in order to inhabit the role accurately. Her hard work was rewarded with the 2002 Academy Award for Best Actress.

GAME 12

6. Who tied Katharine Hepburn for a Best Actress Oscar in 1969?

a. Mia Farrow

b. Barbra Streisand

c. Julie Andrews

d. Faye Dunaway

GAME 12 Q5 ANSWER c

Starring Tom Hanks as the kid whose wish to be "big" comes true, this heart-warming comedy was directed by Penny Marshall—Garry's sister. It made her the first female to direct a movie that grossed over $100 million at the box office. An instant hit, *Big* is ranked #42 on American Film Institute's "100 Years …100 Laughs" list.

GAME 32

6. Which film series features Frank, a tough-talking pug?

a. *Babe*

b. *X-Men*

c. *The Rescuers*

d. *Men in Black*

GAME 32 Q5 ANSWER a

Day performed "Secret Love" in the 1953 Western comedy *Calamity Jane*, in which she played the title character. Day also recorded a single of the song, which reached #1 on multiple music charts in 1954. Many artists, including Freddy Fender, George Michael, and Mandy Moore, have recorded cover versions of this popular song.

GAME 52

6. In which black comedy does Winona Ryder play an unwitting murderer?

a. *Mermaids* (1990)

b. *Edward Scissorhands* (1990)

c. *Beetlejuice* (1988)

d. *Heathers* (1988)

GAME 52 Q5 ANSWER d

The title track to Ivan Reitman's spooky smash hit film, "Ghostbusters" was written and performed by Ray Parker, Jr., and earned him an Oscar nod for Best Song. Parker, however, was sued for plagiarism by musician Huey Lewis, who felt that the song's intro melody was a rip-off of his tune "I Want a New Drug." The case was settled out of court.

GAME 72

6. Which 1967 film marks Gene Wilder's big screen debut?

a. *The Graduate*

b. *Cool Hand Luke*

c. *Thoroughly Modern Millie*

d. *Bonnie and Clyde*

GAME 72 Q5 ANSWER c

Wood began her acting career as a child, coming to prominence in the Christmas classic *Miracle on 34th Street* (1947). Her role in this angst-filled Nicholas Ray film helped marked her transition into a mature actress and resulted in her first Oscar nomination. She went on to appear in such movies as *West Side Story* (1961) and *Gypsy* (1962).

GAME 9

8. Who directed the first *Harry Potter* movie?

a. Alfonso Cuarón

b. Chris Columbus

c. Mike Newell

d. David Yates

GAME 9 Q7 ANSWER b

Roman Polanski earned a Best Director Oscar nomination for *Chinatown*, and won the Golden Globe Award for this category. He appears briefly in *Chinatown* as a thug who slices Jack Nicholson's nose with a knife. Legendary director John Huston is also in the film, which features an Oscar-winning screenplay by Robert Towne.

GAME 29

8. Which 1929 picture is recognized by many as Hollywood's first complete musical?

a. *Big Business*

b. *Dance Hall*

c. *Top Hat*

d. *The Broadway Melody*

GAME 29 Q7 ANSWER c

The Jazz Singer (1927) was the first "talkie," heralding a new age of film. Al Jolson was not first choice for the title role, but was given the lead only after negotiations failed with Eddie Cantor and George Jessel. Although Jolson was to make many more movies, he was always best known for his portrayal of jazz singer Jack Robin.

GAME 49

8. *The Final Conflict* is the subtitle to the third film in which horror series?

a. *The Omen*

b. *A Nightmare on Elm Street*

c. *Halloween*

d. *The Exorcist*

GAME 49 Q7 ANSWER c

Based loosely on the 1898 Henry James novella *The Turn of the Screw*, *The Others* stars Nicole Kidman as a mother in post-World War II Britain who feels she and her two children are haunted by ghosts. Two years earlier, Kidman and then-husband Tom Cruise starred as a tormented couple in Stanley Kubrick's final film *Eyes Wide Shut* (1999).

GAME 69

8. Which writer's life is portrayed in 1980's *Heart Beat*?

a. Jack Kerouac

b. Truman Capote

c. F. Scott Fitzgerald

d. Charles Bukowski

GAME 69 Q7 ANSWER c

The versatile actor nabbed an Academy Award nomination for his portrayal of Charlie Kaufman (the real-life author of the film's screenplay) and Kaufman's fictional twin brother Donald. Though the role did not win Cage an Oscar, costar Chris Cooper did take home the Academy Award for Best Supporting Actor for his performance in this eccentric movie.

GAME 12

5. Which film was *not* directed by Garry Marshall?

a. *Pretty Woman* (1990)

b. *The Other Sister* (1999)

c. *Big* (1988)

d. *The Princess Diaries* (2001)

GAME 12 Q4 ANSWER c
After appearing in films for over two decades, Bullock earned her first Oscar for her role as Leigh Anne Tuohy in *The Blind Side*—a 2009 Best Picture nominee. Ironically, for her work that same year in *All About Steve,* she was given the Worst Actress Razzie. And for *The Proposal,* her third film that year, she received a Golden Globe nod.

GAME 32

5. Who sang the Oscar-winning song "Secret Love"?

a. Doris Day

b. Marilyn Monroe

c. Jane Russell

d. Betty Grable

GAME 32 Q4 ANSWER c
Despite starring in only three movies, James Dean is an acting legend. His career was cut short when he died in a tragic car accident at age twenty-four. Dean was the first actor to receive a posthumous Academy Award nomination for Best Actor, and the only actor to have two posthumous nominations—for 1955's *East of Eden* and 1956's *Giant.*

GAME 52

5. Which movie's theme song reached #1 on the Billboard charts?

a. *The Goonies* (1985)

b. *Goldfinger* (1964)

c. *Pretty in Pink* (1986)

d. *Ghostbusters* (1984)

GAME 52 Q4 ANSWER a
The large ensemble cast of this Oscar-winning drama also includes Terrence Howard, Ryan Phillippe, Thandie Newton, and Brendan Fraser. In a surprise upset, this dark horse Oscar nominee beat the odds-on favorite *Brokeback Mountain* for Best Picture, and also took home the honors for Best Original Screenplay and Best Editing.

GAME 72

5. Who plays James Dean's girlfriend in 1955's *Rebel Without a Cause*?

a. Paula Prentiss

b. Ann-Margret

c. Natalie Wood

d. Angie Dickinson

GAME 72 Q4 ANSWER a
Directed by Penny Marshall, this fictionalized comedy-drama is about the real all-girl pro baseball league that was formed during WWII. Tom Hanks, Madonna, and Geena Davis are among its stellar cast. (Marshall's daughter Tracy Reiner plays "Betty Spaghetti.") The real-life players appear in the scene at the Hall of Fame and during the end credits.

GAME 9

9. Who directed the 1969 counterculture film classic *Easy Rider*?

a. Jack Nicholson
b. Bob Rafelson
c. Peter Fonda
d. Dennis Hopper

GAME 9 Q8 ANSWER b
Chris Columbus directed the first two *Home Alone* movies in the '90s for writer/producer John Hughes. He also directed the first two films in the *Harry Potter* series—*Harry Potter and the Sorcerer's Stone* (2001) along with *Harry Potter and the Chamber of Secrets* (2002). Columbus's credits also include *Mrs. Doubtfire* (1993) and *Rent* (2005).

GAME 29

9. What was the first commercial color-film system?

a. Daguerrotype
b. Kodachrome
c. Fujitsu
d. Kinemacolor

GAME 29 Q8 ANSWER d
Harry Beaumont directed this musical, which includes the George M. Cohan classic, "Give My Regards to Broadway." *The Broadway Melody* was MGM's first musical, Hollywood's first all-talking musical (*The Jazz Singer* was only a partial "talkie"), and the first sound film to win an Academy Award for Best Picture. It even included a Technicolor sequence.

GAME 49

9. Which actor is shot to death in *Salem's Lot: The Movie* (1979)?

a. Elisha Cook, Jr.
b. James Mason
c. Marie Windsor
d. Fred Willard

GAME 49 Q8 ANSWER a
Before playing heroic paleontologist Dr. Alan Grant in Steven Spielberg's hit *Jurassic Park* (1993), Sam Neill won the attention of moviegoers in *The Omen III: The Final Conflict* (1981). In it, he plays Damien Thorn, the grown son of Satan who rises in the world of politics to prevent the second coming of Jesus, as prophesied in the Bible.

GAME 69

9. Which actor plays journalist John Reed in *Reds* (1981)?

a. Dustin Hoffman
b. Elliott Gould
c. Warren Beatty
d. James Caan

GAME 69 Q8 ANSWER a
Nick Nolte plays Kerouac's free-spirited friend Neal Cassady in this movie based on the Beat Generation literary movement. Despite Nolte's realistic performance, Beat poet Allen Ginsberg objected to the movie from the outset. The character of Ira was created to represent Ginsberg, who did not want his name associated with the project.

4. Who won a Best Actress Oscar and a Razzie in the same year?

a. Meryl Streep
b. Halle Berry
c. Sandra Bullock
d. Hilary Swank

GAME 12

GAME 12 Q3 ANSWER a
Mel Gibson plays the Scottish warrior in the 1995 historic drama *Braveheart*. He also directed and produced the film, which received ten Academy Awards nominations and earned five, including Best Director and Picture. The movie also generated increased tourism in Scotland, particularly those places where Wallace fought.

---

4. Which actor played both Cal Trask and Jett Rink?

a. Clark Gable
b. Rock Hudson
c. James Dean
d. Spencer Tracy

GAME 32

GAME 32 Q3 ANSWER b
McQueen plays "The Kid," a budding poker player who challenges the more experienced Lancey Howard to a game. Many professional poker players have commented on the film's final hand, in which The Kid's full house loses to Howard's straight flush, saying that the odds of those hands appearing in the same deal are worse than 45 million to 1.

---

4. Which film stars Matt Dillon, Don Cheadle, and Sandra Bullock?

a. *Crash* (2004)
b. *Babel* (2005)
c. *Mulholland Drive* (2001)
d. *Love Actually* (2003)

GAME 52

GAME 52 Q3 ANSWER c
Wayne won the only Oscar of his career for his performance as US Marshal Reuben "Rooster" J. Cogburn in the 1969 Western *True Grit*. The sixty-two-year-old actor famously accepted the Best Actor award by saying, "If I had known this, I would've put that patch on thirty-five years ago." The film also earned an Oscar nod for Best Song "True Grit."

---

4. Which movie gives us "Betty Spaghetti" and "All-the-Way May"?

a. *A League of Their Own* (1992)
b. *Some Like It Hot* (1959)
c. *Waitress* (2007)
d. *Talladega Nights* (2006)

GAME 72

GAME 72 Q3 ANSWER c
Lewis wrote, starred in, and directed this 1960 black-and-white comedy (his first) about the antics of a helpful but clumsy bellboy at a luxurious hotel. The movie was shot at Miami Beach's beautiful Fontainebleau Resort. Filming took place during the day and Lewis performed in the Fontainebleau's nightclub in the evenings.

GAME 9

10. Which gangster saga was *not* directed by Brian De Palma?

a. *The Cotton Club* (1984)

b. *The Untouchables* (1987)

c. *Scarface* (1983)

d. *Carlito's Way* (1993)

GAME 9 Q9 ANSWER d
Directed by Dennis Hopper, *Easy Rider* was based on a script written by Hopper and Peter Fonda together with hipster novelist Terry Southern. Shot on a shoe-string budget, this movie earned Jack Nicholson his first Best Supporting Actor Oscar nomination. Hopper's second film, *The Last Movie* (1971), was never re-leased commercially in the US.

GAME 29

10. Who was the first black performer to win an Academy Award?

a. Sidney Poitier

b. Hattie McDaniel

c. Butterfly McQueen

d. Bill "Bojangles" Robinson

GAME 29 Q9 ANSWER d
Developed in England by George Albert Smith and Edward R. Turner, and then launched by Charles Urban, Kinemacolor worked by photographing and projecting black-and-white film strips behind alter-nating green and red filters. The process was used commercially between 1908 and 1914, and was very successful in Europe, but less so in the United States.

GAME 49

10. The real-life *Amityville Horror* house stands in which US state?

a. New York

b. Texas

c. California

d. Wisconsin

GAME 49 Q10 ANSWER b
Mason's character Straker is shot at the end of the film by David Soul's character Ben Mears. Interestingly, James Mason shot Peter Sellers dead in Stanley Kubrick's 1962 film *Lolita*—and in 1956, Elisha Cook, Jr. shot Marie Wind-sor (both later appeared with Mason in *Salem's Lot*) in another Kubrick film called *The Killing*.

GAME 69

10. What does the title character attempt to write in *Barton Fink* (1991)?

a. A novel

b. A play

c. An opera

d. A screenplay

GAME 69 Q9 ANSWER c
In addition to his nomination for Best Ac-tor, Beatty received Oscar nods for writ-ing, directing, and producing the film. After Orson Welles, the multi-talented star is the second person ever to be con-sidered for awards in all four categories for a single film. He is the *only* person, however, to do so twice, thanks to 1978's *Heaven Can Wait*.

GAME 12

3. Which epic film hero's last word is "Freee-dommmmm!"?

a. William Wallace

b. Maximus Meridius

c. Judah Ben-Hur

d. Spartacus

GAME 12 Q2 ANSWER d

All these films were nominees, but it was the musical adaptation of Charles Dickens' *Oliver Twist* that won the award. To date, it is the only G-rated film (since the MPAA rating system was established in 1968) to win an Oscar. *The Wizard of Oz* lost to *Gone With the Wind; The Yearling* lost to *The Best Years of Our Lives;* and *Babe* lost to *Braveheart*.

GAME 32

3. What role does Steve McQueen play in 1965's *The Cincinnati Kid*?

a. A fighter pilot

b. A high-stakes gambler

c. A gunslinger

d. A cat burglar

GAME 32 Q2 ANSWER b

The romantic comedy *As Good as It Gets* also stars Helen Hunt, who took home an Academy Award for her leading role as waitress Carol Connelly. Hunt also won a Golden Globe and an Emmy that year, making her the second actress to accomplish that feat. (Liza Minnelli was the first in 1973, and Helen Mirren became the third in 2007.)

GAME 52

3. Who wore an eye patch in his Oscar-winning role?

a. Michael Douglas

b. Marlon Brando

c. John Wayne

d. Jack Lemmon

GAME 52 Q2 ANSWER c

Willis' big break came in the role of David Addison on the 1980's TV show *Moonlighting*. After a few unsuccessful turns on the big screen, the actor shot to fame as Officer John McClane in 1988's *Die Hard*. Coincidentally, the part was initially offered to his future Planet Hollywood business partners, Arnold Schwarzenegger and Sylvester Stallone.

GAME 72

3. In which Jerry Lewis film does his character never speak?

a. *The Big Mouth* (1967)

b. *Hardly Working* (1980)

c. *The Bellboy* (1960)

d. *Cinderfella* (1960)

GAME 72 Q2 ANSWER a

Claire Danes portrays aspiring artist Mirabelle Buttersfield, who works as a salesgirl behind a glove counter at a Beverly Hills department store. The movie is based on a somewhat autobiographical novella written by actor-comedian Steve Martin, who wrote the screenplay and also stars in the film as one of Mirabelle's love interests.

GAME 9

11. Which film did Rob Reiner both appear in and direct?

a. *A Few Good Men* (1992)

b. *This Is Spinal Tap* (1984)

c. *When Harry Met Sally* (1989)

d. *The American President* (1990)

GAME 9 Q10 ANSWER a
Paired again with *Godfather* producer Robert Evans, director Francis Ford Coppola did his best to recreate the Harlem jazz world of the 1930s in this film with only marginal success. Meanwhile, Brian De Palma had major success with *The Untouchables*, which brought Sean Connery an Oscar for Best Supporting Actor.

GAME 29

11. What was the first Western to win the Academy Award for Best Picture?

a. *The Last Outlaw* (1936)

b. *Cimarron* (1931)

c. *The Virginian* (1929)

d. *Riders of the Purple Sage* (1931)

GAME 29 Q10 ANSWER b
At the 1940 Academy Awards ceremony, Hattie McDaniel accepted the Best Supporting Actress award for her role as Mammy in the epic film *Gone With the Wind* (1939). Over twenty years later, Sidney Poitier became the first black performer to win the Best Actor award for his portrayal of itinerant worker Homer Smith in *Lilies of the Field* (1963).

GAME 49

11. In 2007's *Sweeney Todd,* which character dies first?

a. Beadle Bamford

b. Judge Turpin

c. Adolfo Pirelli

d. Mrs. Lovett

GAME 49 Q10 ANSWER a
Located in the Long Island town of Amityville, NY, this house inspired the 1979 movie, a 2005 remake, and a number of sequels. California is the location of the Bates Motel in the *Psycho* films, and Texas is home to *The Texas Chainsaw Massacre* carnage. Interestingly, both stories were influenced by Wisconsin's real-life serial killer Ed Gein.

GAME 69

11. Who is William Holden's character in *Sunset Boulevard* (1950)?

a. Jack Towne

b. Jim Thomas

c. Joe Gillis

d. Jerry Scott

GAME 69 Q10 ANSWER d
Loosely based on 1930s playwright Clifford Odets, the part of Barton Fink was written specifically for actor John Turturro. In order to appear comfortable using a typewriter, Turturro diligently learned how to touch type. The skill went relatively unappreciated, however, as his character suffers from writer's block throughout most of the movie.

GAME 12

2. Which of the following family films won a Best Picture Oscar?

a. *The Wizard of Oz* (1939)
b. *The Yearling* (1946)
c. *Babe* (1995)
d. *Oliver!* (1968)

GAME 12 Q1 ANSWER d
In this romantic comedy, written and directed by Nancy Meyers, Nicholson plays a "sixty-something" bachelor with a eye for much younger women . . . until he meets a divorcée (Diane Keaton) who is much closer to his age. In an ironic real-life twist, Keaton is the one who has never been married, and Nicholson is the divorcée.

GAME 32

2. In what film does Jack Nicholson say, "You make me want to be a better man"?

a. *Five Easy Pieces* (1970)
b. *As Good as It Gets* (1997)
c. *Anger Management* (2003)
d. *The Shining* (1980)

GAME 32 Q1 ANSWER c
Reynolds rejected the role of Garrett Breedlove in 1983's *Terms of Endearment* so that he could play the title character in this film. Jack Nicholson was cast in *Endearment* instead, and won the Best Supporting Actor Oscar for his performance. In fact, *Endearment* won five Academy Awards, including Best Picture, while *Stroker Ace* was a complete bomb.

GAME 52

2. What is the setting for the Bruce Willis film *Die Hard 2* (1990)?

a. A high-rise office building
b. Streets of Manhattan
c. An airport
d. The Pentagon

GAME 52 Q1 ANSWER b
While Clint Eastwood turned it down, the role made Charles Bronson a household name. The tough guy actor would go on to star in four sequels to this crime drama. Coincidentally, Bronson had turned down the part of the Man with No Name in Sergio Leone's "Dollars Trilogy" of Westerns years earlier—the role that first made Clint Eastwood famous.

GAME 72

2. What does Claire Danes sell in *Shopgirl* (2005)?

a. Gloves
b. Scarves
c. Lingerie
d. Swimwear

GAME 72 Q1 ANSWER b
Although a number of projects were planned for these two screen legends, *Easter Parade* is the only movie in which they appeared together. Astaire's most notable film partner was Ginger Rogers, who starred with him in ten movie musicals. He costarred with Betty Hutton in 1950's *Let's Dance*, and with Leslie Caron in 1955's *Daddy Long Legs*.

GAME 9

12. Who directed the war movies *Paths of Glory* (1957) and *Full Metal Jacket* (1987)?

a. Stanley Kubrick
b. Sam Fuller
c. Robert Aldrich
d. Sam Peckinpah

GAME 9 Q11 ANSWER b
Appearing along with the great comedic actors Harry Shearer, Michael McKean, and Christopher Guest, Rob Reiner—son of comedian/actor/writer Carl Reiner—plays a "rockumentary" filmmaker named Marty DiBergi. Fred Willard also appears in this film as an Air Force lieutenant.

GAME 29

12. What was the first full-length cel-animated motion picture?

a. *Snow White*
b. *Cinderella*
c. *Lady and the Tramp*
d. *Pinocchio*

GAME 29 Q11 ANSWER b
Despite the fact that America was struggling through the Depression, RKO invested more than $1.5 million in the production of *Cimarron*. The resulting Western was praised by critics, received nominations for more than six Academy Awards, and won three Oscars, including Best Picture. Nevertheless, RKO was never able to recoup its investment.

GAME 49

12. Who stars in the 1953 horror flick *House of Wax*?

a. Boris Karloff
b. Lon Chaney
c. Christopher Lee
d. Vincent Price

GAME 49 Q11 ANSWER c
Pirelli is played by Sacha Baron Cohen, who is best known for his outrageous movie characters Borat and Brüno. The actor brings some light comedy and singing to director Tim Burton's dark horror version of this 1979 Stephen Sondheim musical. His brutal murder at the hand of Sweeney Todd (Johnny Depp) sets the tone for the rest of the film.

GAME 69

12. Which author does Johnny Depp portray in *Finding Neverland* (2004)?

a. J.M. Barrie
b. Dr. Seuss
c. Lewis Carroll
d. Oscar Wilde

GAME 69 Q11 ANSWER c
Holden plays a struggling screenwriter in this classic Hollywood tale directed by Billy Wilder. After a lengthy period of struggle in his own career, Holden was brought back into the limelight by his Oscar-nominated performance in the film. Though he did not win the award that year, he would soon take home the prize for his role in 1953's *Stalag 17*.

GAME 12

1. Which film pairs Jack Nicholson with Diane Keaton?

a. *Heartburn* (1986)

b. *Terms of Endearment* (1983)

c. *As Good As It Gets* (1997)

d. *Something's Gotta Give* (2003)

The answer to this question is on:

page 232,
top frame,
right side.

GAME 32

1. Who stars in the 1983 film *Stroker Ace*?

a. Charles Bronson

b. Clint Eastwood

c. Burt Reynolds

d. Chuck Norris

The answer to this question is on:

page 232,
second frame,
right side.

GAME 52

1. Which film features a vigilante named Paul Kersey?

a. *First Blood* (1982)

b. *Death Wish* (1974)

c. *F/X* (1986)

d. *Darkman* (1990)

The answer to this question is on:

page 232,
third frame,
right side.

GAME 72

1. Who is Fred Astaire's costar in the 1948 holiday classic *Easter Parade*?

a. Ginger Rogers

b. Judy Garland

c. Betty Hutton

d. Leslie Caron

The answer to this question is on:

page 232,
bottom frame,
right side.

GAME 10
War Films

*Turn to page 237
for the first question.*

Turn to page 237
for the first question.

GAME 9 Q12 ANSWER a
A master chess player with a legendary obsession for detail, Stanley Kubrick's first war movie was *Paths of Glory,* which starred Kirk Douglas and was set during World War I. Thirty years later, Kubrick recreated the Vietnam War in *Full Metal Jacket.* He even satirized the fear of nuclear warfare in *Dr. Strangelove* (1964).

GAME 30
Film Noir

*Turn to page 237
for the first question.*

Turn to page 237
for the first question.

GAME 29 Q12 ANSWER a
In 1934, Walt Disney announced that he was producing his first feature film, *Snow White and the Seven Dwarfs.* Disney had to fight to get the film made, and even mortgaged his house to help finance it. But when the movie went into general release in 1938, it was a major success, and by May 1939, it had become the most successful film of all time.

GAME 50
From Comic Book to Silver Screen

*Turn to page 237
for the first question.*

Turn to page 237
for the first question.

GAME 49 Q12 ANSWER d
This horror film classic is a remake of an earlier 1933 film *Mystery of the Wax Museum* (starring once-famous *King Kong* heroine Fay Wray). Decades before *Avatar* would resurrect the 3-D cinema craze in 2010, *House of Wax* was the first 3-D color movie released in the US. A remake of the film featuring Paris Hilton in a small part was released in 2005.

GAME 70
Orson Welles

*Turn to page 237
for the first question.*

Turn to page 237
for the first question.

GAME 69 Q12 ANSWER a
Depp scored a Best Actor nomination at the Oscars for playing the author of *Peter Pan, or The Boy Who Wouldn't Grow Up* in this period piece. It was his second nomination in as many years, having been named in the same category one year prior for his role as Captain Jack Sparrow in the 2003 film *Pirates of the Caribbean: The Curse of the Black Pearl.*

GAME 12

GRAB BAG

*Turn to page 234
for the first question.*

GAME 11 Q12 ANSWER a

Actually, Fallon grew up a Mets fan because his father worked for IBM and got free tickets to the games. Later, while working on *Saturday Night Live,* he became a Yankees fan after regularly attending games with his boss Lorne Michaels. However, when the filming of *Fever Pitch* started, Fallon claimed he was really rooting for the Red Sox.

GAME 32

GRAB BAG

*Turn to page 234
for the first question.*

GAME 31 Q12 ANSWER All

In 1942, the Academy of Motion Picture Arts and Sciences had one documentary category and presented awards to *four* of the nominees. Since World War II had been raging for several years, it should come as no surprise that each of the winning films either examined events that led up to the war or showed troop actions, including actual battle footage.

GAME 52

GRAB BAG

*Turn to page 234
for the first question.*

GAME 51 Q12 ANSWER c

It is where Toula (Nia Vardalos) first sees her future "non-Greek" husband (John Corbett). The story was first developed by Vardalos as a one-woman play. When actress Rita Wilson (who has a Greek heritage) saw it, she convinced husband Tom Hanks to produce the movie, which was a sleeper hit that inspired a brief 2003 TV series *My Big Fat Greek Life.*

GAME 72

GRAB BAG

*Turn to page 234
for the first question.*

GAME 71 Q12 ANSWER c

"Terry" the dog played Dorothy's adorable pet in this film classic. Although the pooch had appeared a few years earlier in Shirley Temple's *Bright Eyes* (1934), it was her role in *The Wizard of Oz* that solidified her star quality. Her weekly salary of $125 was larger than that of many of the actors in the film. The Munchkins, for instance, were paid $50.

GAME 10	**1.** In which war movie does Robert De Niro play Russian roulette? **a.** *The Deer Hunter* (1978) **b.** *Casualties of War* (1989) **c.** *Full Metal Jacket* (1987) **d.** *Apocalypse Now* (1979)	The answer to this question is on: **page 239, top frame, right side.**
GAME 30	**1.** Which actor plays the central character in *D.O.A.* (1950)? **a.** Robert Mitchum **b.** Wendell Corey **c.** Dana Andrews **d.** Edmond O'Brien	The answer to this question is on: **page 239, second frame, right side.**
GAME 50	**1.** Who does Spidey square off against in 2002's *Spider-Man*? **a.** Doctor Octopus **b.** Green Goblin **c.** The Riddler **d.** The Sandman	The answer to this question is on: **page 239, third frame, right side.**
GAME 70	**1.** Who plays a Mexican drug agent in Orson Welles' *Touch of Evil* (1958)? **a.** Paul Newman **b.** Charlton Heston **c.** Marlon Brando **d.** Burt Lancaster	The answer to this question is on: **page 239, bottom frame, right side.**

GAME 11

12. Jimmy Fallon plays a big fan of which baseball team in the 2005 film *Fever Pitch*?

a. Boston Red Sox
b. New York Yankees
c. Los Angeles Dodgers
d. Chicago Cubs

GAME 11 Q11 ANSWER a
Playing one of Cameron Diaz's many boyfriends, three-time MVP Brett Favre has a short cameo in the film. Troy Aikman appeared in *Jerry Maguire* (1996); Jim Brown was one of the "dirty dozen" in the 1967 movie of the same name; and Timmy Brown had roles in a number of movies, including *M*A*S*H* (1972), *Nashville* (1975), and *Frequency* (2000).

GAME 31

12. What was the first film to win an Oscar for best documentary?

a. *The Battle of Midway* (1942)
b. *Kokoda Front Line!* (1942)
c. *Moscow Strikes Back* (1942)
d. *Prelude to War* (1942)

GAME 31 Q11 ANSWER b
Surfer/skateboarder Stacy Peralta wrote, directed, and narrated this critically acclaimed 2004 documentary on the sport of big wave riding. The film—which includes archival footage, still photos, home movies, and interviews with renowned surfers—has the distinction of being the first documentary to ever open the Sundance Film Festival.

GAME 51

12. What's the name of the restaurant in *My Big Fat Greek Wedding* (2002)?

a. Christos Place
b. Souvlaki Central
c. Dancing Zorbas
d. Parthenon Palace

GAME 51 Q11 ANSWER b
When teacher Howard Bracket (Kline) is "outed" on TV by a former student (Matt Dillon), he starts to wonder if he actually *is* gay. This 1997 film was inspired by Tom Hanks' Oscar acceptance speech for his role in *Philadelphia* (1993). In it, he proudly spoke of his gay high school drama teacher and a former classmate, whom he mentioned by name.

GAME 71

12. What breed of dog is Toto in *The Wizard of Oz* (1939)?

a. Beagle
b. Maltese
c. Cairn terrier
d. Chihuahua

GAME 71 Q11 ANSWER b
Thumper isn't in Felix Salten's *Bambi*—the book on which the film is based. Walt Disney created the lovable rabbit specifically for the movie. Bambi and Thumper were such good friends, the two names are often linked together. For instance, a pair of asteroids are named after the duo, as are two characters in *Diamonds are Forever* (1971).

GAME 10

2. Which war is the backdrop for the 2004 remake of *The Manchurian Candidate*?

a. Korean War

b. Gulf War

c. Vietnam War

d. Civil War

GAME 10 Q1 ANSWER a
De Niro plays soldier Michael Vronsky in this critically acclaimed Vietnam War film for which he earned a Best Actor Oscar nomination. The movie itself won five Oscars, including Best Picture and Director (Michael Cimino). The American Film Institute ranked it #53 on its list of the "100 Greatest American Movies of All Time."

GAME 30

2. In which city is 1941's *The Maltese Falcon* set?

a. New York

b. Chicago

c. Cincinnati

d. San Francisco

GAME 30 Q1 ANSWER d
As a boy in New York, O'Brien got his first taste of show business from his neighbor Harry Houdini, who would teach the youngster magic tricks. Though the actor won a Best Supporting Actor Oscar for his performance in 1954's *The Barefoot Contessa*, it is for his role as the poisoned Frank Bigelow in this film noir that he is perhaps best remembered.

GAME 50

2. How does the Joker get his famous grin in 1989's *Batman*?

a. Ravaged by rats

b. Disfigured by chemicals

c. Burned in a fire

d. Botched plastic surgery

GAME 50 Q1 ANSWER b
Nicolas Cage, Robert De Niro, and John Malkovich were all offered the role of the Green Goblin, but Willem Dafoe—who had actually lobbied for the opportunity—landed the part. Dafoe performed most of his own stunts and enjoyed the filming so much that he convinced director Sam Raimi to include him in a cameo in the 2004 sequel, *Spider-Man 2*.

GAME 70

2. Which film did Orson Welles direct right after *Citizen Kane* (1941)?

a. *Mr. Arkadin*

b. *The Third Man*

c. *The Stranger*

d. *The Magnificent Ambersons*

GAME 70 Q1 ANSWER b
Heston plays Detective Vargas, who investigates corrupt police chief Hank Quinlan (played by Welles) in this crime-drama, which was also written and directed by Welles. *Touch of Evil* is considered a classic—in the 1995 comedy *Get Shorty*, film-obsessed mobster Chili Palmer (John Travolta) is shown watching it in a movie theater.

GAME 11

11. Which NFL star appears in *Something About Mary* (1998)?

a. Brett Favre
b. Jim Brown
c. Troy Aikman
d. Timmy Brown

GAME 11 Q10 ANSWER b
Cobb (1994) stars Tommy Lee Jones as the legendary Ty Cobb, whose career was with the Detroit Tigers and Philadelphia Athletics. William Bendix played Yankee great Babe Ruth in *The Babe Ruth Story* (1942), while John Goodman portrayed Ruth in *The Babe* (1992). *The Pride of the Yankees* (1942) starred Gary Cooper as Yankee Lou Gehrig.

GAME 31

11. What is the subject of director Stacy Peralta's documentary *Riding Giants*?

a. Big-rig racing
b. Surfing
c. Skateboarding
d. Whitewater rafting

GAME 31 Q10 ANSWER d
Based on the book of the same name, *Touching the Void* tells the story of Joe Simpson, who was climbing the Siula Grande in the Peruvian Andes when fellow climber, Simon Yates, cut the rope that connected the two men in order to save his own life. The film shows what led to Yates's action as well as the amazing events that occurred afterwards.

GAME 51

11. Why can't Kevin Kline's character say his wedding vows in *In and Out*?

a. He loves someone else
b. He thinks he's gay
c. He's already married
d. He thinks he's too old

GAME 51 Q10 ANSWER d
Roberts plays the commitment-phobic Maggie Carpenter, who keeps leaving her grooms at the altar in this romantic comedy that was in development for ten years! Directed by Garry Marshall, the film also stars Richard Gere and Héctor Elizondo. In 1990, Roberts, Gere, and Elizondo starred together in *Pretty Woman* —another Garry Marshall flick.

GAME 71

11. In Disney's 1942 film *Bambi,* what type of animal is Thumper?

a. Deer
b. Rabbit
c. Skunk
d. Chipmunk

GAME 71 Q10 ANSWER c
Based on John Grogan's autobiographical book, *Marley & Me: Life and Love with the World's Worst Dog,* this film features the antics of a very special golden Lab. Twenty-two dogs played Marley during the various stages of his life. To get the dogs to "kiss" them, costars Jennifer Aniston and Owen Wilson put ham-flavored baby food on their faces.

GAME 10

3. Major Major is a character in which 1970 war film?

a. *Tora! Tora! Tora!*

b. *Catch-22*

c. *MASH*

d. *Kelly's Heroes*

GAME 10 Q2 ANSWER b
In the original 1962 John Franken-heimer-directed film, a group of soldiers returning from the Korean War had been brainwashed and programmed to kill. In the Jonathan Demme-directed remake, the action took place during Operation Desert Storm. The storyline was also altered from a Communist conspiracy to an anti-corporation scheme.

GAME 30

3. Which "Big" film stars Humphrey Bogart?

a. *The Big Heat* (1953)

b. *The Big Sleep* (1946)

c. *The Big Combo* (1955)

d. *The Big Clock* (1948)

GAME 30 Q2 ANSWER d
Based on Dashiell Hammett's novel of the same name, this Oscar-nominated film features Humphrey Bogart as detective Sam Spade. Hammett based the character on his own experiences while working for the Pinkerton Detective Agency. While his performance is a classic, Bogart bears no resemblance to the tall, blond Spade of the book.

GAME 50

3. Which character is a member of the *Fantastic Four* (2005)?

a. Captain America

b. Elektra

c. Human Torch

d. Plastic Man

GAME 50 Q2 ANSWER d
Although chemicals are responsible for his white skin and green hair, Nicholson's iconic Joker smile resulted from a botched surgical attempt to fix a gunshot wound. Coincidentally, the film's prop dental tools were also used on Bill Murray's character in 1986's *Little Shop of Horrors*—a part Nicholson had in the film's original 1960 version.

GAME 70

3. Who plays Orson Welles' wife in *The Stranger* (1946)?

a. Loretta Young

b. Ruth Warrick

c. Jeanette Nolan

d. Rita Hayworth

GAME 70 Q2 ANSWER d
Based on the 1918 Pulitzer Prize-winning novel by Booth Tarkington, Welles considered his 131-minute version of *The Magnificent Ambersons* (1942) to be better than *Citizen Kane*. However, RKO cut more than 40 minutes from the film and shot a new "happy ending" while Welles was making a documentary in Brazil for the US government.

GAME 11

10. Which of the following actors did *not* portray a New York Yankee?

a. Gary Cooper

b. Tommy Lee Jones

c. William Bendix

d. John Goodman

GAME 11 Q9 ANSWER d
In this movie, originally called *Underdog*, the actors had some real physical challenges. Justin Long's eyebrow was cut open when it was hit with a rubber wrench. Ben Stiller hit his wife (actress Christine Taylor) in the face with a ball and broke three cameras. The actors said the hardest part of filming was not flinching when they were about to be hit.

GAME 31

10. Which film tells the story of a mountain climber who cut his friend's rope?

a. *The Man Who Skied Down Everest* (1975)

b. *Have You Seen Andy?* (2001)

c. *Beyond Gravity* (2000)

d. *Touching the Void* (2003)

GAME 31 Q9 ANSWER a
Directed by Michael Apted, this 1985 documentary chronicles the making of Sting's first album as a solo performer. In addition to presenting recording sessions, the film provides insights into the lives of Sting and his band members, including saxophonist Branford Marsalis, pianist Kenny Kirkland, bassist Darryl Jones, and drummer Omar Hakim.

GAME 51

10. Who plays the *Runaway Bride* (1999)?

a. Hilary Swank

b. Cameron Diaz

c. Charlize Theron

d. Julia Roberts

GAME 51 Q9 ANSWER a
After looking through his old journals, screenwriter Richard Curtis realized that over a ten-year period, he had attended over seventy weddings! This inspired him to write the Oscar-nominated *Four Weddings and a Funeral*. At the time, the movie (which took just thirty-five days to film) was the highest-grossing British film in cinema history.

GAME 71

10. In which movie do the Grogans adopt a "spirited" Labrador retriever?

a. *My Dog Skip* (2000)

b. *Old Yeller* (1957)

c. *Marley & Me* (2008)

d. *Beethoven* (1992)

GAME 71 Q9 ANSWER a
Seabiscuit was named "Horse of the Year" after his victory over War Admiral in this 1938 race. The 2003 film, based on a book by Laura Hillenbrand, recounts the true story of Seabiscuit—an "underdog" of a racehorse, whose unlikely victories lifted the nation's spirits during the Great Depression. It earned seven Oscar nods, including Best Picture.

GAME 10

4. Who directed the 1953 World War II film *From Here to Eternity*?

a. Robert Aldrich

b. William Wyler

c. Stanley Kubrick

d. Fred Zinnemann

GAME 10 Q3 ANSWER b
Bob Newhart plays the role in this Mike Nichols-directed adaptation of the Joseph Heller novel. The movie stars Alan Arkin as Captain John Yossarian—a B-25 bombardier whose goal is to be declared insane so he can go home. Despite its stellar cast, the movie was overshadowed by Robert Altman's *M*A*S*H*, which came out the same year.

GAME 30

4. Which latter-day film noir features the character Evelyn Mulwray?

a. *After Dark, My Sweet* (1990)

b. *The Last Seduction* (1994)

c. *Chinatown* (1974)

d. *Body Heat* (1981)

GAME 30 Q3 ANSWER b
This film noir marks the second on-screen appearance of Bogart and future wife Lauren Bacall. Bogey (who was married) had begun a romantic relationship with his nineteen-year-old costar while filming 1944's *To Have and Have Not*. They tied the knot after his divorce, and then worked together again in *Dark Passage* (1947) and *Key Largo* (1948).

GAME 50

4. Which Jim Carrey movie was adapted from a comic book?

a. *The Mask* (1994)

b. *Ace Ventura: Pet Detective* (1994)

c. *The Truman Show* (1998)

d. *Dumb & Dumber* (1994)

GAME 50 Q3 ANSWER c
After appearing in such movies as *Not Another Teen Movie* (2001) and *Cellular* (2004), Chris Evans signed on to play the youngest member of Marvel's "first family" in this film directed by Tim Story. Rounding out the team are Jessica Alba as the Invisible Woman, Ioan Gruffudd as Mr. Fantastic, and Michael Chiklis as the ever-lovin' blue-eyed Thing.

GAME 70

4. What was the first Shakespearean role that Orson Welles played in a film?

a. Hamlet

b. Macbeth

c. King Lear

d. Richard III

GAME 70 Q3 ANSWER a
In *The Stranger*, Young slowly discovers that Welles' character is an escaped Nazi. Meanwhile, *All My Children* TV soap star Ruth Warrick plays wife to Welles' Charles Foster Kane in *Citizen Kane*; Jeanette Nolan plays Lady Macbeth in his film of *Macbeth* (1948); and Rita Hayworth was actually married to Welles from 1943 to 1948.

GAME 11

9. Which comedy stars Rip Torn as a coach who throws wrenches at his players?

a. *The Replacements* (2000)

b. *Leatherheads* (2008)

c. *Necessary Roughness* (1991)

d. *Dodgeball* (2004)

GAME 11 Q8 ANSWER c
When an injury prematurely ended his basketball career in the mid-'80s, Marques Johnson looked to Hollywood. In addition to his cameo in *White Men Can't Jump,* Johnson appeared in the basketball flicks *Blue Chips* (1994) and *Forget Paris* (1995). He also guest starred on several network television shows, such as *LA Law.*

GAME 31

9. Which artist is the focus of the rock film *Bring on the Night*?

a. Sting

b. Bono

c. David Bowie

d. Bob Marley

GAME 31 Q8 ANSWER c
This film about two aspiring basketball players is one of the highest-grossing documentaries ever made. *Hoop Dreams* was so popular with moviegoers and critics that when it failed to draw an Academy Award nomination for Best Documentary, a controversy was sparked that eventually resulted in a revised process of nomination within that category.

GAME 51

9. In which movie does Hugh Grant declare love for Andie MacDowell?

a. *Four Weddings and a Funeral* (1994)

b. *Nine Months* (1995)

c. *About a Boy* (2002)

d. *Mickey Blue Eyes* (1999)

GAME 51 Q8 ANSWER d
Steve Martin plays father of the bride George Banks in this remake of the 1950 film classic starring Spencer Tracy. Both versions had sequels in which the daughter (played by Elizabeth Taylor in the original and Kimberly Williams in the remake) has a baby. In the 1995 sequel, the mother of the bride (played by Diane Keaton) has a baby as well.

GAME 71

9. *Seabiscuit's* "Match of the Century" pits which horse against Seabiscuit?

a. War Admiral

b. Secretariat

c. Whirlaway

d. Citation

GAME 71 Q8 ANSWER d
Robert Shaw played the professional shark hunter in this 1975 blockbuster. Actor Lee Marvin had also been considered for the role but turned it down, claiming he would rather go fishing. As a point of interest, just like their characters, Shaw and costar Richard Dreyfuss didn't get along. This resulted in great tension during their scenes.

GAME 10

5. In which film does Bruce Willis play a Vietnam vet?

a. *Gardens of Stone* (1989)
b. *Jacknife* (1989)
c. *Coming Home* (1978)
d. *In Country* (1989)

GAME 10 Q4 ANSWER d
Zinneman earned the Best Director Oscar for this film classic, which won a total of eight Oscars including Best Picture. Robert Aldrich directed the 1967 war film *The Dirty Dozen*, while William Wyler directed 1946's *The Best Years of Our Lives*. Kubrick's *Paths of Glory*, set during World War I, was banned in France due to its anti-French sentiment.

GAME 30

5. Who plays psychopath Max Cady in 1962's *Cape Fear*?

a. Peter Lorre
b. Robert Mitchum
c. Robert Ryan
d. Alan Ladd

GAME 30 Q4 ANSWER c
This Roman Polanski classic received eleven Oscar nominations. The film's script earned writer Robert Towne the Oscar for Best Original Screenplay and was the first part of an intended trilogy starring Jack Nicholson. The second installment—1990's *The Two Jakes*—fared so poorly, however, that plans for a third movie were abandoned altogether.

GAME 50

5. Who created the comic book on which 2005's *Sin City* is based?

a. Mike Mignola
b. Robert E. Howard
c. Frank Miller
d. Stan Lee

GAME 50 Q4 ANSWER a
Carrey began his career as a stand-up comic in his native Canada. For his very first performance, the then teenager wore a yellow suit and tails that his mother had made for him. The performance was a disaster, but the suit would inspire the costume worn by his character in *The Mask*—the second of his three films that year to debut at #1.

GAME 70

5. In which film did Orson Welles direct *Psycho* star Anthony Perkins?

a. *F for Fake* (1974)
b. *Touch of Evil* (1958)
c. *The Trial* (1962)
d. *Chimes at Midnight* (1965)

GAME 70 Q4 ANSWER b
Initially, Welles had been interested in creating a screen adaptation of Shakespeare's *Othello*, but was unable to gain financial backing for the project. When he suggested a movie of *Macbeth*, Republic Pictures—which was trying to raise the level of its films—was willing to provide the director/actor with a small but sufficient budget.

GAME 11

8. Which former hoops star plays a gun-toting psycho in *White Men Can't Jump* (1992)?

a. Kareem Abdul-Jabbar
b. Wilt Chamberlain
c. Marques Johnson
d. Robert Parish

GAME 11 Q7 ANSWER c
Glen Ford plays the legendary golfer in this biographical film that follows Hogan's career from the time he was a young caddy working to help support his family to his courageous comeback after being seriously hurt in a tragic car accident. Through fan support and sheer determination, Hogan recovers and goes on to become a golfing great.

GAME 31

8. Which film relates the struggles of two Chicago high school students?

a. *Down and Out in America* (1986)
b. *Scared Straight* (1978)
c. *Hoop Dreams* (1994)
d. *Roger & Me* (1989)

GAME 31 Q7 ANSWER d
Written and directed by Barbara Kopple, this award-winning documentary focuses on the 1972 strike of 180 coal miners against the Duke Power Company of Harlan County, Kentucky. An interesting feature of the film is that Kopple did not choose to use narration, but allowed the participants' own words and deeds to tell the story of the event.

GAME 51

8. In *Father of the Bride* (1991), what does George Banks' company produce?

a. Basketballs
b. Coffee makers
c. Candy
d. Sneakers

GAME 51 Q7 ANSWER c
In this Mike Nichols film, Hoffman is seduced by Mrs. Robinson (Ann Bancroft); but falls in love with her daughter, whose wedding he disrupts. Although part of Simon and Garfunkel's song "Mrs. Robinson" is heard in the film, it wasn't written for the movie. It was actually a work in progress, originally called "Mrs. Roosevelt" (about Eleanor Roosevelt).

GAME 71

8. In *Jaws*, what is the name of Quint's boat?

a. *SS Minnow*
b. *Amity*
c. *The Aurora*
d. *Orca*

GAME 71 Q7 ANSWER c
During filming of this screwball comedy, Katharine Hepburn was fearless around Nissa the leopard (Baby). Cary Grant, on the other hand, wasn't fond of the leopard at all, and demanded a double for his scenes with her. To minimize the cat's proximity to the actors, a number of optical tricks, such as rear projection and split screen, were used.

GAME 10

6. Who plays Major John Reisman, leader of *The Dirty Dozen* (1967)?

a. Lee Marvin
b. George Kennedy
c. Ernest Borgnine
d. Robert Ryan

GAME 10 Q5 ANSWER d
Willis's portrayal of an emotionally battered war vet proved his worthiness as a serious actor in this Norman Jewison-directed film. In *Gardens of Stone*, James Caan plays a veteran soldier who must prepare his men for the realities of war; in *Jacknife*, Robert De Niro is a Vietnam vet, as is John Voight in *Coming Home*.

GAME 30

6. Which Humphrey Bogart movie features the gangster Johnny Rocco?

a. *Beat the Devil* (1954)
b. *Key Largo* (1948)
c. *High Sierra* (1941)
d. *In a Lonely Place* (1950)

GAME 30 Q5 ANSWER b
Mitchum terrorizes Gregory Peck throughout the film, but it was Peck whom the studios initially wanted for the bad guy role. Peck preferred to stick to his familiar hero persona and asked Mitchum to play Cady instead. When Mitchum turned him down, Peck—also the film's producer—sent the actor a bottle of bourbon, which helped to change his mind.

GAME 50

6. Which actor plays Wolverine in *X-Men* (2000)?

a. Alan Cumming
b. James Marsden
c. Hugh Jackman
d. Anna Paquin

GAME 50 Q5 ANSWER c
Because Miller was so involved in this comic book movie's creation, director Robert Rodriguez insisted on giving him a director's credit, and resigned from the Directors Guild of America when it refused the request. Rodriguez also asked friend and filmmaker Quentin Tarantino to shoot a segment of the film, crediting him as "special guest director."

GAME 70

6. Who is Orson Welles' character in *The Third Man* (1949)?

a. Harry Lime
b. Charles Foster Kane
c. Hank Quinlan
d. Mr. Rochester

GAME 70 Q5 ANSWER c
Two years before Alfred Hitchcock had Janet Leigh's character stay alone at a deserted motel in *Psycho* (1960), Welles had Leigh's character do the same in *Touch of Evil*. Welles then directed Anthony Perkins in his film of Kafka's *The Trial*. In 1970, Welles and Perkins both appeared in Mike Nichols' anti-war satire *Catch-22*.

GAME 11

7. Which sports film focuses on the life of golfer Ben Hogan?

a. *Golden Boy* (1939)

b. *Bang the Drum Slowly* (1973)

c. *Follow the Sun* (1951)

d. *Inside Moves* (1980)

GAME 11 Q6 ANSWER d
This revolutionary film, which follows two surfers around the world in search of the perfect wave, gave birth to the "surf and travel" culture, which emphasized two things—meeting new people and riding the perfect wave. The movie's title signifies that with enough time and money, you could follow summer around the world, essentially making it "endless."

GAME 31

7. What is the subject of the 1976 documentary *Harlan County USA*?

a. Political corruption

b. Desegregation

c. Textile mills

d. Coal mining

GAME 31 Q6 ANSWER b
Environmental activist Laurie David persuaded Al Gore to write *An Inconvenient Truth* after watching him present a ten-minute slide show on the dangers of global warming. In addition to being a huge box office success, this film was the first documentary to garner two Academy Awards—one for Best Documentary Feature and one for Best Original Song.

GAME 51

7. In which film does Dustin Hoffman's character disrupt a wedding?

a. *The Other Sister* (1999)

b. *The Marrying Man* (1991)

c. *The Graduate* (1967)

d. *Tootsie* (1982)

GAME 51 Q6 ANSWER b
Meryl Streep stars in this romantic 2008 film that is adapted from the stage musical of the same name, and based on the songs of the Swedish pop group ABBA. When Pierce Brosnan signed on for the project, he knew only that it was being filmed in Greece and Meryl Streep was in it. He claimed he would have signed on for *any* project involving Streep.

GAME 71

7. In 1938's *Bringing Up Baby*, what kind of animal is Baby?

a. Dog

b. Chimpanzee

c. Leopard

d. Horse

GAME 71 Q6 ANSWER a
The Pushmi-Pullyu is just one of the many fantastical creatures in this Academy Award-winning musical starring Rex Harrison as the eccentric doctor who is able to speak in hundreds of animal languages. The film received a number of Oscar nominations including Best Picture. It won two—Best Special Effects and Best Song, "Talk to the Animals."

GAME 10

7. Robin Williams plays which real-life disc jockey in *Good Morning, Vietnam*?

a. Robert Weston Smith
b. J.P. Richardson
c. Alan Freed
d. Adrian Cronauer

GAME 10 Q6 ANSWER a

Kennedy, Borgnine, and Ryan are officers in this box office smash, but it is Marvin who leads the twelve recruited criminals on the WWII suicide mission. Marvin based his character on a close personal friend who served with him in the Marine Corps during WWII. Marvin enjoyed the movie, but felt that it was "crap" and had nothing to do with war.

GAME 30

7. Who plays the femme fatale in *The Lady from Shanghai* (1947)?

a. Rita Hayworth
b. Lauren Bacall
c. Gene Tierney
d. Barbara Stanwyck

GAME 30 Q6 ANSWER b

Known for his tough-guy roles, Edward G. Robinson plays the fugitive mobster in this stormy tale. It would be his last time starring opposite Bogey on the big screen. In addition to this John Huston crime film, they worked together in *Bullets or Ballots* (1936), *Kid Galahad* (1937), *The Amazing Dr. Clitterhouse* (1938), and *Brother Orchid* (1940).

GAME 50

7. What is shown collapsing at the end of 1978's *Superman*?

a. The Capitol
b. The Brooklyn Bridge
c. The Hollywood sign
d. The Hoover Dam

GAME 50 Q6 ANSWER c

Though it is Jackman who flashes the famous claws in this superhero flick, each of these actors can call themselves a member of the X-Men. In the same film, Marsden plays team leader Cyclops alongside Paquin, who sports a streak of white hair as new recruit Rogue; and Cumming appears as the blue-skinned Nightcrawler in *X2: X-Men United* (2003).

GAME 70

7. Which of these films did Orson Welles make first?

a. *Citizen Kane*
b. *The Hearts of Age*
c. *The War of the Worlds*
d. *Heart of Darkness*

GAME 70 Q6 ANSWER a

Although many consider it an "Orson Welles picture," *The Third Man* was actually directed by Carol Reed. The film paired Welles with *Citizen Kane* co-star Joseph Cotten, and it won an Oscar in 1950 for Best Black and White Cinematography. The movie's instrumental theme song was a chart-topping hit in the US during 1950.

GAME 11

6. Which famous surfing movie did pioneer filmmaker Bruce Brown release in 1966?

a. *Hanging Ten*

b. *The Forever Coast*

c. *Back to the Beach*

d. *The Endless Summer*

GAME 11 Q5 ANSWER b

Although George Foreman was the defending champ heading into 1974's "Rumble in the Jungle," there is no doubt that Muhammad Ali not only stole the show, but also regained his title. In addition to providing stirring fight footage, the documentary shows Ali's goal to illustrate the plight of the black man in Zaire during the 1970s.

GAME 31

6. Which documentary was written by a vice president of the United States?

a. *Fight for the Planet* (2009)

b. *An Inconvenient Truth* (2006)

c. *American Jobs* (2004)

d. *Faces of Gore* (1999)

GAME 31 Q5 ANSWER a

This 1922 documentary on Inuit life in the Canadian Arctic had a long run in Broadway theaters, and was so successful that filmmaker Robert Flaherty was asked to "make another Nanook"—this time, by filming village life in Samoa. Unfortunately for Flaherty and his distributor, Paramount Pictures, *Moana* (1926) was a box office failure.

GAME 51

6. Which actor does *not* play one of the "possible dads" in *Mamma Mia?*

a. Colin Firth

b. Gabriel Byrne

c. Stellan Skarsgård

d. Pierce Brosnan

GAME 51 Q5 ANSWER d

In this movie, which is supposedly based on Alda's personal experiences with his own daughter's wedding, Molly Ringwald plays Betsy, who doesn't want the lavish affair that her dad is planning. Although the movie was a flop at the box office, it is said to have launched the career of Anthony LaPaglia, who plays a mobster in the film.

GAME 71

6. In 1967's *Doctor Dolittle,* the "Pushmi-Pullyu" is a two-headed:

a. Llama

b. Donkey

c. Snake

d. Dog

GAME 71 Q5 ANSWER c

After his mom dies, the piglet lives on the farm with a family of border collies and learns how to herd. Nominated for seven Oscars including Best Picture (the last G-rated movie to date to do so), *Babe* won Best Visual Effects for its impressive use of real and animatronic animals. (Forty-eight live pigs were used for the role of Babe alone!)

GAME 10

8. Who is Dana Andrews' true love interest in *The Best Years of Our Lives*?

a. Virginia Mayo
b. Myrna Loy
c. Teresa Wright
d. Gene Tierney

GAME 10 Q7 ANSWER d
Williams received an Oscar nomination for his role as the enormously popular Armed Forces Radio DJ in this 1987 Barry Levinson film. As for the other answer choices, all were famous DJs as well. Robert Weston Smith was better known as Wolfman Jack; J.P. Richardson was The Big Bopper; and Alan Freed was the DJ who pioneered rock and roll.

GAME 30

8. Who plays detective Philip Marlowe in the 1947 film *Lady in the Lake*?

a. Humphrey Bogart
b. Robert Montgomery
c. Dick Powell
d. Robert Mitchum

GAME 30 Q7 ANSWER a
Hayworth was cast by then-husband Orson Welles, who not only produced the film, but directed and starred in it as well. In desperate need of some quick cash for a play he was staging, Welles called the head of Columbia Pictures with an offer to produce, write, and direct the movie in exchange for an immediate payment of $55,000, which he received.

GAME 50

8. Who has the title role in 2004's *The Punisher*?

a. James Caviezel
b. Thomas Jane
c. Vince Vaughn
d. Vin Diesel

GAME 50 Q7 ANSWER d
Christopher Reeve had appeared on the big screen only once (in 1978's *Gray Lady Down*) before winning the role of Superman in director Richard Donner's film. In preparation for the part, the former Julliard student put on thirty pounds and trained with British weight-lifting champion David Prowse—also known as Darth Vader in 1977's *Star Wars*.

GAME 70

8. Which Orson Welles drama climaxes with a shootout in a hall of mirrors?

a. *The Lady from Shanghai* (1947)
b. *The Stranger* (1945)
c. *Touch of Evil* (1958)
d. *Citizen Kane* (1941)

GAME 70 Q7 ANSWER b
At age nineteen, Welles co-directed this short film in 1934 with his college chum William Vance. Welles' first wife, Virginia Nicholson, appears in the film as a mysterious old woman, while Welles shows his taste for morbidity by playing the part of Death. In 1941, he began *Citizen Kane* by dying in the first scene.

GAME 11

5. Which boxing match is spotlighted in the 1996 documentary *When We Were Kings*?

a. "The Thrilla in Manila"

b. "The Rumble in the Jungle"

c. "I Shook Up the World"

d. "No Mas"

GAME 11 Q4 ANSWER d
Legendary actor Paul Newman plays Reggie Dunlop, the coach and player of a failing minor-league hockey team, who helps them find success through constant fighting and violence during the games. Newman has often said that of all the movies he has starred in, this is his favorite. It's also the one he had the most fun making.

GAME 31

5. What was the first commercially successful documentary film?

a. *Nanook of the North* (1922)

b. *The Louisiana Story* (1948)

c. *Olympia* (1938)

d. *Man of Aran* (1934)

GAME 31 Q4 ANSWER c
In 2003, Morgan Spurlock, a young filmmaker, ate nothing but McDonald's fast food for thirty days. His documentary *Super Size Me* not only chronicles his month-long experiment but also examines the many health disorders—included obesity, hypertension, mood swings, and sexual dysfunction—that too often result from America's supersized diet.

GAME 51

5. Alan Alda wrote, directed, and starred in which "wedding" movie?

a. *American Wedding* (2003)

b. *Muriel's Wedding* (1994)

c. *Monsoon Wedding* (2001)

d. *Betsy's Wedding* (1990)

GAME 51 Q4 ANSWER a
McConaughey plays Steve in this 2001 film, which costars Jennifer Lopez. Steve reasons that chocolate is brown, so brown M&Ms have less artificial coloring. The movie opened at #1 at the box office —the same week, Lopez's album *J.Lo* debuted at #1 on the *Billboard* 200. She's the first performer to have a #1 film and album released in the same week.

GAME 71

5. What is Babe the pig's job in the 1995 movie *Babe*?

a. Protecting the farmer

b. Hunting mice

c. Herding sheep

d. Gathering corn

GAME 71 Q4 ANSWER d
Butkus—named after Chicago Bears linebacker Dick Butkus—was actually Sylvester Stallone's real-life bullmastiff. Times were tough early in Stallone's career, and he was forced to sell Butkus. Six months later, when *Rocky* was in the works, Stallone was able to buy his dog back. Butkus Stallone appears in *Rocky* (1976) and *Rocky II* (1979).

9. Which film was *not* part of director Oliver Stone's "Vietnam Trilogy"?

a. *Platoon* (1986)

b. *Born on the Fourth of July* (1989)

c. *Heaven & Earth* (1993)

d. *Casualties of War* (1989)

GAME 10 Q8 ANSWER c
When Fred Derry (Andrews) returns home after serving in WWII, he realizes that he has little in common with his war bride (Virginia Mayo). Eventually, he falls in love with Peggy (Teresa Wright), who shares his love of home and family. This 1946 drama, which follows the lives of three returning servicemen, won seven Oscars, including Best Picture.

9. What sport features prominently in the 1947 film *Body and Soul*?

a. Football

b. Boxing

c. Golf

d. Bowling

GAME 30 Q8 ANSWER b
While Montgomery plays the famous Raymond Chandler private eye in this murder mystery, each of these actors has appeared on camera as the gumshoe. Bogart plays him in *The Big Sleep* (1946); Dick Powell takes the case in *Murder, My Sweet* (1944); and Robert Mitchum fills the role in 1975's *Farewell, My Lovely* and 1978's *The Big Sleep.*

9. Which monster film was based on a comic book of the same name?

a. *Screamers* (1995)

b. *Slugs* (1988)

c. *Slither* (2006)

d. *Swamp Thing* (1982)

GAME 50 Q8 ANSWER b
Though the character of Frank Castle—aka the Punisher—marks the only superhero entry on his résumé, Jane's no stranger to the world of comic book movies. He was rumored for the role of Harvey "Two-Face" Dent in 2008's *The Dark Knight;* and was offered the part of the Comedian in 2009's *Watchmen,* but turned it down due to scheduling issues.

9. In which novel did Orson Welles' character Father Mapple originate?

a. *The Thorn Birds*

b. *The Scarlet Letter*

c. *The Golden Bowl*

d. *Moby Dick*

GAME 70 Q8 ANSWER a
Born Margarita Carmen Cansino, Rita Hayworth played Elsa Bannister in this film. She and Welles married in 1943; but by the time they started making the movie in 1946, they were on the road to divorce. Welles caused a furor in Hollywood by demanding that Hayworth cut her famous red hair and bleach it blonde for the film.

GAME 11

4. Which hockey movie follows the exploits of the Charlestown Chiefs?

a. *Mystery, Alaska* (1999)

b. *Miracle* (2004)

c. *Youngblood* (1986)

d. *Slap Shot* (1977)

GAME 11 Q3 ANSWER d
Gaelic for "my darling" or "my blood," Macushla was the term of endearment given to aspiring boxer Maggie Fitzgerald (Hilary Swank) by her trainer and father figure Frankie Dunn (Clint Eastwood). Nominated for seven Oscars, the film won four—Best Picture, Best Director (Eastwood), Best Actress (Swank), and Best Supporting Actor (Morgan Freeman).

GAME 31

4. Which documentary includes footage of gastric bypass surgery?

a. *The Last Party* (1993)

b. *The Big One* (1997)

c. *Super Size Me* (2004)

d. *Answering the Call* (2006)

GAME 31 Q3 ANSWER b
Filmmakers George Hickenlooper and Fax Bahr combined behind-the-scenes footage with cast and crew interviews to produce this documentary on the making of Francis Ford Coppola's *Apocalypse Now*. *Hearts of Darkness* (1991) recounts Coppola's many production problems, including extreme weather, health crises, and skyrocketing costs.

GAME 51

4. In *The Wedding Planner,* which color M&Ms does Matthew McConaughey eat?

a. Brown

b. Yellow

c. Orange

d. Red

GAME 51 Q3 ANSWER d
In this box office hit, Barrymore is a waitress who falls in love with a jilted wedding singer (Adam Sandler). A stage adaptation of the film opened on Broadway in 2006. Among Barrymore's many roles, she has played an investigator in the *Charlie's Angels* movies, a journalist in *Never been Kissed* (1999), and a songwriter in *Music and Lyrics* (2007).

GAME 71

4. In the *Rocky* series, what's the name of Rocky's dog?

a. Ditka

b. Nietzsche

c. Huff

d. Butkus

GAME 71 Q3 ANSWER b
Willy—a killer whale—escapes captivity in this film with the help of a young boy. Keiko, the whale who played Willy and who also lived in captivity, experienced his own freedom after the film's debut. The movie inspired The Keiko Project—a movement sponsored by The Humane Society that helped release Keiko to his native waters.

GAME 10

10. In which war film did John Lennon play Musketeer Gripweed?

a. *The Visitors* (1972)

b. *Oh, What a Lovely War* (1969)

c. *How I Won the War* (1967)

d. *Coming Home* (1978)

GAME 10 Q9 ANSWER d

Stone wrote *Platoon,* winner of the Best Picture Oscar, based on his own experiences in Vietnam. For *Born on the Fourth of July*—the story of Vietnam vet Ron Kovic—Stone won the Best Director Oscar. Stone also wrote *Heaven & Earth,* based on the true-life story of a Vietnamese girl named Le Ly Hayslip. *Casualties* was directed by Brian De Palma.

GAME 30

10. Who appears opposite Alan Ladd in 1942's *This Gun for Hire*?

a. Madeleine Carroll

b. Gene Tierney

c. Veronica Lake

d. Lucille Ball

GAME 30 Q9 ANSWER b

The film was hailed as revolutionary in its treatment of fight sequences. Innovative cinematographer James Wong Howe was able to capture a fluid realism by wearing roller skates while shooting scenes in the ring. The movie earned its star John Garfield an Oscar nomination and went on to inspire director Martin Scorsese's work in *Raging Bull* (1980).

GAME 50

10. Which comic book movie was directed by Jon Favreau?

a. *Ghost Rider* (2007)

b. *The Incredible Hulk* (2008)

c. *Blade* (1998)

d. *Iron Man* (2008)

GAME 50 Q9 ANSWER d

After achieving cult status by directing such horror movies as *The Last House on the Left* (1972) and *The Hills Have Eyes* (1977), filmmaker Wes Craven decided to bring this DC Comics monster to theaters. In addition to starring in the film's sequel, Swamp Thing has appeared in his own live-action TV show, an animated series, and numerous comics.

GAME 70

10. Who plays Charles Foster Kane's mother in *Citizen Kane* (1941)?

a. Agnes Moorehead

b. Deborah Kerr

c. Dorothy Comingore

d. Joan Fontaine

GAME 70 Q9 ANSWER d

Featuring a script co-written by director John Huston and legendary sci-fi novelist Ray Bradbury, this 1956 film of the classic Herman Melville novel stars Oscar-winning actor Gregory Peck as the revenge-obsessed Captain Ahab. In 1998, Peck played the part of Father Mapple himself in a TV-movie adaptation starring Patrick Stewart as Ahab.

GAME 11

3. What is embroidered on Maggie's robe in *Million Dollar Baby* (2004)?

a. M'eudail
b. Gaolach
c. Misneach
d. Macushla

GAME 11 Q2 ANSWER d
Bill Murray is Carl Spackler, a country club greenskeeper whose objective is to rid the course of a pesky gopher. Along with Murray, the cast included comics Rodney Dangerfield and Chevy Chase, who, with director Harold Ramis, created a rowdy working atmosphere. Some cast members, including Ted Knight, didn't appreciate the "constant shenanigans."

GAME 31

3. Which motion picture is the focus of the documentary *Hearts of Darkness*?

a. *Heaven's Gate* (1980)
b. *Apocalypse Now* (1979)
c. *The Godfather* (1972)
d. *In Cold Blood* (1967)

GAME 31 Q2 ANSWER d
In one segment of Michael Moore's documentary on handgun violence in the US, Moore and two Columbine victims visited Kmart's headquarters—supposedly to get a refund for bullets that remained lodged in the students' bodies. As a result of this and other actions taken by Moore, the superstore decided to phase out its sale of handgun ammunition.

GAME 51

3. What is Drew Barrymore's occupation in *The Wedding Singer* (1998)?

a. Private investigator
b. Journalist
c. Song lyricist
d. Waitress

GAME 51 Q2 ANSWER a
In the famous scene, this special effect was created by mounting the camera on the floor of a special room that was built on a revolving cage. Astaire danced on the floor as the room turned, giving the impression that he was actually on the walls and ceiling. The same technique allowed singer Lionel Richie to "dance on the ceiling" in a music video.

GAME 71

3. Michael Jackson's "Will You Be There" is heard during which film's credits?

a. *Andre* (1994)
b. *Free Willy* (1993)
c. *Flipper* (1996)
d. *Buddy* (1997)

GAME 71 Q2 ANSWER a
Robert Redford costars with Jane Fonda in this Sidney Pollack-directed film. He plays Norman "Sonny" Steele—a former rodeo star whose intention is to return an old race horse to the wild. A noted equestrian, Redford performed all of his own riding stunts in the film. And when the movie's production was completed, he bought Rising Star.

GAME 10

11. Which war film includes a mission to kidnap a Vietnamese general?

a. *The Green Berets* (1968)

b. *Full Metal Jacket* (1987)

c. *Apocalypse Now* (1979)

d. *Three Kings* (1999)

GAME 10 Q10 ANSWER c
Directed by Richard Lester, who also directed John and the Beatles in *A Hard Day's Night* (1964) and *Help!* (1965), this dark comedy stars Michael Crawford as an inept British lieutenant in charge of a WWII outfit. Their mission? To set up a cricket field behind enemy lines. During filming, Lennon wrote "Strawberry Fields Forever."

GAME 30

11. Screenwriter Joe Gillis is a central character in which film noir classic?

a. *Railroaded!* (1947)

b. *Sunset Boulevard* (1950)

c. *Double Indemnity* (1944)

d. *The Maltese Falcon* (1941)

GAME 30 Q10 ANSWER c
This was the first of four movies in which Lake shared the big screen with Alan Ladd. The couple appeared together again later that same year in an adaptation of Dashiell Hammett's *The Glass Key* (1942), went on to shoot the Raymond Chandler-penned *The Blue Dahlia* in 1946, and finished by costarring in the 1948 drama *Saigon.*

GAME 50

11. Who plays Catwoman in *Batman Returns*?

a. Sean Young

b. Michelle Pfeiffer

c. Roseanne Arnold

d. Rebecca De Mornay

GAME 50 Q10 ANSWER d
Favreau first appeared on Hollywood's radar after writing and starring in the 1996 comedy *Swingers*. After a brief stint on TV's *Friends*, the multi-talented star moved into the director's chair for 2001's *Made* (also written by and starring Favreau). In addition to the first *Iron Man* film, he also helmed its sequel, 2010's *Iron Man 2.*

GAME 70

11. Orson Welles plays which Shakespearean character in *Chimes at Midnight*?

a. Falstaff

b. Macbeth

c. Othello

d. King Lear

GAME 70 Q10 ANSWER a
Agnes Moorehead was one of many actors whom Welles brought from New York's Mercury Theatre to appear in his films. After playing Kane's mother in *Citizen Kane*, Moorehead portrayed Aunt Fanny in Welles' second movie *The Magnificent Ambersons* (1942). She also appeared with Welles and Joan Fontaine in *Jane Eyre* (1944).

GAME 11

2. "Au revoir, gopher," is a line from which golf movie?

a. *Tin Cup* (1996)

b. *Happy Gilmore* (1996)

c. *The Legend of Bagger Vance* (2000)

d. *Caddyshack* (1980)

GAME 11 Q1 ANSWER c
Robert Redford plays Roy Hobbs, who slams a game-winning run into the overhead lights, causing sparks to fly and stadium lights to explode as he runs the bases. The scene was inspired by Boston Braves outfielder Bama Rowell. In 1946, he smashed a ball into the clock over the Ebbets Field scoreboard, causing shattered glass to rain on the field below.

GAME 31

2. What film chronicled Kmart's policy change on the sale of gun ammunition?

a. *The Big One* (1997)

b. *An Inconvenient Truth* (2006)

c. *It's All True* (1993)

d. *Bowling for Columbine* (2002)

GAME 31 Q1 ANSWER a
Through interviews, archival footage, and Cabinet recordings of conversations, *The Fog of War* follows ex-Secretary of Defense Robert McNamara from his birth in San Francisco, California to his involvement in the Vietnam War under Presidents John Kennedy and Lyndon Johnson. This film won the 2003 Academy Award for Best Documentary Feature.

GAME 51

2. In *Royal Wedding* (1951), Fred Astaire thrilled audiences by dancing:

a. On the walls and ceiling

b. On a frozen pond

c. On a tightrope

d. With his daughter

GAME 51 Q1 ANSWER c
In the 2005 comedy *Wedding Crashers*, Chazz (Will Ferrell) was the boys' mentor. (He eventually moved on to crashing funerals to meet women!) The movie sparked *The Real Wedding Crashers*—an NBC reality series in which couples let real crashers pull pranks at their weddings to make them memorable. After three episodes, the show "crashed."

GAME 71

2. Rising Star is a lightning fast thoroughbred in which movie?

a. *The Electric Horseman* (1979)

b. *Seabiscuit* (2003)

c. *National Velvet* (1944)

d. *The Black Stallion* (1979)

GAME 71 Q1 ANSWER a
This first film in a series of nine stars "Higgins the Dog," who had been on TV's *Petticoat Junction* for years. He came out of retirement to star in *Benji*. (His daughter replaced him in the sequels.) Higgins expressed emotions so well that several industry papers ran ads recommending him as an Oscar contender; but he wasn't nominated.

GAME 10

12. Which actor does *not* have a cameo in *The Thin Red Line* (1998)?

a. George Clooney

b. Woody Harrelson

c. Tommy Lee Jones

d. John Travolta

GAME 10 Q11 ANSWER a
This pro-war film starring John Wayne was his tribute to the soldiers serving in Vietnam. Released during the conflict itself, the film met with much criticism due to the anti-war sentiment of the time. The movie was noted for its realistic sets of Vietnamese villages, which were later used by the Army for training soldiers bound for Vietnam.

GAME 30

12. Which actor stars in the 1990 neo-noir *The Hot Spot*?

a. Alec Baldwin

b. Jack Nicholson

c. Mickey Rourke

d. Don Johnson

GAME 30 Q11 ANSWER b
For this sordid Hollywood tale, the film's co-writer and director Billy Wilder took home the Best Screenplay Oscar. Throughout his career, Wilder received an astounding twenty-one Oscar nominations. He earned eight nominations as a director, twelve for screenwriting, and one as a producer of his 1960 film *The Apartment.*

GAME 50

12. Which 2005 movie is based on a series of comic books by Alan Moore?

a. *Sin City*

b. *Batman Begins*

c. *Kingdom of Heaven*

d. *V for Vendetta*

GAME 50 Q11 ANSWER b
Annette Bening was originally cast as the leather-clad villain in this 1992 sequel to *Batman* (1989), but had to drop out of filming due to pregnancy. Both Susan Sarandon and Sean Young expressed interest in the part. Young even showed up unannounced at the film studio dressed in a homemade Catwoman costume, but her plan backfired.

GAME 70

12. Which actress did *not* appear in *Touch of Evil* (1958)?

a. Zsa Zsa Gabor

b. Janet Leigh

c. Jeanne Moreau

d. Marlene Dietrich

GAME 70 Q11 ANSWER a
Orson Welles created *Chimes at Midnight* (1965), which is also known as *Falstaff*, by combining text from five plays by William Shakespeare—primarily, *Henry IV, Parts 1 and 2*. Welles took the lead role of Sir John Falstaff, Keith Baxter played Prince Hal, John Gielgud portrayed Henry IV, and Jeanne Moreau filled the role of Doll Tearsheet.

260

<table>
<tr>
<td>GAME 11</td>
<td>**1.** Which baseball film ends with a spectacular home run?

a. *The Bad News Bears* (1976)
b. *Eight Men Out* (1988)
c. *The Natural* (1984)
d. *Bull Durham* (1988)</td>
<td>The answer to this question is on:

**page 258,
top frame,
right side.**</td>
</tr>
<tr>
<td>GAME 31</td>
<td>**1.** Who is the subject of the 2003 documentary *The Fog of War*?

a. Robert S. McNamara
b. Lyndon B. Johnson
c. Franklin D. Roosevelt
d. Donald H. Rumsfeld</td>
<td>The answer to this question is on:

**page 258,
second frame,
right side.**</td>
</tr>
<tr>
<td>GAME 51</td>
<td>**1.** Who taught Owen Wilson and Vince Vaughn the art of crashing weddings?

a. Brad Beckwith
b. Lance Grey
c. Chazz Reinhold
d. Zach Armstrong</td>
<td>The answer to this question is on:

**page 258,
third frame,
right side.**</td>
</tr>
<tr>
<td>GAME 71</td>
<td>**1.** In which movie does a lovable stray dog save two kidnapped kids?

a. *Benji* (1974)
b. *Dusty* (1983)
c. *That Darn Cat* (1965)
d. *The Magic of Lassie* (1978)</td>
<td>The answer to this question is on:

**page 258,
bottom frame,
right side.**</td>
</tr>
</table>

GAME 11

Sports Films

*See page 260
for the first question.*

GAME 10 Q12 ANSWER c
Terrence Malick returned to filmmaking after a twenty-year absence to direct this Oscar-nominated World War II film about the Battle of Guadalcanal. Clooney, Harrelson, and Travolta (as well as other notable actors like Adrien Brody, John Cusack, and Jared Leto) agreed to cameos just for the opportunity to work with the legendary director.

GAME 31

Documentaries

*See page 260
for the first question.*

GAME 30 Q12 ANSWER d
Johnson costars with Virginia Madsen in this Dennis Hopper-directed film based on the book *Hell Hath No Fury* by Charles Williams. After years of struggling to make a name for himself, Johnson found success playing police detective Sonny Crocket on the popular '80s TV series *Miami Vice*. The part earned him an Emmy nomination in 1985.

GAME 51

Wedding Movies

*See page 260
for the first question.*

GAME 50 Q12 ANSWER d
Though Moore refuses to watch them, many movies have been adapted from the legendary writer's comic books, including *From Hell* (2001), *The League of Extraordinary Gentlemen* (2003), and *Watchmen* (2009). Another film, 2005's *Constantine*, is also based on a character Moore created during his groundbreaking run with the *Swamp Thing* comic series.

GAME 71

Animal Flicks

*See page 260
for the first question.*

GAME 70 Q12 ANSWER c
French actress Jeanne Moreau appeared in Welles' films *The Trial* (1962) and *Chimes at Midnight* (1965). In *Touch of Evil* (1958), Janet Leigh played Charlton Heston's young wife, Susan Vargas. Actresses Zsa Zsa Gabor and Marlene Dietrich each had a small role in the film as well.

FRED WILLARD

Fred Willard, a four-time Emmy nominee, radiates a unique charm that has established him as one of our generation's most gifted comic actors. A master of sketch comedy, Fred is most heralded for his quick wit and improvisational expertise, which he has demonstrated in hundreds of appearances on stage, on the big screen, and on a wide range of television shows.

An alumnus of the famed Second City comedy troupe, Fred was also a founding member of the Ace Trucking Company sketch/improv group, where he honed his comedic skills. Of course, movie audiences know him best for his work in over seventy films. From *Silver Streak* with Gene Wilder and Richard Pryor to his most recent film, *Youth in Revolt*, starring Michael Cera, Ray Liotta, Steve Buscemi, and Jean Smart, he has worked with Hollywood's best. He danced with Jane Fonda in *Fun with Dick and Jane* and played a presidential advisor in *First Family*, starring Bob Newhart, Gilda Radner, and Madeline Kahn. He appeared with James Mason in *Salem's Lot*, with Jennifer Lopez in *The Wedding Planner*, and with

Steve Martin and Daryl Hannah in *Roxanne*. Fred's improvisational performances in *Waiting for Guffman* and *Best in Show* earned him an American Comedy Award nod for Funniest Supporting Actor, and won him the Boston Film Critics Award, the American Comedy Award, the Sierra Award, and a tribute from the American Film Institute (AFI). His filmography also includes *This Is Spinal Tap, Anchorman: The Legend of Ron Burgundy, A Mighty Wind, For Your Consideration,* the Academy Award-nominated *Monster House,* and the Academy Award-winning short film *Ray's Male Heterosexual Dance Hall.* Fred starred as the only human in the Oscar-winning film *WALL-E,* which *The New York Times* named the best film of the decade. He was honored by AFI for contributing to America's cultural legacy.

Fred's stage work includes off-Broadway productions of Jules Feiffer's *Little Murders,* Dan Greenburg's *Arf and the Great Airplane Snatch,* and Mary Willard's *Elvis and Juliet.* He has also performed in *Mame* at the Hollywood Bowl, and in the Los Angeles Reprise Theatre productions of *Promises, Promises, Anything Goes,* and *L'il Abner.* Fred won an Inland Empire Music Award for Outstanding Actor in a Musical for his role in Mary Willard and Marty Stuart's *Moon Shine!* His "one-man show" (with a cast of ten)—*Fred Willard, Alone At Last!*—earned the comic actor two Los Angeles Artistic Director Awards.

A favorite on TV talk shows, games shows, and series, Fred has appeared in over one thousand television episodes, from the variety *Tom Jones Show* to his recent appearances on *Modern Family.* He and Martin Mull co-starred in Norman Lear's innovative TV cult classic *Fernwood 2 Night.* He was a regular on *Sirota's Court, D.C. Follies* (again the only human!), *Maybe It's Me, A Minute with Stan Hooper,* and *Back to You.* Fred garnered three Emmy nominations for his performance as

Amy's Dad on *Everybody Loves Raymond*. His work on *What's Hot, What's Not* earned him a daytime Emmy nomination for Outstanding Talk Show Host. He has also made over one hundred appearances on *The Tonight Show with Jay Leno*.

Fred donates a great deal of his time to charitable endeavors. For his work with Big Brothers/Big Sisters, City of Hope, and Actors and Others for Animals, he received a commendation from the City of Los Angeles, and Mayor Antonio Villaraigosa praised him for "outstanding humanitarian and philanthropic work."

Fred and his playwright wife, Mary Willard, make their home in Los Angeles.

JOE FRANKLIN'S GREAT ENTERTAINMENT TRIVIA

Here's the book that will put your knowledge of movies, radio, music, and television to the test. New York's famous talk- and variety-show host Joe Franklin, whose guest list over the years reads like a who's who of celebrity royalty, has drawn on his own unique knowledge and personal experiences to create *Great Entertainment Trivia*. Not only is the book jam-packed with challenging questions, but it also provides lots of interesting information along with the answers.

Guaranteed fun, dozens of individual games, each with twelve questions, will both challenge and amuse. But unlike other books of this type, which reveal the answers below the questions or group them together with all of the other answers, this book cleverly formats the games in a way that allows the reader to see only one answer at the appropriate time. This way, the reader can play along. In addition to the questions, Franklin shares some of his favorite memories in fascinating insets that are peppered throughout the book.

From cover to cover, *Great Entertainment Trivia* is pure entertainment. And who better to create such a book than Joe Franklin, with his decades-long involvement in the business that he so dearly loves—and that so dearly loves him.

$7.95 • 288 pages • 4 x 7-inch paperback • ISBN 978-0-7570-0038-6

MICKY DOLENZ'
ROCK 'N ROLLIN' TRIVIA

Here he comes, walking down the street . . .
For nearly forty years now, Micky
Dolenz has pleased millions of fans
throughout the world by playing a
role in rock 'n roll history as a member
of The Monkees. And in that time, he
has also played a number of other
roles—actor, director, writer, producer,
brother, husband, father, and even
radio DJ. Now he's ready to play a
brand-new role as trivia maven—and
in *Micky Dolenz' Rock 'n Rollin' Trivia*,
you're invited to play a role, too!

From Elvis in America to The Beatles in England; from
doo-wop to punk rock; from MTV to MP3; it's all here in one big
collection of over 900 questions hand-picked by Micky himself
to tease and please any rock 'n roll fan. Unlike other trivia books
that simply supply the answers to the questions, this book includes interesting information along with each answer. Furthermore, the answers are cleverly formatted in a way that allows
the reader to play alone or with others.

With over 65 million records sold worldwide, Micky Dolenz
remains an important part of rock 'n roll culture. But now he
wants to take a close look at rock 'n roll history, one question at
a time. Micky's ready—are you? Pick up this book and find out
for yourself.

$7.95 • 288 pages • 4 x 7-inch paperback • ISBN 978-0-7570-0289-2

DICK VAN PATTEN'S
TOTALLY TERRIFIC TV TRIVIA

So you think you're a whiz at TV trivia—
an expert on everything from *I Love
Lucy* to *Seinfeld* to *Saturday Night Live*.
Well, here is the perfect book to put
your knowledge to the test. Created by
beloved television actor Dick Van Patten, this unique book of trivia is guaranteed to provide hours of enjoyment
for those who love to be quizzed on
their "small screen" expertise.

Packed with over 900 thought-pro-
voking questions, *Dick Van Patten's To-
tally Terrific Trivia* covers a wide range of
topics. You'll find questions on both classic and contemporary sitcoms, talk shows, made-for-TV movies, prime-time soaps, spinoffs,
game shows, and much, much more. It's all here in one enormous
collection that is sure to challenge, entertain, and inform. Adding to
the book's uniqueness is that unlike most other trivia books, which
simply supply the answers to the questions, this one includes interesting information along with each answer—you'll actually learn
as you play! As an added bonus, the answers are cleverly formatted
in a way that allows the reader to play alone or with others.

While other trivia books may get their information from published references, this one was lovingly compiled by Dick Van Patten, who has been entertaining television viewers for many years.
Let Dick take you on a tour of TV history—one question at a time.

$7.95 • 288 pages • 4 x 7-inch paperback • ISBN 978-0-7570-0231-1

RICK BARRY'S SUPER SPORTS TRIVIA

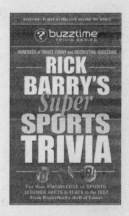

Irascible, opinionated, and absolutely brilliant, Rick Barry was named one of the fifty greatest players to have ever competed in professional basketball. A natural on the court, he possessed the physical ability, quick mind, and God-given talent to play among the best. Now, Basketball Hall of Famer Rick Barry challenges all those who pride themselves on their knowledge of sports with his unique book of trivia.

Drawing information from the history, legends, and lore of basketball, baseball, football, boxing, hockey, auto racing, and more, Barry has created a series of quizzes that are guaranteed to provide hours of entertainment and fun. But unlike other trivia books that simply supply the answers to the questions, this book includes interesting information along with each answer—you'll actually learn as you play! Furthermore, the answers are cleverly formatted in a way that allows the reader to play alone or with others. Each game is guaranteed fun—challenging, informative, and amusing.

Rick Barry's knowledge of sports results in a trivia book with a spin that's more challenging than a curveball. If you're ready for a game that is interesting, educational, and always fun to play, *Rick Barry's Super Sports Trivia* is the way to go.

$7.95 • 288 pages • 4 x 7-inch paperback • ISBN 978-0-7570-0134-5

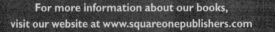

**For more information about our books,
visit our website at www.squareonepublishers.com**

FOR A COPY OF OUR CATALOG, PLEASE CALL TOLL FREE:
877-900-BOOK, ext. 100

ABOUT
BUZZTIME

NTN Buzztime, Inc. (NYSE Amex: NTN) is one of the most popular interactive entertainment networks in North America. For over twenty-five years, Buzztime has developed trivia, card, and sports games that are broadcast on the Buzztime Network to more than 4,000 restaurants, bars, and pubs throughout the United States and Canada. Over 1 million registered players use a blue Playmaker or an Apple iPhone® to compete in more than 4.5 million games each month. Players eagerly spread the word, inviting friends and family to their favorite Buzztime locations to enjoy an evening of fun and competition or simply to unwind after a hectic day. Buzztime boosts the fun factor, turning visitors into regulars, and attracting new players every day of the week.

For more information about Buzztime trivia games,

visit
www.buzztime.com